CHAMPIONSHIP TRACK AND FIELD FOR WOMEN

Other Books by the Authors

How They Train
by Fred Wilt (Tafnews Press, Inc.)

Run-Run-Run
by Fred Wilt (Tafnews Press, Inc.)

The Jumps: Contemporary Theory, Technique and Training
by Fred Wilt (Tafnews Press, Inc.)

The Throws: Contemporary Theory, Technique and Training
by Fred Wilt (Tafnews Press, Inc.)

Motivation and Coaching Psychology
by Fred Wilt and Ken Bosen (Tafnews Press, Inc.)

International Track and Field Coaching Encyclopedia
by Fred Wilt and Tom Ecker (Parker Publishing Company, Inc.)

Illustrated Guide to Olympic Track and Field Techniques
by Tom Ecker and Fred Wilt (Parker Publishing Company, Inc.)

Olympic Track and Field Techniques
by Tom Ecker, Fred Wilt and Jim Hay (Parker Publishing Company, Inc.)

Championship Track and Field
by Tom Ecker (Prentice-Hall, Inc.)

Championship Football
by Tom Ecker with Paul Jones (Prentice-Hall, Inc.)

Pista y Campo de Campeonato
by Tom Ecker (Editorial Diana, Mexico)

Track and Field Dynamics
by Tom Ecker (Tafnews Press, Inc.)

Track and Field: Technique Through Dynamics
by Tom Ecker (Tafnews Press, Inc.)

The Biomechanics of Sports Techniques
by Jim Hay (Prentice-Hall, Inc.)

CHAMPIONSHIP TRACK AND FIELD FOR WOMEN

Edited by

Fred Wilt,
Tom Ecker
and
Jim Hay

Parker Publishing Co., Inc.
West Nyack, NY

© 1978, *by*

PARKER PUBLISHING COMPANY, INC.

West Nyack, N.Y.

Library of Congress Cataloging in Publication Data
Main entry under title:

Championship track and field for women.

    Includes bibliographies.
    1. Track-athletics for women. 2. Track-athletics
coaching. 3. Sports--Physiological aspects. 4. Sports--
Psychological aspects. I. Wilt, Fred. II. Ecker, Tom.
III. Hay, James G.
GV1060.8.C4   796.4'2   77-10520
ISBN 0-13-127845-2

Printed in the United States of America

ACKNOWLEDGEMENT

For sharing her expertise and her valued time with us during the final preparation of the manuscript, we are beholden to Dr. N. Peggy Burke of the University of Iowa.

FOREWORD

Championship Track and Field for Women is a book of physiological, psychological and biomechanical information for track and field coaches and competitors. It is also a how-to-do-it manual for the individual track and field events. And it is something more—an important something. That something, as indicated in its title, is its focus on the female as a competitor.

Athletics for girls and women are here to stay. Enforcement of existing legislation will ensure that opportunity, but legislation does not ensure encouragement for the individual girl or woman who aspires to be athletically great. Encouragement will come only when those surrounding the female athlete become educated to the "rightness" of her struggle for human excellence in pitting her body against time and space and, indeed, educated to her ability to achieve such excellence. This book serves such educating functions by helping to remove one important obstacle for the female athlete—her invisibility in sports literature.

The editors, renowned scholars and authors in the area of track and field, have chosen not to write this book, but rather to find capable women scholars, competitors and coaches, and male coaches who have worked directly with female athletes. Their understanding of the female athlete is evident.

There are numerous illustrations of women as competitors, and when times and distances are cited, they are women's times and distances. Further, the reader is spared the constant use of masculine pronouns and references to adult women as "girls."

Yes, the focus is on women, but the techniques are universal and even members of the "other sex" can profit from the information contained in this fine text.

Dr. N. Peggy Burke
National President
Association for Intercollegiate
   Athletics for Women

WHAT THIS BOOK OFFERS YOU

Here at last is a *complete* book on the coaching of women's track and field. This remarkable volume is a compilation of the latest available information on the many aspects of this growing sport, presented in a range extending from fundamental technique and training all the way through to the most advanced (sometimes revolutionary) technical know-how.

The book's contributors were chosen because of their proven ability, their scientific knowledge, their coaching expertise, their years of experience and their hundreds of successes in coaching women's track and field. Acknowledged experts in the areas for which they have been selected to write, the contributors have provided the practical, common-sense explanations that can benefit women's track and field coaches everywhere.

We have done some editing on the contributed material—mostly for clarity and consistency. However, for the most part each chapter represents the knowledge and the individual style of the contributing author. The views of the contributors are their own, of course, and not necessarily those of the other contributors or of the editors, who frequently disagree with each other on some matters of track and field. We view such disagreement as a healthy state of affairs leading ultimately to a more complete understanding of the sport.

Leading off the book are comprehensive discussions of biomechanics, physiology and psychology, followed by a complete analysis of each of the women's track and field events. The contributors have provided penetrating examinations of sprinting, middle and long distance running, hurdling, relay racing, long jumping, high jumping, shot putting, discus throwing and javelin throwing.

Chris Murray, one of America's most respected women's distance coaches, confirms that girls and women can greatly increase their mileage during weekly practice sessions, producing amazing improvements in their times in the middle and long distance races.

Bert Lyle, whose relay teams have held every national collegiate record, explains how to select relay personnel and outlines the techniques and strategy necessary for improving relay exchanges.

Eleanor Rynda, a noted authority in several areas of women's track and field, covers the technique and training for shot putting that will increase the strength and power necessary for longer puts.

Also included is an in-depth chapter on weight lifting for women, an essential yet often neglected part of women's track and field coaching.

And there are six more information-packed event chapters that will provide the coach with ideas and programs that have been successfully tested at every level of competition.

Each event chapter also contains photo sequences of champion women performers, complete with technical analyses of each athlete's techniques. From there, the coach will learn to recognize the major technique changes that might turn an average athlete into a champion, or to recognize the refinements that will improve an already outstanding performer. Though the reproduction of a few of these photographic sequences may be of less than ideal clarity, the editors feel that they aptly convey the essence of form and technique of the individuals in actual competition.

This single volume has it all—the scientific background, the explanations of technique and strategy, the teaching stages, the training programs for each event, strength training programs, and illustrative photo sequences.

We are pleased to have been able to put it all together!

Fred Wilt

Tom Ecker

Jim Hay

CONTENTS

What This Book Offers You 9

Chapter 1.   **Biomechanical Considerations** 17
Christine Brooks

Chapter 2.   **Physiological Considerations** 35
Emily Haymes

Chapter 3.   **Social-Psychological Considerations** 47
Penny McCullagh

Chapter 4.   **The Sprints** 76
Maurice Sipes

Chapter 5.   **The Middle and Long Distances** 93
Chris Murray

Chapter 6.   **The Hurdles** 120
Patricia Brown

Chapter 7.   **The Relays** 141
Bert Lyle

Chapter 8.   **The Long Jump** 155
David Rodda

13

Chapter 9.   **The High Jump** 168
                Jim Santos

Chapter 10.   **The Shot Put** 182
                Eleanor Rynda

Chapter 11.   **The Discus Throw** 202
                Olga Connolly

Chapter 12.   **The Javelin Throw** 217
                Jessica Dragicevic

Chapter 13.   **Weight Training
                for Girls and Women** 236
                John Jessee

                Bibliography 261

CHAMPIONSHIP
TRACK AND FIELD
FOR
WOMEN

1 Christine Brooks

BIOMECHANICAL CONSIDERATIONS

Author: **Christine Brooks** is a women's track and cross-country coach and the holder of a research appointment in the Biomechanics Laboratory at Pennsylvania State University. A former high jumper and hurdler, she competed at club, regional and national levels in New Zealand before coming to the United States in 1970. Her present dual appointment as coach and researcher—she is currently engaged in biomechanics research dealing with women's track—is unique in U.S. track and field.

The practical application of biomechanics is becoming increasingly important in this country, not only in track and field, but in all sports. For instance, the United States used to be a weight-lifting power, but this situation has drastically changed in recent years. In an effort to upgrade performances on an international level, American weight-lifters are now using mechanical analysis of the different lifts in an attempt to find more efficient lifting techniques.

It is becoming apparent to coaches in most countries that they can no longer rely on large numbers of participants trying out for the national teams and expect to compete successfully on an international level. Something further must be done to help the athletes perform to their maximum potential whether it is (a) through a system of training centers where athletes are able to train and have all the necessary facilities and coaching available to them, or (b) through sports research centers established to help the athletes perform to their optimum mechanical efficiency. An example of how research has helped the status of sport in a country can be seen in recent developments in East Germany (DDR). Some years ago when the DDR ranked low in world-level swimming performances, researchers from that country filmed and studied the American swimmers, and as a direct result of upgrading their knowledge in swimming, the DDR is now one of the top swimming nations in the world. Indeed, they have taken over world supremacy from the Australians and Americans as far as the women's performances are concerned.

The immediate reaction of some American coaches is that this is not what sport is all about and that it is for the fun and enjoyment of our youth. To some extent this is true, but if international success in sport did not mean anything to the United States, we would not be in the process of attempting to establish a "higher sports council" which would be responsible for upgrading sport in this country. According to Smith (1976), "a nation develops a pride through its international sports teams and is a good substitute for war," and this, together with the fact that U.S. youths fall behind their European counterparts in physical fitness, is a sound reason for the upgrading and the development of sport in this country. It is of interest to note that one of the suggestions of the President's Council on Sport may be to include research centers along with the proposed training centers.

The question being asked, therefore, is no longer, "Why is research necessary and scientific knowledge required in order to be a good and effective coach?" but rather, "How can research be developed to help sport in this country?" In the past the innovative athlete has come up with a new technique and the researcher has then analyzed it and arrived at reasons why it is a better method of performing a specific movement. What is needed today are researchers who are primarily concerned with the optimization of technique and who can suggest new techniques to be used by athletes.

If a coach has a basic knowledge of mechanics, errors in technique coaching should be virtually nonexistent. An example of a typical coaching error brought about by a lack of knowledge of mechanics concerns the dive straddle style of high jumping and the problem of clearing the bar with the trail leg. In this regard, it has frequently been recommended that the athlete drive the arm that is already over the bar down and back under the bar. This was supposed to increase rotation of the body around the bar and thus assist in clearing the trailing leg. Unfortunately, this advice is in direct conflict with sound mechanics. Instead the athlete should have been told to raise the arm that was already over the bar up and back, an action which would result in a reaction in the trail leg causing it to be lifted up and away from the bar. This was the very technique used by Brumel.

Before any upgrading of women's track and field can be done in this country, a study of the top American and world female athletes must be performed in an attempt to pinpoint areas where the U.S. athletes may improve. If it is established that the errors observed in this process are a result of coaching, technique or a combination of these two factors, then the researcher and the coach can work together and attempt to solve the problems.

It is obviously impossible to cover all aspects of mechanics in track and field in the short space of a chapter when complete books have been written on the topic. This chapter will therefore be confined to a discussion of two concepts in mechanics that are of a great concern in track and field—the concepts of speed and force.

SPEED

Speed is the distance traveled in any direction divided by the time taken by the athlete to travel that distance. Velocity is different only in that the distance traveled is in a specified direction. Most research will use the term "velocity" in preference to speed but the two terms essentially have the same meaning. Acceleration is another important term and is the rate with which an athlete increases her velocity and, in contrast, deceleration is the rate with which she decreases her velocity.

Speed of movement is very important in all the events. For instance, in the 100 m. dash, the ability of the athlete to maintain maximum speed for as long as possible and to slow down the least determines who gets to the finish line first. In the 1500 m., sustained speed determines who the winner will be and in the throwing events the objective is to make the implement go as fast and, thus, as far, as possible. In the jumping events the speed of approach plays a very significant role in determining the height or distance with which the athlete is eventually credited.

Components of Running Speed

The ability of an athlete to run fast depends, to a large extent, on the ratio of red and white muscle fibers in her muscular system, and this is an inherent factor. The red fibers are the endurance fibers and the white fibers are the speed fibers and research has indicated fairly conclusively that sprinters have a higher proportion of white muscle fibers in their muscle than the middle-distance or distance runners who, in turn, have a higher proportion of red fibers. The term that "sprinters are born" is, therefore, basically accurate since at the present time it appears impossible to train an athlete with a low number of white muscle fibers to be a world-class sprinter. It can be said fairly conclusively, therefore, that these are the physiological factors involved in speed where very few changes can be made. However, if two athletes have the same number of white muscle fibers, the biomechanical factors of speed may possibly be changed to enhance the performance of one athlete and as a result make her faster than the other.

Since running speed is determined by the product of just two biomechanical factors (stride length and stride frequency), it may be increased in any one of three ways:

(a) by keeping the stride length the same, and increasing the stride frequency

(b) by keeping the stride frequency the same, and increasing the stride length

(c) by increasing both the stride length and the stride frequency.

Obviously, if increasing speed were as simple as that, there would be a larger number of world record holders in this country. Unfortunately, it is much more involved than simply telling an athlete that she must increase stride frequency or stride length. First, the coach must know the stride length that the girl should be aiming for, what stride frequency is equivalent to world-class, and what mechanical errors are noticeable when the athlete is sprinting. It is relatively easy for a sprinter to attain a longer stride length, but in most cases this occurs at the expense of technique and consequently there is a resulting loss of speed.

STRIDE FREQUENCY

Stride frequency is the number of strides that the athlete takes in one second and it is obvious that the faster the athlete runs, the higher her stride frequency will be. It also follows that the ability of an athlete to maintain a high stride frequency depends, to a large extent, on the number of white muscle fibers in her muscles. There appears to be a limit to the maximum stride frequency that a sprinter can attain, and the question as to whether this limit was the result of neuromuscular functions of the body was investigated by Slater-Hammel (1941). He established that the legs were capable of a much higher frequency than was observed during sprint running and concluded that stride frequency was not limited by neuromuscular functions but by "the weight the muscles must move." The observations of Slater-Hammel were borne out by the actions of cyclists who are able to move their legs at a much faster rate than is possible in sprint running.

The stride frequency is affected by many factors including leg length, stride length, leg strength, and the height of the heel in the kickup of the recovery leg as it is brought forward in preparation for the next stride. The maximum stride frequency of top American female sprinters, who have times of between 10.3 and 10.6 seconds for the 100-yard dash, fall between 3.9 and 4.55 steps/second (Brooks, 1976).

If stride length is short and the athlete wishes to maintain the same speed as an athlete who has a longer stride length, she must increase her stride frequency accordingly. However, since research has indicated that there is a limit to how much stride frequency can be increased, this alone is not the most efficient way of improving speed. World-class runners appear to have found the best ratio of stride length to stride frequency for their height and leg length. If the athlete has a relatively slow stride frequency compared to other athletes of the same height and leg length, then two biomechanical errors may be the cause of the problem. The first and most common error is a low heel kickup height. Although this was once thought to be a waste of energy, most of the top sprinters in the world have a heel kickup which is very close to the buttocks and which, therefore, enables the leg to be brought forward at a much faster rate than an athlete with a lower kickup (Figure 1-1). The biomechanical principle involved here is the conservation of angular momentum and is easily demonstrated by the ice skater who brings her arms in close to her body in order to turn faster during a pirouette and stretches her arms back out in order to slow down.

To increase the angular velocity of a body or a body part, such as a leg or an arm, it is necessary to bring as much mass as possible close to the axis about which the body is rotating. For instance, when the ice skater stretches her arms

FIGURE 1-1

out, she has, in effect, increased the rotary inertia of her body (i.e. the resistance to rotary movement) since she has increased the distance of her body parts from the axis about which she is rotating. The turning velocity is still there, but it is being reduced by her large rotary inertia. The long jumper faces a problem of forward rotation at take-off and, therefore, makes use of a large rotary inertia by stretching herself out while she is in the air. This serves to slow her rotation and thus allows her to obtain an effective landing position. In contrast, one reason why a straight lead leg swing at take-off does not work for a Fosbury-flop jumper is that it tends to slow her rotation about her long axis and thus makes it difficult for her to be in the correct position at the peak of the flight. In relation to these examples, since the sprinter wants to have a fast movement of her leg as it is being swung through in preparation for the next stride, and since a high kickup brings the mass of the limb close to the hip joint about which it is rotating, such an action allows for a faster forward motion of the recovery leg.

The second biomechanical error which may affect the stride frequency of the athlete is a forward motion of the foot at the instant of touchdown. This has the effect of repeatedly braking the forward motion of the athlete. This action is usually noticeable in athletes who are overstriding and have their foot landing well out in front of their center of gravity at the instant of touchdown. Injuries such as shin splints appear to be more common in athletes who have this type of foot motion since, in most cases, they tend to land on the front part of the foot which places constant pressure on the muscles down the front of the leg. The athlete must be taught to drop onto her foot so that it is always in the strongest driving position.

Runners other than sprinters have much longer stride frequencies and these appear to vary according to the event that the athletes specialize in. This, however, is probably more indicative of the fact that distance runners do not have as many white muscle fibers and are, therefore, physiologically unable to move their legs as fast as the sprinter. It is also of interest to note that films of the top distance runners in this country show that most have never been taught sound running technique. This may well effect their stride frequency at fast speeds and consequently have a detrimental effect on their performances.

STRIDE LENGTH

Stride length may be divided into two categories—(a) stride length at maximum speed and (b) stride length at sub-maximum speed.

Stride Length at Maximum Speed. At maximum speed the most effective stride length appears to be one that is as long as mechanically possible. Hoffman (1972) has obtained a stride length-to-height ratio of 1.28:1–1.33:1 for world-class female athletes and gives values of maximum stride lengths for Rudolph (USA) and Szewinska (Poland) of 90.25 in. (Both of these athletes were relatively tall—5 ft. 10 in. and 5 ft. 9¾ in. respectively.) Studies on American runners are in relative agreement with this ratio even though American female sprinters are not considered to be world-class. Stride length is a "place to start" since it becomes an immediate and tangible technique problem that has a solution. In addition, it is apparent that data on athletes who are closer to world-level performances more closely resemble the data obtained on the world-level athletes than does the data on athletes of lesser abilities.[1] It is of interest to note that the hurdlers have a somewhat shorter stride length than the sprinters and the reason for this is probably related primarily to the placement of the hurdles. The 100 m. hurdles do not allow a normal stride length between them and most hurdlers must chop their strides in order to be in the most effective take-off position for the next hurdle. The technique of running between the hurdles, therefore, may be somewhat different than normal sprinting and the suggestion by some coaches of "shuffling the strides" between the hurdles may have some merit.

Due to obvious differences in the length of the leg, it appears that leg length may be a better indicator of stride length than is an athlete's height. According to Hoffman, world-class female sprinters have stride lengths between 2.38 and 2.50 times their leg length. However, this is a more difficult measurement for a coach to make and for practical purposes, the ratio of stride length to height is a much more valuable method and gives a relatively good indication of the stride length for which an athlete should be aiming.

The length of the stride, however, must not be achieved at the expense of sound mechanical running technique. Strength development in the legs is probably the single most important factor for improving stride length and if the athlete attempts to increase stride length without strength, she will understandably develop serious mechanical errors. Since the indication of research is that the world-class sprinter is not only characterized by a high recovery leg and knee lift,

[1]Data obtained from athletes at the U.S. Women's Olympic Training Camp, Gainesville, FL, Dec. 1975. The project was partially funded by the U.S. Olympic Development Committee.

but also by placement of the foot as closely as possible beneath the center of gravity at the instant it strikes the ground, stride length should only be increased as long as the foot placement is in a sound driving position.

Stride Length at Sub-maximum Speeds. The optimum stride length at sub-maximum speeds is uncertain, and in fact, a controversial subject. There are excellent coaches in this country who maintain that stride length should always be a maximum length, at least up to the 880 yd., and some even suggest that stride length should not decrease even after that distance. The argument is that the 440 yd. is a sprint and that the 880 yd. is fast becoming a sprint and, therefore, there should be no difference in running technique between these races and the shorter dashes. Szewinska, the world record holder in the 400 m., had an average speed of 26.3 ft./sec. during that 400 m. race, an average speed of 29.56 ft./sec. during her best 100 m. race, and very close to that (29.16 ft./sec.) during her best 200 m. race. Since she starts from zero, the estimate for her maximum speed would be somewhat higher than 30 ft./sec. There is no comparison, therefore, between her maximum speed and her speed during the 400 m. race, even though she may be attempting to maintain maximum speed—actually a physiological impossibility. The fact that 400 m. hurdlers usually add strides between the hurdles during the latter portions of the race is a sure indication that as the body becomes physically tired the athlete is incapable of maintaining maximum stride length. If the athlete insists on maintaining a maximum stride length, then she must as a result place her foot forward of her center of gravity at each touchdown and, in turn, cause a repeated retarding effect on her forward motion. However, it is doubtful, even at the insistence of the coach, that an athlete can maintain maximum stride length throughout a 400 m. race. The question then becomes, "What is the optimum stride length for sub-maximum speeds?" Nelson and Gregor (1975) found in a study performed with male middle-distance runners that over a 4-yr. period their stride length decreased and their stride frequencies increased as they improved their performances. While it is generally felt by the scientists working in this area that there is some optimum stride length for different speeds that is the most efficient for each particular speed, and that it may be independent of leg length, more work must be done before any definite conclusions can be reached.

Stride Length Out of the Blocks. There is very little information available on the stride lengths of world-class women sprinters as they move out of the blocks. Information on the top male athletes indicates that the first stride is at least as long as the second stride and is the best indication of a good start, but little work has been done to give the coach an indication on how long the first stride should be. Gagnon (1976) found in studies on the standing start that the first stride was shorter than the second stride and maintained that this was "a pattern which is ineffective for high velocity development." However, when succeeding strides were taken into account, the standing start allowed the athlete to achieve her normal stride at a much faster rate than the kneeling start. Gagnon's results were inconclusive with regard to whether this was an advantage over the kneeling start since the kneeling start permits the sprinter to exert more force in the horizontal direction and the resultant inclination of her body may prevent her from obtaining

*Table 1-1: STRIDE LENGTHS OF TOP SPRINTERS EXECUTING SPRINT START**

Athlete	Stride Length (in.)							Maximum Stride Length (in.)	Time 100 yd. (sec.)
	1	2	3	4	5	6	7		
Sandra Upshaw	34	34	45	55	57	63		78	10.6
Mattline Render	36	45	44	46	51	57	58	85	10.3
Teresa Montgomery	38	38	47	52	57	63	64	80	10.4
Rochelle Davis	42	33	45	52	58	62		82	10.3
Steve Williams	41	42	55	59	70	70			

*Brooks, unpublished data.

the knee lift necessary to obtain normal stride length. Stride patterns out of the blocks obtained for top American female sprinters indicate that, while many manage to have a first stride that is at least as long as the second stride, the distance covered by the first and second stride varies considerably (Table 1-1).

Sandra Upshaw had a very short first stride out of the blocks and it was probably the cause of her "popping up" as she moved into her first stride—a fault which caused her coach considerable concern. Her stride length characteristics at maximum speed indicated that she had a short stride for her height and this in turn may have been due to a lack of leg strength. If the legs are not strong, the ability of the athlete to apply the necessary force on the blocks and to remain in the low driving position during the initial strides may be affected. Although Steve Williams was not considered to be a great starter when compared to other male athletes, he did show the characteristics of the top male sprinters out of the blocks.

The optimum length of the first stride for women is still not certain and would undoubtedly depend on the leg length and leg strength of the athlete concerned. An extreme example of the first stride length is seen in Carol Thomson, one of the top 100 m. hurdlers in the United States. Thomson's first stride is 4 ft. and this is probably due to the fact that she takes seven strides to the first hurdle rather than the eight strides typical of most female sprint hurdlers. It is doubtful, however, if many female sprinters could effectively perform a first stride length of 4 ft. and the optimum is probably somewhere between 3 ft. and 4 ft. A good rule of thumb, however, is to have the athlete attempt to obtain a first stride that is at least as long as the second stride. If this situation does not occur, it is probably due to inefficient use of the starting blocks and the athlete must learn how to apply the maximum amount of force to the blocks in order to develop an effective start.

Speed Curve

A speed curve presents the pattern of the speed throughout the race graphically and allows the coach or the athlete to determine where the weakest part of her race may be. Researchers have maintained for a number of years that the most efficient method of running a distance race, which included the 440 yd., was to maintain an even pace throughout. Up to the present time few world-class athletes have run the 440 yd. this way—the first 220 yd. is usually run much faster than the second 220 yd. It is physically impossible to accelerate maximally from start to finish even in a short race such as the 100 m., and it appears to be equally impossible to maintain maximum speed for any long period of time.

Although data on the speed curves for various distances are somewhat limited, the work that has been done on the 100 m. race by Ikai (1968) indicates that an athlete reaches maximum speed around the 30-40 m. mark and maintains that speed through to 70-80 m., (Figure 1-2). At this point in the race Ikai reported a

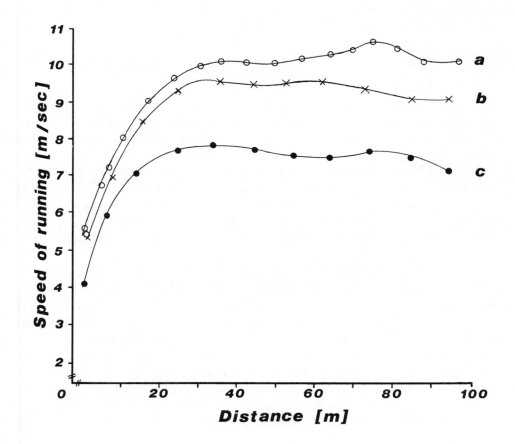

FIGURE 1-2:   *SPEED CURVE OF 100 M. RUNNING IN TRAINED ATHLETES*
        a) First class sprinter
        b) Second class sprinter
        c) Ordinary student
(After Ikai, M. ''Biomechanics of Sprint Running with Respect to the Speed Curve.'' In Biomechanics: Technique of Drawings of Movement and Movement Analysis, 1968)

second speed peak after which there is a gradual deceleration until the finish of the 100 m. race. Ikai maintained that the differences between trained and untrained sprinters were in (a) the rate of acceleration to the first speed peak, (b) the fact that the untrained runners could not reach a second speed peak at the 70 m. mark and (c) that deceleration was much more marked for the untrained than for the trained runner. In a similar effort to gain some insight into speed distribution, Alabin and Maishutovich (1975) studied speed curves for U.S. male intermediate hurdlers in an attempt to determine why Soviet hurdlers were not having the same international success as U.S. hurdlers. They found that the U.S. hurdlers were able to reach higher speeds than the Soviet hurdlers at 80 m. and to maintain it for 200 m., after which there was a gradual drop-off in speed. Their conclusions were that the Soviet hurdlers had to solve three problems before they would be capable of competing on the international level. These were:

(a) Improve the special endurance of the hurdlers,
(b) Correct the rhythm of running strides (13-15 running strides),
(c) Gain mastery over hurdle clearance technique.

There has been considerable argument over the years as to the best way to run a race and win. The 100 m. seemed relatively simple: the instructions were to run as fast as possible for the whole race, and the fastest shall be first. However, even in this race, coaches are beginning to recognize that it is not the fastest out of the blocks who ultimately wins the race, or even the fastest athlete, it is the athlete who manages to maintain speed for the longest period of time and *decelerates the least*. In recent years, therefore, emphasis has been placed on speed endurance and a concentration on an attempted "pickup" at the 70-80 m. point in the race—a "pickup" which Ikai's speed curve of the 100 m. dash indicates may indeed be possible to perform.

The speed curve of the 400 m. dash has proved to be an even more debatable issue than that for the 100 m. or 200 m. sprint. Athletes are still experimenting with speed during various portions of the 400 m. race and it is doubtful that they will ever stop experimenting until scientific evidence provides them with the ultimate answer. According to Doherty (1971), Lee Evans attempted to run the 400 m. slightly differently in Mexico in 1968 than he had been running it prior to the Games. Here he ran the first 100 m. hard, the backstretch as relaxed as possible without losing momentum, picked up the pace in the third 100 m. and attempted to relax and maintain this pace into the finish. He was almost beaten by Larry James who had an entirely different approach to the race. Doherty sums up the speed curve for the 400 m. by the following, "The only sound tactic in running the 400 is to get there first."

Although the study of speed curves is still in the early stages and not much information has really been gained through either scientific or athletic experimentation, the results of a study by Franklin Henry (1952) on the efficiency of running indicates that the method which will ultimately produce the fastest times is one that is run at a steady pace.

Effect of the Start on the Speed Curve

What the athlete does at the start of a 100 m. race may ultimately affect her speed during other parts of the race. The conclusion reached by Gagnon (1976) when she looked at the various portions of the 50 m. sprint was that "the plotting of average velocities during each 10 m. interval of the 50 m. sprint reveals that the type of starting technique utilized by the sprinter can affect the development of her velocity during the entire sprinting race and that its effects are not limited to the first strides of the race." Henry (1952) reported similar findings in his study of the effect of bunch, medium, and elongated starting positions on the block clearance time and on times to 10 yd. and 50 yd. His conclusions were that the bunch start allowed the athlete to leave the blocks sooner but moving at a slower speed and, consequently, the time advantage obtained at the start was lost by the 10 yd. line. The elongated start allowed the athlete a longer time in the blocks to generate speed but athletes using this start had slower times at the 10 yd. and 50 yd. lines than athletes using the medium start. Although the medium start did not allow the same time advantage out of the blocks as the bunch start, it allowed the athlete to reach the 10 yd. and 50 yd. mark faster, and was therefore considered to be the best of the starts tested.

The question as to the effect that the start has on the remainder of the race was of concern to Gagnon (1976) in her study of the differences between the standing and kneeling start techniques. Her results indicated that while the standing start allowed the athlete to reach maximum speed sooner (20-30 m. for the standing start and 30-40 m. for the kneeling start) the athletes using the standing start experienced a greater loss of speed during the latter portions of the race than those using the kneeling start. Gagnon used relatively inexperienced female athletes who were definitely well below world-class. In the light of Ikai's (1968) data on the speed curve for the 100 m. race, it seems feasible that an experienced athlete might be trained to maintain speed for a period of time and that, as a consequence, it may be an advantage to reach that speed earlier in the race. If, however, the second velocity peak and, thus, the deceleration part of the curve are reached earlier, the standing start would be a definite disadvantage. Unfortunately, very little research is available on this and therefore a definite conclusion is not yet possible.

FORCE

The three laws of motion involving force that a coach should be familiar with are: (1) the Law of Inertia (b) the Law of Acceleration, and (c) the Law of Reaction.

Law of Inertia

Inertia is the resistance of a body to change what it is doing. In the words of Doherty (1971) referring to the shot, it prefers "above all else staying where it's at.'' Athletes are well aware that it is difficult to get a weight moving at the start of a weight lifting movement, but once it is moving, the task at hand becomes much easier. This resistance to movement or resistance to change in movement is called the inertia of the object. An experienced shot putter knows that to get the shot moving across the circle she must use her heavier lower body which is stronger but slower than her upper body. Once the shot is moving then she must use the faster, smaller muscles of the trunk and the arm to continue to accelerate the shot across the circle to the point of release. The biggest error among beginners is that they waste the initial part of the motion by stopping the shot after the glide which then leaves the smaller and weaker muscles to overcome the inertia of the shot once more. Something similar occurs in sprint running when the result of overstriding is a braking effect on forward velocity. In effect the athlete is constantly overcoming the inertia of her body and must therefore use much more energy than a more efficient runner.

To overcome inertia and get a body moving in the desired direction, an athlete will generally adopt an unstable position from which she can exert strong forces to get her moving in that direction. The sprint start is an example of this process of overcoming inertia. The athlete who sits back in the blocks is in a very stable position and as a result she has considerable difficulty overcoming her inertia. Placement of the weight well forward over the hands serves the purpose of making the starting position more unstable and thereby makes it easier to overcome the inertia of the body. Jackson and Cooper (1970) studied the effect of the 8 in. and the wide hand spacing on starting performance and found that the 8 in. hand spacing put the athlete in a more unstable position than the wide hand spacing. These same authors also found that although there was no difference in the times recorded over a 10 yd. and a 30 yd. distance when back-knee angles of 90 deg. and 135 deg. were used, the hips were in a lower position when the knee angle was at 90 deg. The 90 deg. back-knee angle is a feature of the position that Winter (1956) called the ''Rocket Sprint Start'' and may help the experienced athlete generate more horizontal force. A beginner, however, may find it more difficult to overcome her inertia with this technique. Raising the hips a little higher, therefore, may be a more efficient start for a beginner since it would serve to increase her ability to overcome the inertia of her body.

Law of Acceleration

For an athlete to increase her speed she must increase the force that she is applying and the rate of increase in speed is directly proportional to the force that is being applied. Here strength is a very important factor, since more strength allows the athlete to apply a larger force over a specific period of time. Strength has played a very significant role in the improvement in male track and field performances but in the time period of 1920-1948 the emphasis was solely on technique since strength was not considered to be of particular importance. According to Doherty (1971) the emphasis changed from technique to strength training around 1952 and the remarkable improvement in the field event records, especially the shot and discus, have been attributed to this shift in emphasis. There is no doubt that increased strength allows for the application of much larger forces which increase the speed either of the implement (in the case of the throwing events) or of the athlete (in the case of the running and jumping events). The question then arises as to the type of strength required, since it would be useless to be extremely strong and yet unable to move the muscles at the fast rate necessary in all track and field events. When Charles Fonville broke the world record for the shot in 1948 at only 195 lb. and 6 ft. 2 in. the reasons given were an "amazing degree of explosive power and quickness of muscle action." Marhold (1974) also maintains that the better shot putters are much faster during the final phase of the put which entails the use of the shoulders and arm. The term "explosive power" therefore becomes important since the aim is not only to have great strength but also to have the speed of movement necessary for athletic success.

Law of Reaction

This law states that to every action there is an equal and opposite reaction. In order for the sprinter to run she must exert a force on the ground which, in turn, exerts an equal and opposite force against the athlete. In mid-air, however, there is nothing to exert a force against, and thus, if something is done with one part of the body, a reaction can be expected somewhere else in the body. For instance, a high jumper using the Fosbury flop style does not drop her head back when attempting to clear her feet over the bar since this would cause her heels to go further underneath the bar and result in it being knocked off. Instead, a coach with some knowledge of mechanics would be able to give the athlete sound advice and tell her to bring her head and shoulders forward which will result in an equal and opposite reaction in the lower limbs and cause them to rise up and over the bar.

An example of minimizing actions (and, thus, reactions) is seen in a new hurdling technique used by some top U.S. hurdlers. Female hurdlers have copied male high hurdlers for numerous years and it seemed reasonable to believe that there was really no difference between the most efficient methods of clearing the high and the low hurdles. The classical style of hurdling with the straight lead arm out in front, the straight lead leg and the lateral-sweeping trail leg is now considered by some coaches to be an inefficient method of hurdle clearance for the 100 m. hurdles. The latter, they maintain, are low enough that the typical lay-out position is not necessary. Some of the top hurdlers in this country are experimenting with a technique of bringing the trail leg through in a normal stepping action and just turning the foot sideways at the last minute to clear the hurdle. In the words of one coach, "You try to bite your knee and turn your toes sideways to the sky." This trail leg technique also has the effect of reducing upper body rotation in reaction to the more orthodox lateral-sweeping trail leg since the limbs are kept as close as possible to the longitudinal axis of the body. No research on hurdling techniques over low hurdles has been done in any detail yet and as a result athletes have again taken the initiative in an attempt to find more efficient methods.

Impulse

Although force in itself is an important factor in athletic performance, the product of the force and the time over which it acts is proving to be an even more significant factor. This combination of force and time is called impulse, and the two factors have a direct bearing on the speed produced at the end of the movement. This is shown in the equation

$$\text{Force} \times \text{Time} = \text{Change in (Mass} \times \text{Speed)}$$

It can be seen from this equation that, if the mass of the athlete or the implement remains constant, the speed may be increased—(a) by exerting a small force over a long time or (b) by exerting a large force over a short time. Recent research suggests that the second method allows generation of a much greater speed. For instance, Gagnon (1975) found that the application of large forces on the starting blocks over short times was one of the most important characteristics of a good start. Cooper (1973) concluded that good long jumpers had much shorter take-off times than less successful jumpers and in the high jump, Lance (1935) concluded from his results that as the athlete jumped higher he spent a shorter time executing the take-off. Nelson *et al* (1976) reached a similar conclusion when they studied the best technique for performing the spike in volleyball—they found that a short ground contact time improved the height that the volleyballers were able to jump. In discussing the two methods for producing vertical velocity by varying the time of application of force, they concluded that:

> Although either of the . . . methods could theoretically yield the same impulse the technique may actually involve a process of optimization from the point of view of energy storage. Since it is hypothesized that a muscle must be actively contracting to store energy, muscle contraction to produce a large reaction force would facilitate the storage of elastic energy. Furthermore, a short time on the plate would limit the loss of elastic energy due to relaxation, thus allowing a greater amount of stored energy to be regained.

In short, the muscles may be better able to use the energy stored by contracting maximally over a short time than by contracting maximally over a longer time. This tends to support what was said earlier—that it was not strength alone that was important in force application but a combination of strength and speed of movement.

PRACTICAL APPLICATIONS

One of the underlying problems with women's track and field in this country is the lack of basic information that may aid the coach in guiding girls into the events for which they have the greatest potential. At the present time most athletes are placed in an event on pure guesswork or by a process of elimination from other events. However, as further information is gained about what our athletes can be expected to do as far as performances are concerned, the task of coaching the female athlete should become somewhat simpler. In the meantime coaches should use the best available scientific knowledge to help them remove some of the guesswork from coaching. For instance, it is a fairly easy process to measure running speed, but the most valuable information would be gained from some measure of maximum speed, since from this information the coach can obtain a good indication as to whether a girl has the potential to be a sprinter or whether she should set her sights on one of the longer races. In order to reach world-class an athlete must be prepared to train very hard for many years and it is essential she be in the event for which she has the most potential.

Measurement of Maximum Speed

A stopwatch and a premeasured distance are all that are necessary for the coach to quickly obtain a measure of the maximum speed of each athlete, and thereby to determine the sprint potential of the team. A distance, which is short enough to insure that speed and not endurance is being measured, should be marked off with a hurdle at the beginning and at the end of the test zone (Figure 1-3). Sixty feet is suggested since this allows more accuracy of timing than a shorter distance. The athlete should be allowed at least a 40-yd. approach so that she has ample time to reach maximum speed prior to reaching the beginning of the 60-ft. test zone.

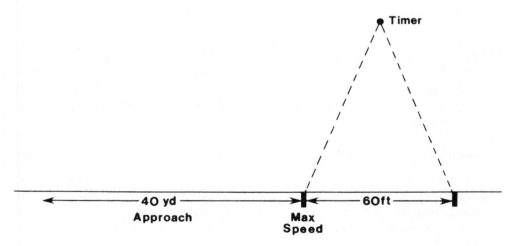

FIGURE *1-3: Measurement* *of maximum speed, stride length and stride frequency*

The athlete is timed over the 60-ft. test distance and the time obtained is matched with the speed chart (Table 1-2). For instance, if an athlete covers the distance in 2.0 sec. then the speed chart indicates that she traveled at 30 ft./sec. Already it is apparent that this particular athlete would probably not make a

Table 1-2: MAXIMUM RUNNING SPEED BASED ON TIME OVER 60 FT*

Time (sec.)	Speed (ft./sec.)
3.5	17.1
3.4	17.7
3.3	18.2
3.2	18.8
3.1	19.4
3.0	20.0
2.9	20.7
2.8	21.4
2.7	22.2
2.6	23.1
2.5	24.0
2.4	25.0
2.3	26.1
2.2	27.3
2.1	28.6
2.0	30.0
1.9	31.6
1.8	33.3
1.7	35.3
1.6	37.5

*Adapted from Nelson and Gregor (1975)

world-class sprinter but does have the speed necessary for a quarter- and a half-miler. Although the effects of ''sharpening'' on speed are still uncertain, it is now possible for each coach to keep a check on the maximum speed of the sprinters. A marked reduction in maximum speed may indicate faulty training programs that should, therefore, be revised.

Measurement of Stride Length and Stride Frequency

Measurements of stride length and stride frequency are also easily obtained and give the coach an even greater insight into the technique optimization of each athlete. An assistant should count the number of strides (to the nearest half stride) taken to cover the 60-ft. distance. The stride length is then obtained by referring to Table 1-3.

The value obtained here can be compared with a predicted stride length that the athlete should be capable of attaining, using height as the criterion. (The obtained stride length should lie between 1.28 and 1.33 times the athlete's height.) Once maximum speed and stride length have been found, stride frequency can be calculated from Table 1-4. The left hand column gives the maximum speed and the numbers at the top of the page indicate the stride length. For example, if an athlete has a maximum speed of 33.3 ft./sec. and a stride length of 7.5 ft., her stride frequency is 4.4 steps/sec.

Table 1-3: *STRIDE LENGTH BASED ON NUMBER OF STRIDES TO RUN 60 FT**

Number of Strides	Stride Length (ft.)
13	4.6
12.5	4.8
12	5.0
11.5	5.2
11	5.5
10.5	5.7
10	6.0
9.5	6.3
9.0	6.7
8.5	7.1
8.0	7.5
7.5	8.0
7.0	8.6
6.5	9.2

*Adapted from Nelson and Gregor (1975)

Table 1-4: *STRIDE FREQUENCY BASED ON RUNNING SPEED AND STRIDE LENGTH IN RUNNING 60 FT.**
(Steps/sec.)

Running Speed (ft./sec.)	Stride Length (ft.)												
	8.6	8.0	7.5	7.1	6.7	6.3	6.0	5.7	5.5	5.2	5.0	4.8	4.6
37.5	4.4	4.7	5.0	5.3	5.6	6.0	6.3	6.6	6.8	7.2	7.5	7.8	8.2
35.3	4.1	4.4	4.7	5.0	5.3	5.6	5.9	6.2	6.5	6.8	7.1	7.4	7.6
33.3	3.9	4.2	4.4	4.7	5.0	5.3	5.6	5.8	6.1	6.4	6.7	6.9	7.2
31.6	3.7	3.9	4.2	4.5	4.7	5.0	5.3	5.5	5.8	6.1	6.3	6.6	6.8
30.0	3.5	3.8	4.0	4.2	4.5	4.8	5.0	5.2	5.5	5.8	6.0	6.2	6.5
28.6	3.3	3.6	3.8	4.0	4.3	4.5	4.8	5.0	5.2	5.5	5.7	6.0	6.2
27.3	3.2	3.4	3.6	3.9	4.1	4.3	4.5	4.8	5.0	5.2	5.5	5.7	5.9
26.1	3.0	3.3	3.5	3.7	3.9	4.1	4.3	4.6	4.8	5.0	5.2	5.4	5.7
25.0	2.9	3.1	3.3	3.5	3.8	4.0	4.2	4.4	4.6	4.8	5.0	5.2	5.4
24.0	2.8	3.0	3.2	3.4	3.6	3.8	4.0	4.2	4.4	4.6	4.8	5.0	5.2
23.1	2.7	2.9	3.1	3.3	3.5	3.7	3.8	4.0	4.2	4.4	4.6	4.8	5.0
22.2	2.6	2.8	3.0	3.2	3.3	3.5	3.7	3.9	4.1	4.3	4.4	4.6	4.8
21.4	2.5	2.7	2.9	3.0	3.2	3.4	3.6	3.8	3.9	4.1	4.3	4.5	4.6
20.7	2.4	2.6	2.8	2.9	3.1	3.3	3.5	3.6	3.8	4.0	4.1	4.3	4.5
20.0	2.3	2.5	2.7	2.8	3.0	3.2	3.3	3.5	3.7	3.8	4.0	4.2	4.3
19.4	2.3	2.4	2.6	2.7	2.9	3.1	3.2	3.4	3.5	3.7	3.9	4.0	4.2
18.8	2.2	2.3	2.5	2.7	2.8	3.0	3.1	3.3	3.4	3.6	3.8	3.9	4.1
18.2	2.1	2.3	2.4	2.6	2.7	2.9	3.0	3.2	3.3	3.5	3.6	3.8	4.0
17.6	2.1	2.2	2.4	2.5	2.6	2.8	2.9	3.1	3.2	3.4	3.5	3.7	3.8
17.1	2.0	2.1	2.3	2.4	2.6	2.7	2.9	3.0	3.1	3.3	3.4	3.6	3.7
16.7	1.9	2.1	2.2	2.4	2.5	2.6	2.8	2.9	3.1	3.2	3.3	3.5	3.6
16.2	1.9	2.0	2.2	2.3	2.4	2.6	2.7	2.8	3.0	3.1	3.2	3.4	3.5
15.8	1.8	2.0	2.1	2.2	2.4	2.5	2.6	2.8	2.9	3.0	3.2	3.3	3.4
15.4	1.8	1.9	2.1	2.2	2.3	2.4	2.6	2.7	2.8	2.9	3.1	3.2	3.3
15.0	1.8	1.9	2.0	2.1	2.2	2.4	2.5	2.6	2.8	2.9	3.0	3.1	3.2

*Adapted from Nelson (1976)

Now the coach has the following information for each of the girls on the team:

1. Maximum speed
2. Stride frequency at maximum speed
3. Predicted stride length at maximum speed
4. Actual stride length at maximum speed

This is the beginning of a biomechanical profile of the athlete and may serve to identify flaws in technique as well as help in picking out the potentially best sprinters on the team. If stride frequency is slow, check heel kickup of the recovery leg, foot placement at touchdown, arm action and perhaps include downhill running in the training program. A short stride length is usually an indication of lack of leg strength and a weight training program should be included to improve this weakness. Nelson (1976) has further suggestions for building on a profile if the coach wishes to gather further information on the team and thereby have a greater insight into each individual runner.

SUMMARY

Some practical applications of biomechanics to track and field have been suggested with a special emphasis on speed and the application of force. It is felt that measurements such as predicted stride length, actual stride length, stride frequency and speed are easily obtained and could contribute a great deal to eliminating errors in technique and to eliminating some of the guesswork of coaching. The art of coaching will never be replaced since this is a human element, but there is no doubt that coaches of women's track and field in this country need to make some effort to find possible sources of error that may be contributing to the lack of international success.

Emily Haymes

PHYSIOLOGICAL CONSIDERATIONS

Author: **Emily Haymes** is an assistant professor in the Department of Physical Education at the University of Colorado. A graduate of Drury College, Missouri (A.B.), Florida State University, Tallahassee (M.S.) and Pennsylvania State University (Ph.D.), she is actively engaged in research on physiological problems of concern to women in sport.

In order to excel in athletics the body must function at a maximal level. Muscles must contract with an optimal force at precisely the right time in events demanding explosive power. In events lasting more than a few seconds, the cardiovascular and respiratory systems must assist the muscles in carrying out their prescribed tasks. With prolonged activity, the body's store of nutrients becomes important. In warm weather, the excretory system plays a major role in maintaining body temperature during performance.

Physiology is the study of the functioning of the body. Exercise physiology is the study of how the body functions during exercise, of how functions change due to training, and of the effects of body functioning on performance. This chapter is intended primarily as a review of basic exercise physiology and research related specifically to track and field.

MUSCLE FUNCTION

The function unit of the muscle is the motor unit composed of a single motor neuron and the muscle fibers innervated by it. In muscles that are involved primarily in gross movements (e.g., rectus femoris, vastus lateralis) a motor neuron will innervate hundreds of muscle fibers. Muscles that are involved in very fine movements (e.g., muscles of the eye) will have only a few muscle fibers innervated by a motor neuron.

Each muscle fiber is a single cell. Contained within the muscle fiber are myofilaments composed of two proteins, actin and myosin, and mitochondria which supply most of the high energy phosphates necessary for contraction. According to the Huxley Sliding Filament Theory, the actual contraction of the muscle occurs when crossbridges link the proteins actin and myosin and the actin slides over the myosin. The sliding together of the proteins allows the overall length of the muscle fiber to decrease.

In order to supply the energy for contraction, a high energy phosphate (ATP) must break off one of its phosphate groups:

$$ATP \rightarrow ADP + P_i + energy$$

The splitting of the bond between the phosphate and the remainder of the ATP molecule results in the liberation of a tremendous amount of energy, only a fraction of which will be used for the actual contraction.

Only a very small amount of ATP is stored in the muscle fiber. It is necessary to resynthesize ATP for sustained muscle contractions. Another high energy phosphate compound, creatine phosphate (CP), is also stored in the muscle and is used in the resynthesis of ATP:

$$ADP + CP \rightarrow APT + creatine$$

There is enough ATP and creatine phosphate stored in the muscles to supply the energy for a few seconds of exercise.

Glycogen is also normally stored within each muscle fiber. Glycogen is composed of glucose units which are strung together and is the storage form for carbohydrates within the body. Through a series of chemical reactions called glycolysis, glycogen is broken down to a simpler compound called pyruvic acid. If there is no oxygen present in the muscle fiber, pyruvic acid will be converted to lactic acid. The small amount of energy liberated during glycolysis will resynthesize a small amount of ATP. Since oxygen is not needed to form lactic acid or in the breakdown of ATP and creatine phosphate these processes are anaerobic.

The accumulation of lactic acid within the muscle in some way interferes with the contraction process. Only a limited amount of lactic acid can be tolerated before the muscle fatigues.

In the presence of oxygen, pyruvic acid will break down completely to carbon dioxide and water in the mitochondria with the liberation of a large amount of energy and the synthesis of 18 to 19 times as much ATP as occurs when lactic acid is produced. Because oxygen must be present, the complete breakdown of pyruvic acid to carbon dioxide and water is an aerobic process.

Field events (e.g., high jump, shot put, javelin throw) which are explosive power events lasting only a few seconds rely exclusively on the breakdown of ATP and creatine phosphate for energy. The resynthesis of the high energy phosphates will occur during the rest period between trials. The sprints are largely anaerobic with the breakdown of glycogen to lactic acid for energy. As the distance increases the amount of energy that must be supplied aerobically increases. Events lasting 1 min. (400 m.) are approximately 60% anaerobic and 40% aerobic while those lasting 2 min. (800 m.) are approximately 40% anaerobic and 60% aerobic (Gollnick and Hermansen, 1973). The mile is approximately 80% aerobic and events lasting 10 min. or longer are supplied over 90% by aerobic processes.

There are two types of fibers in human muscles. White muscle fibers are fast twitch fibers and red fibers are slow twitch (slow contractile speed). Individual muscles are a mixture of the two types of fibers with some muscles being predominantly red and others predominantly white. Red muscle fibers have a high aerobic capacity and a low anaerobic capacity which means they must be supplied with oxygen so that glycogen can be completely broken down. White muscle fibers have a high anaerobic capacity which means these fibers work quite well in the absence of oxygen. Samples of tissue from selected muscles indicated that the percentage of slow twitch fibers is about 60% in athletes involved in endurance activities (i.e., swimming, running, cycling). Weight lifters were found to have approximately equal numbers of the two types of fibers (Saltin, 1973).

The actual number of slow twitch and fast twitch fibers cannot be changed through training. Endurance type training will cause the slow twitch (red) fibers to increase in size and aerobic capacity. Anaerobic training will increase the size of the fast twitch (white) fibers and their anaerobic capacity. Genetics determines whether a person has the potential to be good in endurance or power type activities. Proper training allows the athlete to reach full potential.

Strength is the force exerted by the muscles. *Power* is the force exerted times the distance moved and divided by the time it takes to complete the movement. The faster a movement can be completed the greater the power. Throwing and jumping events demand explosive power. The shorter sprints are also power events. Two sprinters of equal body weight run 50 m. The sprinter with the faster time has the greater power because the force necessary to lift the body weight is equal as is the distance moved.

Because all of the field events are power events, strength is a very important factor in these events. Strength is also an important factor in sprinting. The cross section of the muscle is directly proportional to the strength. There appears to be little difference qualitatively between the strength of males and females, although quantitatively males have greater strength due to their greater amount of muscle tissue. When the muscle increases in strength, the diameter of the muscle fiber increases. Both the protein content and the sacroplasm of the muscle fiber increase.

Training for strength involves the overload principle. The muscle must be stressed in order to increase in strength. In practice there are several different methods of strength training. One of the most popular forms is progressive resistance exercise. Weight training belongs in this category. Some women athletes have avoided weight training because they do not wish to develop bulky muscles. Wilmore (1974) found smaller increases in the girth of the arms and shoulders of women after ten weeks of weight lifting than among men. Similar increases in relative body strength were found in both groups. The largest gain in girth for the women was 0.6 cm. or 0.25 in. The reason for the smaller increase in muscle size in the female is most likely the very small amount of the sex hormone testosterone present in the female. Males produce far greater quantities of testosterone, a hormone which stimulates the growth of muscle tissue. It is unlikely that lifting weights or other forms of strength training will increase the muscle bulk of the female to the same extent as the male.

Flexibility training can also be beneficial to track and field performers. Flexibility exercises stretch the connective tissue covering the muscle. The range of motion at the joint increases and it is believed the length of stride may be increased. Research findings have not always found improved running perform- ance following flexibility training. Positive results are more likely to be found if flexibility training is used in addition to rather than instead of sprint training.

Increasing the temperature of the muscle decreases the viscosity of the tissue. This lowers the resistance to movement and is the physiological basis of warming up. Warm-up is also thought to lower the resistance to stretching in the antagonis- tic muscles and thus to prevent injury. Unfortunately research studies have not supported warm-up as either improving performance or preventing injury. The beneficial aspect of warm-up may in part be psychological. In any event, warm- up should not be abandoned as nonessential. One case in which warm-up may be detrimental is warming up extensively before a long distance event on a hot day which will raise the body temperature. Further increase in temperature during the race may lead to the development of hyperthermia, a topic to be discussed in a later section.

CARDIOVASCULAR AND RESPIRATORY FUNCTION

As long as the exercise (event) can be performed anaerobically no particular strain is placed on the cardiovascular and respiratory systems. When the muscles' demand for oxygen increases, both the cardiovascular and respiratory systems become involved. The respiratory system is responsible for exchanging gases between the air and the blood. Oxygen is taken in and carbon dioxide is removed. Increasing the intensity of exercise results in an increase in lung ventilation. Once the oxygen enters the blood, transport to the muscles is the function of the cardiovascular system.

The oxygen taken up by the muscles is dependent upon the amount of blood flowing through the muscles and the amount of oxygen extracted from the blood. Blood flowing through the muscles is determined by the amount of blood pumped out of the heart and the percentage of the flow which is distributed to the muscles. Cardiac output, the amount of blood pumped out of the heart per minute, is equal to the heart rate times the stroke volume, the amount of blood pumped out of the heart per beat. Within limits, an increase in intensity of exercise results in an increase in cardiac output. Both stroke volume and heart rate increase initially but the stroke volume levels off. Heart rate will continue to increase as the intensity of the exercise increases.

Distribution of blood flow changes as the intensity of the exercise increases. At rest only 15 to 20% of the blood flow is distributed to the muscles. During exercise as much as 80 to 85% of the blood flow will be distributed to the muscles and skin. This is accomplished by reducing the amount of blood sent to the kidneys and organs of the digestive system. The end result of both an increase in cardiac output and the redistribution of blood flow is a much larger blood flow through the muscles during exercise and a greater oxygen supply to the muscles.

The amount of oxygen removed from the blood by the muscle is determined by the percentage of oxygen extracted (coefficient of utilization) and the amount of oxygen carried in the blood. The coefficient of utilization. increases as the demand for oxygen in the muscle increases. Oxygen content of the blood is determined by the hemoglobin content of the blood. Men carry approximately 15.5 g. hemoglobin per 100 ml. blood while the average woman has only 14 g. hemoglobin per 100 ml. blood. In order to compensate for the lower oxygen content of the blood, the female must increase cardiac output or increase the coefficient of utilization to achieve the same oxygen uptake as the male. For a given intensity of exercise the female may have a slightly higher heart rate. On the basis of available data, the maximal oxygen uptake will be reached sooner by the female and at a lower intensity of exercise.

Training of the cardiovascular system increases the cardiac output and the amount of oxygen removed from the blood by the muscles. The increase in cardiac output is due to an increase in stroke volume as maximal heart rate remains relatively constant. Resting stroke volume also increases with training, resulting in a lower heart rate at rest. Trained individuals will be able to work at the same intensity as in the untrained state with a low heart rate after training. Again this is due to a larger stroke volume. The reason training increases stroke volume is that the cardiac muscle is strengthened. A stronger cardiac muscle allows the heart to pump more blood with each beat. As discussed earlier, increases in the amount of oxygen removed from the blood by the muscle are related to the increase in aerobic capacity of the muscle with training.

Endurance training which is begun before puberty results in larger heart and lung volumes (Astrand *et al.*, 1963). Girls who have participated in age group track programs before puberty may have an advantage in events requiring predominantly aerobic capacity because of their larger cardiac output.

During exercise the stroke volume increases as the blood flow through the veins back to the heart increases. This is aided by contraction of skeletal muscles which help push the blood back to the heart. At the end of strenuous exercise with the majority of blood flow in the muscles and skin, the pumping action of the skeletal muscles is lost if the athlete comes to a complete standstill. This will reduce the blood flow back to the heart and stroke volume will decrease rapidly. If not enough blood is pumped out of the heart to supply the brain, the athlete will faint. To avoid this situation the athlete should continue to move at the end of a race, either jogging or walking for several minutes. The longer the race the more time that will need to be spent cooling down because the body temperature will be higher in the longer races and more blood vessels in the skin will have dilated.

TRAINING THE ATHLETE

The particular type of training necessary for each event is dealt with more completely in the remaining chapters of this book. There are, however, some general principles which pertain to all the events. Training can best be accomplished by overloading the system. This principle has already been discussed with respect to strength. It applies equally well to training the ATP-creatine phosphate, lactic acid and aerobic systems.

Training is specific. Strength can be improved by lifting weights, but repetition of the movements in the shot put and high jump is necessary to gain maximal use of this strength. Through repetition of the movement, neuromuscular coordination is improved. The proper timing of the muscle contractions can only be gained by repeating the movement. An example is the shot putter who lifts weights to increase upper body strength. Strength will be gained on both the left and right sides, but the side normally used will still be superior in the shot put. Strength training should be used in addition to rather than in place of practice in the event.

Specificity of training also applies to the anaerobic and aerobic systems. The hurdler who has just completed the basketball season will still have to get in shape for track because of the different sets of muscles involved and the longer distance to be sprinted. Overdistance training will improve aerobic capacity but will not help the distance runner develop a kick at the end of the race.

The amount of time devoted to aerobic and anaerobic training depends on the event. Events lasting only a few seconds rely on the ATP-creatine phosphate system for energy. This system can be trained by repeated bouts of activity with short rest pauses between bouts. Since nearly all of the field events involve the development of power in the legs, (e.g., approach in the long jump, high jump, javelin) repeated short sprints will aid this development. Repeats of 50 m. sprints will improve the use of the ATP-creatine phosphate system (Mathews and Fox, 1971). The speed of the sprint should be approximately 1.5 sec. slower than the individual's best time for 50 m. from a running start (Wilt, 1968). Rest intervals between bouts should be long enough for the heart rate to drop below 140 beats per min. (Mathews and Fox, 1971).

Lengthening the distance to 100 and 200 m. will improve not only the ATP-creatine phosphate system but also the body's ability to use lactic acid. The time for completing the sprint should also be increased as the distance increases. For 200 m. the individual should add 5 sec. to her best time from a running start (Wilt, 1968). The heart rate should reach 180 beats per min. at the end of each sprint. Heart rates should be allowed to drop below 140 beats per min. between intervals. The number of repeats is determined by the distance. At least 1.5 miles should be covered for the greatest effect (Mathews and Fox, 1971). This would require 24 100 m. repeats or 12 200 m. repeats.

Intervals of up to 1000 m. can be used to improve anaerobic capacity. Time for the interval should be a little slower than the runner's best time for that distance but fast enough to achieve a heart rate of 180 beats per min. Longer intervals will also tax the aerobic system. Improvements in aerobic capacity can be achieved through both interval training and overdistance work.

Distance is the key to the percentage of time that should be devoted to a particular type of training. Table 2-1 outlines the percentage of time alloted to each type of training according to the distance run. For example, 100 and 200 m. sprinters should devote 95% of their time to speed work and developing the ATP-creatine phosphate system, 3% of their time developing speed and the lactic acid system and 2% to training the aerobic system (Wilt, 1968). Training for 1500 m. necessitates 20% speed work, 55% anaerobic work and 25% aerobic work.

Very little research has been conducted on training young women athletes. Based on findings using young men, improvement in aerobic capacity is directly related to the intensity of the training sessions, i.e., the higher the heart rate during training the greater the improvement. This means that young runners doing overdistance training at a heart rate of 180 beats per min. will improve their aerobic capacity more than runners working at a heart rate of 160 beats per min. if the same distance is run by both groups. If the runners working at 160 beats per min. increase the distance of the run, similar improvements in aerobic capacity will occur. Duration of the training session is also important. If the intensity of the training is held constant, increasing the duration will increase the improvement in aerobic capacity.

Table 2-1: RECOMMENDATIONS FOR TRAINING EMPHASIS ACCORDING TO RACE DISTANCE*

Event	Speed %	Aerobic Endurance %	Anaerobic Endurance %
Marathon	5	90	5
10,000 m.	5	80	15
5000 m.	10	70	20
3000 m.	20	40	40
1500 m.	20	25	55
800 m.	30	5	65
400 m.	80	5	15
200 m.	95	3	2
100 m.	95	2	3

*Adapted from Wilt (1968).

How frequently one should train is still an unanswered question. Many world-class runners train twice daily seven days a week. Improvements in aerobic capacity occur with two training sessions per week. Increasing the frequency of training to four or five times per week increases the improvement.

Many female athletes are only in training for track a few months each year. When training stops, detraining begins even though the female may be participating in recreational activities. Drinkwater and Horvath (1972) found that three months after the track season had ended, the aerobic capacity of a group of female runners had declined 18% and was no different than that of the average female of the same age. Some type of maintenance program is desirable in the months when active practice is not being held to avoid this effect.

Overtraining is a problem faced by many coaches and athletes. It is often referred to as staleness. The exact physiological mechanism involved is unclear but it may be related to the Stage of Exhaustion in Selye's General Adaptation Syndrome. The body is no longer able to resist the stress imposed upon it by training and the athlete appears to be exhausted. Symptoms include failure of the heart rate to drop below 140 beats per min. between intervals, failure of the heart rate to return to normal after overdistance runs, and poorer times and performances in the various events. The only cure is rest. An athlete should discontinue the workout for that day and either rest for several days or severely reduce the intensity and duration of the workout for several days.

GYNECOLOGICAL CONSIDERATIONS

Surveys of women athletes indicate that the menstrual cycle is normal in 85% of the women [Erdeli (1962), Zaharieva (1965)]. Only a few of the young women reported absence of the menses with hard training (Erdelyi, 1962). Menstrual irregularities were more frequent in the younger competitors. Greater than normal flows were reported by 15% of the women athletes during training while 58% reported that they sometimes had dysmenorrhea (Zaharieva, 1965).

Zaharieva (1965) reported that among women athletes competing in the 1964 Tokyo Olympics, competition during the menses had no effect on performance in 37% of the women, a variable effect on 28%, and always a bad effect on 17% of the participants. Poorer performances in the premenstrual period were reported by 15% of the women. In Erdelyi's survey of a much larger sample of Hungarian women athletes, 45% of the women competing during the menses reported no effect on performance, 14% reported better performances and 33% reported poorer performances. More of the Hungarian women reported poorer performances during the premenstrual period and better performances in the postmenstrual period. During the premenstrual period there will likely be a greater retention of water by the body which may affect performance. The change in hormone levels immediately before the menses may also affect the emotional state of the competitor. Responses during different phases of the cycle vary among individuals, and the coach should deal with each athlete individually.

There is little evidence that hard physical training has a detrimental effect on pregnancy and childbirth [Erdelyi (1962), Zaharieva (1965)]. Over 90% of the women athletes surveyed by Zaharieva reported normal pregnancies. Training was continued for the first 3 to 4 months of pregnancy by many of the Hungarian women, with fewer threatened abortions than in the normal population (Erdelyi, 1962). Many women athletes resume training 2 to 3 months after childbirth.

NUTRITIONAL CONSIDERATIONS

There are no magic formulas for success in athletics. The list of foods and food supplements tried by athletes in search of the magic formula to improve performance is quite lengthy. Routine vitamin supplementation is expensive and of little value and has led to the observation that American athletes have the "richest urine in the world." Vitamin supplements are valuable if an athlete is deficient in one or more vitamins. For most athletes a well-balanced diet will provide all the nutrients, vitamins and minerals necessary with a few exceptions.

Increasing the activity level during training increases the energy expenditure of the athlete. Normally the appetite increases to balance the increased expenditure of calories. If dietary intake does not increase, the athlete will begin to lose weight. An increase in weight usually indicates an increase in lean body tissue and many women athletes will lose fat and gain lean tissue during training (Lundegren, 1968). With the increase in caloric intake, an increase in vitamin intake is also required, since many of the vitamins are used in the metabolism of food. If the diet is well-balanced the vitamin intake will increase naturally. The daily protein requirement for the growing girl is 2 g. protein per kg. body weight. Mature women athletes need 1 g. protein per kg. body weight.

The mineral most likely to be deficient in the female is iron. The average woman needs 15 mg. iron in her diet daily. Women need 50% more iron than men to replace the amount lost in the menses. Heavy menstrual flow indicates greater iron loss and an increased iron requirement in the diet. Surveys of the dietary intake of iron among American females reported that the average intake was 11 to 12 mg. iron per day (White, 1968). Over a period of time, failure to replace iron lost will result in depletion of the body's iron stores and eventually a reduction in the formation of hemoglobin. Lowering the hemoglobin level will reduce the oxygen carrying capacity of the blood and the individual's aerobic capacity. Impairment of aerobic performance occurs in athletes when the hemoglobin levels drop below normal. Approximately 25% of a sample of highly trained U.S. women field hockey players were found to be deficient in iron and their performance on a maximal aerobic capacity test was affected by the lower hemoglobin concentrations.

It is highly recommended that women athletes who are deficient in iron or hemoglobin take iron supplements. There is some suspicion that hard training may increase the destruction of hemoglobin or increase the loss of iron and result in lower hemoglobin concentrations. Regular checks should be made of all women training for the middle and long distance events to determine if it is advisable to supplement their diets with iron, since these events rely to a greater extent on the aerobic capacity.

Diets high in carbohydrates are beneficial during the 48 hours preceding the event. Hard training which completely depletes the muscles of their stored glycogen immediately before going on the high carbohydrate diet will increase the amount of glycogen stored in the muscles. This type of dietary manipulation is an advantage to all runners—especially if several events are to be performed and the runner may have to compete in heats as well as the final. Glycogen is the fuel used exclusively during anaerobic work. Use of glycogen increases the closer the runner is to working at her maximal aerobic capacity.

Greater amounts of glycogen can be stored if the runner eats a diet high in fat and protein for a few days prior to switching to the high carbohydrate diet. During the high fat and protein diet the muscles will be in a glycogen depleted state which will impair training. Since it takes approximately two hours of hard running to deplete the glycogen stores, the only runners who should seriously consider the high fat and protein diet are those engaged in long distances such as the marathon. When running at a slower pace as in the longer distances fat as well as glycogen supplies the energy needed.

There is no advantage to staying on a high carbohydrate diet all of the time and there may be a disadvantage. The body normally burns both carbohydrates and fats to supply its daily energy needs. Continuation of a high carbohydrate diet may result in a shift to glycogen as the exclusive source of energy. This could result in a more rapid depletion of the glycogen stores during running.

It may be wise for jumpers to avoid using the high carbohydrate diet before competition. According to Astrand and Rodahl (1970), increasing the storage of glycogen results in increased water storage in the muscle which would increase body weight. This could be an important factor in events in which the body weight must be lifted, e.g., high jump, long jump.

The pre-event meal can be almost anything the athlete enjoys eating and digests easily. Eating 3 to 4 hours before the event allows food to clear the stomach. If the meal is light and primarily carbohydrate in nature it can be eaten within 1 hour of the event without any detrimental effects on performance. Foods to avoid in the pre-event meal include those high in fat which slow digestion and those which produce gas.

ENVIRONMENTAL CONSIDERATIONS

Running on a hot day presents an additional problem. During exercise only about one quarter of the energy released by the muscles is used to do work and the remainder is converted to heat which raises the temperature of the body. On a cool day this excess body heat is lost to the environment. Running produces air currents past the body which aid in the heat loss. Heat loss also occurs through the evaporation of sweat.

On days when the air temperature nears or exceeds body temperature (90°F and above), body heat cannot be lost to the environment except through evaporation of sweat. Heat may even be gained through radiation directly from the sun or indirectly off stadium walls, synthetic tracks and roadways. This puts more of a strain on the individual runner, causes increased sweating and increased loss of body fluids. Unless sweating can keep pace with the gain in heat, body temperature will rise, possibly to dangerously high levels.

Even on days when the temperature is not as high (70° and 80° F) but the humidity is quite high, the body will be under more of a strain during exercise. Although the movement of air across the skin will help remove heat, the high moisture content of the air will prevent most of the sweat from evaporating. This allows the body temperature to rise. The same type of effect can be produced by wearing a sweat suit or clothing that is impermeable to moisture. The relative humidity of the air next to the skin will be 100% and no evaporation will take place.

Coaches and athletes should become familiar with the signs of hyperthermia (heat stroke, heat exhaustion). The symptoms of heat stroke are elevated body temperature (105°F), dry skin, chills, tachycardia, and unconsciousness (Buskirk and Grasley, 1974). There are two forms of heat exhaustion: water depletion, which is due to excessive loss of body fluids, and salt depletion, which is due to the failure to replace salt lost through excessive sweating. Symptoms of water depletion heat exhaustion are excessive weight loss with reduced sweating, excessive thirst, weakness, lack of appetite and elevated body temperature. Salt depletion heat exhaustion symptoms include headache, dizziness, fatigue, nausea, muscle cramps and fainting (Buskirk and Grasley, 1974). If such symptoms occur, training should cease and treatment should begin immediately. The team trainer should be equipped to handle the problems of hyperthermia. If heat stroke is suspected, body temperature should be lowered by immersing the individual in water, packing her with ice or sponging the body with alcohol or water. Medical assistance will be needed.

Attention to several precautionary measures should prevent most hyperthermia cases from occurring. Athletes who have not been exercising in the heat are the most likely candidates for heat problems. This is particularly true of the late summer-early fall programs for track and cross country if the runners have not been training during the summer. Runners who have had a fever due to an infection or who recently received an immunization which caused a fever are also susceptible because body temperature regulation will not be normal. Athletes who have had recent episodes of vomiting or diarrhea should be held out of training until body fluid balance has returned to normal. The coach and trainer should be aware of any athlete who has a history of heat illness.

When training on hot or humid days, frequent rest breaks should be taken. Water or fluids containing salt should be readily available and athletes should be encouraged to drink them. Most athletes will only drink until their thirst is quenched and will not replace the body fluid lost (Costill *et al.*, 1970). Athletes should also be encouraged to add extra salt to their food. Clothing should be loose fitting, lightweight and absorbent. Warm-up suits should be avoided.

The American College of Sports Medicine (1975) has issued a position statement on distance races of 16 km. (10 miles) or longer. Races of this length should not be held when the wet bulb globe temperature index exceeds 82.4°F (28°C). The wet bulb globe temperature index is a combination of wet bulb temperature which measures humidity, globe temperature which measures radiation, and dry bulb temperature which measures air temperature. (WBGT = 0.7 wet bulb temperature + 0.2 globe temperature + 0.1 dry bulb temperature.) During those months of the year when ambient temperature often exceeds 80°F it is recommended that distance races should not be scheduled between 9 a.m. and 4 p.m. This was the reason for the late afternoon start of the marathon at the Montreal Olympics. Ten to fifteen minutes before the race, runners should consume 400 to 500 ml. of fluid (approx. 1 pint). Water stations should be provided by the race sponsors every 3.5 to 4 km. (2 to 2.5 miles).

Hypothermia may present a problem if training is done outside in cold weather. Lowering of body temperature will occur if body heat is lost rapidly. If clothing becomes soaked with sweat or wet from rain or snow, body heat will be lost at a faster rate than normal. During very cold weather the wearing of wool mittens and a wool knit cap on the head will cut down the heat loss. Runners should be advised to watch for signs of frostbite, especially if it is cold and windy. Signs of hypothermia include shivering, loss of coordination and drowsiness.

Altitudes of 1600 m. (one mile) above sea level and greater present problems in the middle and long distance (Astrand and Rodahl, 1970). The atmospheric pressure is reduced enough at these altitudes to lower the amount of oxygen that will be picked up by the blood in the lungs. Times in events longer than 1500 m. will be slower in places such as Boulder, Colorado (altitude 1630 m.). At higher altitudes such as Mexico City (2260 m. above sea level) times will be slower for events 800 m. and longer (Astrand and Rodahl, 1970). Field events and the sprints will have an advantage at higher altitudes because of the lower air resistance. Runners from sea level competing in the longer distances will be at a disadvantage when competing above 1600 m. against opponents who are acclimatized to the altitude.

3 Penny McCullagh

SOCIAL-PSYCHOLOGICAL CONSIDERATIONS*

Author: **Penny McCullagh** is an Assistant Professor in the Department of Physical Education at the University of California, Davis. A graduate of the State University of New York, Brockport (B.S.), the University of Washington (M.S.) and the University of Wisconsin (Ph.D.), she is actively engaged in research on the social psychology of motor behavior.

The purpose of this chapter is to review a number of social-psychological variables that can influence a track and field athlete. Social-psychological variables are those factors which influence an individual's behavior as a result of interaction with at least one other person. This interaction may actually occur or merely be anticipated by the individual. The primary emphasis of this chapter is on (a) whether actual performance is affected by the variables discussed and (b) what importance these effects may have on coaching and teaching track and field. Topics such as the presence of others, arousal, cooperation and competition, motivation, demonstration, and the use of verbal comments are included because performance has been shown to be affected by these variables.

Much of the work investigating these factors has been conducted in controlled laboratory settings. Therefore it is oftentimes difficult to prescribe principles that will necessarily hold true in the more erratic environment of an athletic competition. In general, the research evidence has not shown males and females to be extremely or consistently divergent with respect to the influence of these variables. Unless specifically noted, we will presume their influence to be similar

---
*Extreme appreciation is extended to Stephen A. Wallace who made valuable comments through the preparation of this chapter. Some of the practical examples were supplied by Sue Cumnock, Womens' Track Coach, University of California, Davis; and Peter Tegen, Womens' Track Coach, University of Wisconsin, Madison.

on both sexes. No attempt will be made to prescribe specific principles for track and field or other sports. This precaution is taken because many of the ideas reviewed have not been firmly established within experimental settings. Those ideas that have received considerable support have not been adequately tested in naturalistic sport settings. Rather, examples will be given so you can question and experiment with the topics presented.

PRESENCE OF OTHERS

A track and field athlete is required to perform in the presence of other team members and opponents as well as interested spectators. Therefore, it is of interest to determine the effects, if any, that these other people may have on the performance of athletes. In the case of a running event, for example, many people believe that running with another person enhances an athlete's performance. On the other hand, the presence of another person may distract an athlete's attention and cause her to lose pace.

The research evidence available to aid in answering the above issues has been almost entirely conducted in laboratory settings with novel tasks or in very controlled field settings. The subject groups have been fairly restricted and the types of spectator groups (e.g., size, position from subject, etc.) have been quite limited. Therefore applications of the research findings to larger audiences who yell and cheer at a sporting event need to be cautious indeed. It is likely that many of the concerns reviewed here will have more application to practice sessions where the coach can control the presence of others than to actual meet conditions. Some specific track and field situations will be given, but it will be the coach's duty to extract and extend these ideas and experiment with them during the season.

The term social facilitation is commonly used to describe the effect that the presence of others may have on performance and includes two experimental paradigms. Within the audience paradigm an individual is observed by other persons while performing on an individual task (e.g., shot put, discus, high jump, javelin, long jump) whereas a coaction paradigm is created when more than one individual independently performs at the same time on the same task (e.g., running hurdles). In experimentally investigating audience and coaction effects, the influence of extraneous variables is kept to a minimum. Therefore audience members are usually passive and do not interact with the performers. Similarly external factors such as competition and rivalry from coactors are reduced as much as possible.

Although numerous social facilitation investigations occurred in the early part of the century, there was little in the way of theories or hypotheses to guide the researchers' inquiries. Then in 1965, Zajonc attempted to bring coherency to the previous literature and provide testable hypotheses. He did so by proposing a drive theory explanation to account for performance changes in the presence of others. Simply stated, Zajonc's social facilitation hypothesis suggested that the presence of either audience members or coactors produces an increased level of arousal or activation in the individual, which in turn leads to an enhancement of dominant responses. During early learning of a task it is presumed that many more incorrect than correct responses will be made. Thus during these initial trials the incorrect response would be considered dominant and the presence of others would lead to increased incorrect responses; hence, a decrement in performance. Once the task is well learned, the correct response would be dominant. The presence of others would then lead to increased arousal, which would cause more correct responses by the athlete. In this case the presence of others should lead to performance improvements. In the years that followed, numerous studies attempted to test Zajonc's hypothesis in both coaction and audience paradigms.

Coaction

A recent field experiment by Obermeir, Landers and Ester (1976) investigated the effect of running alone versus coaction on 440 yd. dash performances. Predictions were made on the basis of Zajonc's social facilitation hypothesis. Since the male athletes who participated in this study were teenagers who had been in numerous track and field meets, it seemed reasonable to assume that for these subjects running was a correct dominant response. Therefore, according to the hypothesis, athletes running with a coactor should evidence faster times than would these same athletes when running alone. Such an effect would be a result of increased arousal in the presence of others. Results for total running times were in direct support of this prediction. Subjects in the coaction conditions ran 2.2 to 2.5 sec. faster than alone subjects. This result was statistically significant as well as practically important. Analysis of the 110 yd. split times revealed that, regardless of whether subjects were alone or with coactors, their times were not different for either the first or fourth split. However, coacting runners were faster than alone runners in both the second and third splits.

The Obermeir *et al.* study was also interested in performance dependent on lane assignment. Generally, it is thought that athletes have an advantage on the inside lane, since they are provided with visual cues from the outside lane runners during staggered starts. Unfortunately, research studies have not attempted to substantiate this claim. One German study (Bradtke & Oberste, 1975) measured reaction time for athletes leaving the starting blocks and found a slight advantage for those occupying inner lanes. However, the differences were only slight and disappeared when starting signals of considerable intensity were given to all runners simultaneously. In order to test possible lane differences, Obermeir *et al.* compared the variability of each 110 yd. split as well as total running time when athletes were placed on the inside (Lane 2) and outside (Lane 4) lanes.

The notion that lane assignment would produce differences in total running time was not substantiated, since runners performed similarly when on the inside and outside lane. As mentioned before, both coaction conditions produced faster times than times when running alone. The hypothesis that inside lane runners would be more consistent in their 110 yd. splits was also not supported. In fact subjects who ran alone seemed to be the most consistent. However, when runners were asked at the end of the experiment in which condition they preferred to run, subjects preferred the inside lane the most and the outside lane the least. The alone condition fell between. This inside lane preference could be attributed to the fact that in the past coaches have thought the inside positions to be the best.

The above study suggests that running with a coactor produces faster 440 times than running alone. Since athletes in the above experiment were not encouraged to compete against each other, the results may be more applicable to practice as opposed to meet situations. Nevertheless, over 2 sec. reduction in running time seems a tremendous gain in performance and certainly one worth striving for. It may be best to have runners practice at least in pairs for the various track events. If consistency of 110 yd. splits is a specific goal, it seems as though subjects can do this best when alone, at the expense of running slower however. Extended practice pacing alongside others seems to be needed. It would also have been interesting to test the above subjects in a competitive situation to determine if performance could be enhanced even further.

In the above coaction setting, subjects were encouraged not to compete, and rivalry and competition were therefore kept at a minimum. A very early social facilitation study with cyclists introduced a competitive element and similar results were found. In 1897, Triplett had the notion that cyclists performed faster in the presence of other people than when alone. To examine this notion, Triplett compared bicycle racing records for three different types of events—individual efforts, paced efforts behind humans who set the pace and competitive events. Comparison of these events indicated that competitive events were faster than paced events and paced events were in turn considerably faster than conditions wherein the bicyclists rode alone. The comparisons made here are abstracted from a natural sport setting and therefore there were a number of extraneous variables that could have influenced the results. For example, the coach was the last rider on the pacing machine, and spectators shouted encouragement to the riders. In order to control some of these extraneous variables, Triplett designed an experimental laboratory study in which subjects turned fishing reels as fast as possible. They performed either alone or in direct competition with another person. Results were in the same direction as the previously reported cycling results. Subjects performed faster with others as compared to the alone situation.

From the above coaction findings, it seems that for tasks that are well learned (cycling, running) or for very simple tasks (fishing reel winding), the presence of coactors leads to enhancement of these dominant correct responses and hence results in improved performance. If a subject is initially learning a difficult task, however, the results are in the opposite direction. A laboratory experiment by Hunt and Hillery (1973) required subjects to learn a complex maze task. Each subject performed in the presence of two other coactors but shields prevented view of each other's apparatus. Since the task was complex it was presumed that the dominant response during early learning would be incorrect. According to Zajonc's prediction the presence of others should cause decrement in performance. Results were clearly supportive of the prediction. Together subjects performed worse than alone subjects during early learning of a complex task.

The implications of the above experiments for track and field settings are obvious. During the early training season when athletes are learning new skills or perfecting techniques, the influence of the presence of coactors, especially competitive coactors, should be kept at a minimum. Once the skills are well learned and perfected, then athletes may practice alongside other teammates. To improve performance it does not seem necessary that the individuals compete against one another.

Audience

Support for Zajonc's predictions have also been found in audience paradigms. Martens (1969) conducted a laboratory experiment in which subjects were required to accurately learn a timed task. While initially learning this task subjects performed either alone or in the presence of a passive audience and TV camera (Martens, 1968, p. 45). Once the task was reasonably well learned, the alone and audience groups were divided for the second phase of the experiment. Half of each group performed in the presence of an audience and the other half performed alone.

The results were extremely supportive of Zajonc's hypothesis. During early trials, when subjects were initially learning the task (dominant response incorrect), alone subjects performed better than subjects in the presence of an audience. Once the task was well learned (dominant response correct), the presence of an audience enhanced performance above the level achieved by alone subjects. Martens also measured subjects' arousal level by taking samples of each subject's palmar sweat. According to Zajonc, the presence of others produces arousal increments, which in turn leads to the enhancement of dominant responses. In both early learning trials and later learning trials, it was found that subjects in the presence of an audience had a higher degree of sweating than subjects who performed alone. Besides physiological measures, questionnaires have also been used to assess arousal increments in the presence of an audience (McCullagh & Landers, 1976). For a further discussion of arousal, the readers are referred to the following section of this chapter.

Within the audience paradigm, evidence which seems to negate Zajonc's hypothesis has also been reported. Paulus, Shannon, Wilson and Boone (1972) examined the influence of spectators on the gymnastic performance of students enrolled in an advanced class. On the first day of testing all subjects performed alone and on the second day of testing half of the subjects performed alone while the other half performed in the presence of an audience. Results indicated that subjects who performed alone on both testing days performed similarly on both days. However, subjects who performed alone on the first day and in the presence of an audience on the second day had significant decrements in performance.

Since the authors presumed that the correct response was dominant for these gymnastic students, the results were interpreted as nonsupport for Zajonc.

A potential problem in accepting the results of the above and other studies (e.g., Singer, 1970) which claim to have found nonsupport for Zajonc, is in the definition of whether the dominant response was correct or incorrect. The non-support may merely have been due to inadequate delineations of dominant responses. Although the authors in the Paulus study assumed that the dominant response for the gymnasts tested was correct, it may well have been that the stunts performed had not been well perfected. If this was the case and it was instead presumed that the dominant response was incorrect, then the findings that subjects performed worse in the presence of an audience would be clearly supportive of Zajonc's hypothesis. Therefore when testing Zajonc's hypothesis we need to adequately determine the dominant response.

When a task is very simple it can be easily assumed that the correct response is dominant, since there are few incorrect responses which could occur. The determination of whether the dominant response is correct or incorrect is somewhat more difficult for complex skills (see Landers, 1975). During very early learning stages of complex skills it is probably safe to assume that the incorrect response is dominant, since the performer will make many errors. Also, once a very proficient and consistent performance level is attained, it is probably safe to assume that the correct response is dominant, since the performer will make very few errors. But we are still left with the problem of determining whether the correct or incorrect response is dominant for the middle performance range. This is a more difficult question. If a high jumper has near perfect form and good success on two successive trials and then reverts to an incorrect style and then once again progresses to a correct form, do we conclude that the dominant response is correct or incorrect? Landers (1975) has suggested that we may determine which response is dominant on a percentage basis. If the skill is correctly performed at least seven out of ten times, then the correct response is dominant. If performed correctly less than four times out of ten, then the incorrect response is dominant. As can be seen, the determination of the dominant response is often difficult. Unless this distinction can be adequately made, it is difficult to provide an adequate test of Zajonc's hypothesis.

Ability to Evaluate

Zajonc's original hypothesis had focused on a mere-presence-of-others interpretation for social facilitation. In other words it was presumed that other people just had to be physically present while a person was performing in order for arousal increases to occur. Cottrell (1968, 1972) took issue with this mere-presence interpretation and instead suggested that audience members or coactors had to be able to evaluate a subject's performance before arousal increases would occur. By this he meant that audience members who were merely present (e.g., present but blindfolded), and who were not perceived as being able to evaluate the subject's performance, were not considered sufficiently arousing to alter performance. A practical example of a mere-presence audience would be groundskeepers who are marking the track while runners are practicing their starts. To the athletes, these people would probably produce few anticipations of evaluation. Teammates, coaches or spectators who are actively engaged in observing the athletes' performances would be considered an evaluative audience. The evaluation apprehension that a subject experiences in the presence of others is presumed to arise from past occurrences in the individual's life. If we have played well in a game situation, for example, we expect positive outcomes and if we have played poorly we anticipate unfavorable consequences. It is these learned anticipations of positive and negative outcomes following evaluative situations which, according to Cottrell, social facilitation effects. A number of motor performance studies have attempted to differentiate between the mere-presence and the evaluation-apprehension interpretations of social facilitation.

The authors of some motor performance studies have suggested at least limited support for Zajonc's mere-presence interpretation of social facilitation effects (Burwitz & Newell, 1972; Haas & Roberts, 1975) since the mere-presence conditions created in these studies seemed to influence performance. Although the coactors and the audience members in these studies were designed to be nonevaluative, in both experiments it was possible for the subjects' performances to be evaluated. Visual observation of others' performance was eliminated, but auditory cues which could provide some indication of the subject's progress could be heard by the "nonevaluative" others. Therefore a true mere-presence condition was not created. In order to amend this problem, Roberts (1975) eliminated both auditory and visual evaluations by audience members while subjects learned a novel motor skill. Performance for mere-presence subjects was compared to both alone and evaluative audience subjects. Results indicated that subjects initially learning a novel motor skill performed significantly worse when in the presence of evaluative others than when alone. Arousal measures substantiated this finding, since subjects in the evaluative condition were more highly aroused than alone subjects. Performance for subjects in the mere-presence condition fell between the above groups and was not significantly different from either alone or evaluative conditions. This suggests that mere-presence seems to have a slight effect on performance but this effect is not nearly as great as that produced by evaluative others.

Other studies that have manipulated the ability of audience members (Sasfy & Okun, 1974) and coactors (Martens & Landers, 1972) to evaluate subjects' performance have supported an evaluation interpretation. When the ability to evaluate was minimized and others were merely present in the room, then arousal did not increase sufficiently for performance to be affected by the presence of others. Instead of taking either a pure mere-presence or a pure evaluation stance, it seems more reasonable to assume that the two conditions produce similar effects that only differ in intensity (Crandall, 1974). Thus, the effects when subjects can be easily evaluated by an audience or coactors would simply produce more extreme performance effects than if the others were merely present.

Practical Considerations

As can be seen from this condensed review as well as more extensive coverages (Landers, 1975; Landers & McCullagh, 1976; McCullagh & Landers, 1975), the possibility of drawing hard and fast principles is difficult. Nonetheless the following conclusions could be drawn. In the early part of the track and field season, when many individuals are learning new skills or new techniques, it is probably best if they can do so in the absence of spectators or coactors. If this is not possible, then reduction of the possibility of evaluation from others would be advantageous. Spectators should be discouraged from attending early season practice sessions. It may also be best if performance scores are given to the athletes individually rather than creating a highly competitive situation. Later on in the season, once athletes have attained a high and consistent skill level, the presence of others may well aid in the enhancement of performance. At practice sessions at that time it may, therefore, be possible to raise an athlete's performance level by having other team members or bystanders carefully observe her performance in a particular event.

At this time it is difficult to speculate on the effect that large audiences who shout encouragement to athletes may have on performance. Presently there is just no empirical evidence to provide guidance. Besides, coaches have little control over the actions of the spectators at a meet. Cratty (1973) has suggested that coaches must prepare athletes for possible performance changes that may occur in the presence of others. For example, they should be made aware that a runner may perform faster when running alongside others. Then they can be careful not to overpace themselves, especially when running longer distances. Athletes participating in the field events should also be made aware of possible performance changes that may come about. Variables such as audience size (McCullagh & Landers, 1976), their distance from the athletes and the position of spectators are variables which could possibly influence performance. Coaches need to be cognizant of these variables and experiment with them during practice sessions so performance can be enhanced.

AROUSAL

A common concern among coaches is how to get athletes "up" or sufficiently aroused for their athletic contests. For some extremely excitable individuals, it may even be necessary to calm them down before the meet begins. A number of sports psychology and coaching texts reveal numerous principles as to the nature of arousal and how to control it in the athlete (e.g., Cratty, 1973; Singer, 1972). Literature examining the relationship between arousal levels and motor performance will be reviewed in this section in an attempt to determine if specific arousal levels lead to optimum performance.

According to investigators who have extensively researched arousal concepts (Duffy, 1962; Malmo, 1959), behavior is presumed to fluctuate along two dimensions. These are intensity and direction. The direction of behavior is considered to be an individual's tendency to either approach or withdraw from a specific stimulus. Arousal is defined as the intensity of behavior in this approach-withdraw behavior and ranges on a continuum from deep sleep (low arousal) to extreme excitement (high arousal).

A number of methods for measuring arousal have been used in the past and have been classified into three categories (Martens, 1974). One method is to measure electrical activity in the brain. A second is to measure various autonomic responses such as sweating, skin conductance, heart rate or respiration, to name a few. A third way to measure arousal is behaviorally by either having subjects complete pencil and paper tests (e.g., Thayer, 1967) or through various observational techniques where the level of arousal is assumed from the individual's actions or from the situation. Lowe (1973) assessed arousal levels of Little League baseball players through this latter method. If the two opposing teams were very close in the league standings, then game criticalness was considered high. If the scores were very close and the remaining innings in the game were few, then situation criticalness was considered high. The higher the criticalness, the higher the arousal. In addition, Lowe also took physiological arousal measures and observed individual actions while waiting to bat. All of these measures were used to assess arousal in a field situation.

In general, two major hypotheses have been commonly used to explain how arousal affects performance. Simply stated, drive theory predicts that performance is determined by the habit strength (level of learning) of the skill multiplied by the drive or arousal level (Spence & Spence, 1966). Within this formula, habit strength refers to the dominance of correct and incorrect responses, and it is presumed that increases in arousal lead to increased number of dominant responses (see *Presence of Others* section of this chapter for a more detailed explanation of dominant responses). For beginning athletes initially learning a new skill the dominant response would probably be incorrect. Therefore, according to drive theory, increases in arousal would lead to increases in the dominant response and the athlete would make even more mistakes. Once the season progresses and the various skills become well-learned, the dominant response should be correct. Increases in arousal should lead to enhancement of these correct responses, and hence improve performance. Drive theory predicts a linear relationship between arousal levels and performance on well-learned tasks.

The inverted-U hypothesis, however, predicts that the relationship between arousal and performance is curvilinear. That is, when arousal level is low, performance will be poor. As arousal increases to a moderate level, performance improves to its optimal level. Even higher arousal levels lead to decrements in performance. Easterbrook (1959) has proposed that an inverted-U arises from attention alterations that occur with different arousal levels. As arousal increases, the individual focuses more and more on the important cues needed for performance, and this leads to better performance. However if arousal becomes too great, the individual's attention will become too narrowed and performance will decrease.

To adequately test the inverted-U, it is necessary to create at least three levels of arousal. Martens and Landers (1970) created three levels of experimental stress and exposed subjects of low, moderate and high anxiety to these conditions. They measured performance on a tracking task as well as physiological and behavioral measures of arousal. Results indicated that anxiety and situational stress levels independently supported an inverted-U as opposed to linear relationship. Moderately stressed subjects performed better than low and high stress subjects and moderate anxiety subjects performed better than low and somewhat better than high stress subjects.

As can be seen, the two hypotheses make different predictions about the arousal-performance relationship, especially when high levels of arousal are attained. Martens (1974) extensively reviewed the research literature on arousal and motor performance and suggested that drive theory was inappropriate for explaining motor performance, because it was extremely difficult to determine the habit hierarchies (i.e., dominant responses) for motor tasks. Landers (1975) was more optimistic and suggested a number of ways of determining the dominant responses for motor tasks. It would seem safe to predict that when initially learning a skill, the incorrect responses will be dominant, whereas once the skill is well learned, the correct response will be dominant.

Since it may be difficult to create three distinct levels of arousal in a laboratory setting, real life sport situations may provide more accurate tests of the inverted-U. Fenz (1975) reported a number of experiments that had been conducted with sport parachutists, and the findings revealed that experienced jumpers evidenced arousal increases as they approached jump time. Moments before the jump actually occurred, however, physiological arousal levels (heart and respiration rates) were reduced to a moderate level. These studies also revealed that the best jumps were recorded when such decreases in arousal occurred. Thus good performance occurred when arousal levels were moderate, which provides some support for an inverted-U.

Even though limited support for an inverted-U has been mustered, such a relation between arousal and performance is not a stable finding. The most difficult problem in making adequate experimental tests of the hypothesis is that of creating three levels of arousal. More research in naturalistic settings is definitely required. For example, do athletes perform better at a track meet against difficult as opposed to easy opponents? If so, it may be that their arousal levels vary as a function of the importance of the meet. If this is the case, then it would be important for the coach to try to modify individual arousal levels, dependent on the specific situation.

Oxendine (1970) has speculated that the arousal level required for optimal performance depends on the task. He hypothesized that tasks which require speed, strength and endurance are best performed under high levels of arousal. Tasks which require fine muscle control and coordination are presumed to be performed best under low levels of arousal. He therefore speculated that for 220 and 440 yd. sprints the athlete should be maximally aroused, whereas for events such as shot put and high jump, the arousal level should be somewhat less. To modify the athlete's arousal level to correspond with the specific activity she will participate in, Oxendine suggests the use of competition, social reinforcement, rewards, pep talks and even music. Miller (1974) does caution that the individual rather than entire group should be dealt with when using these "psyching up" techniques. Unfortunately there is not a great deal of research to substantiate that these methods can alter arousal level, although the idea is certainly appealing. The coach should attempt to modify arousal levels and determine what level is best for each individual in each specific event.

COOPERATION VERSUS COMPETITION

Track and field is, in part, an individual sport in which athletes compete against the clock and the meter stick as well as another opponent. Athletes typically do not interact with their own teammates to score or win (except in relays). It is also a team sport because in school athletics competition the wins attained by each individual athlete from a particular school are cumulated to determine which school has won the meet. Therefore an important question for coaches is the determination of whether within-group competition or within-group cooperation should be emphasized during the season.

In the late 1940's a prominent psychologist by the name of Deutsch (1949) experimentally investigated the effects of cooperation and competition upon group performance. In the cooperative conditions, subjects were told that each individual in the group would receive the exact same grade determined by how well their group solution to a problem compared with the solutions of other similar groups. In the competitive situations, subjects were advised to submit a group decision, but individual grades would be determined by the relative contribution of each individual in the group. Deutsch assessed individual feelings as well as performance to determine the influence of competition and cooperation. Generally, the findings indicated that cooperative groups had greater "we-feelings," better coordination of efforts and greater productivity than competitive groups.

Subsequent researchers (Hammond & Goldman, 1961) suggested that Deutsch's research design was incomplete if the question of cooperation versus competition was to be effectively answered. Recall that subjects in Deutsch's cooperative groups were told their score would be determined by comparison with other groups. They were therefore cooperative within the group but competitive with other groups. The competitive groups were merely competitive within their own group. To overcome this problem, subjects in the Hammond and Goldman study were assigned to one of four scoring conditions. The comparison of interest was between the group which was competitive within and the group that was cooperative within. Both types of groups seem to be equally task oriented, although the competitive groups evidenced poorer task performance. In support of Deutsch, cooperative groups had greater internal relations as evidenced by better coordination, communication and attentiveness to other members. A subsequent study by Julian and Perry (1967) similarly found that cooperation led to better group relations. In contrast to Hammond and Goldman, competitive groups demonstrated better performance. Julian and Perry therefore suggested that for cooperative groups to be highly motivated they need to be competitive with other groups.

A study by Myers (1962) further investigated the effect of competition, but within a sport setting. Three-man rifle teams either participated in a tournament against other teams, or their performance was compared to some preestablished standards. In neither case were subjects ever made aware of their own individual performances during the experiment, but rather were told how their entire group was doing. Results indicated that competitive teams evidenced better team adjustment and were more unified, at least when successful, than uncompetitive teams.

In most cases it seems that cooperation within a group leads to better internal group relations. The effect of cooperation versus competition on performance is more difficult to extract from the experimental findings. Some suggestions for creating "we-feelings" on a team would be to encourage the athletes to do their best but also to assist each other and contribute for the team's benefit. Total team warm-ups at the beginning of a track meet, in which all school team members are similarly dressed, would seem more conducive for team spirit than individual work-outs at each separate event station. Of course, individual warm-ups will also be required at the time of each specific event. However, bringing a team, not a bunch of individuals, to track meets would possibly ensure a more cooperative attitude among team members. At this time it is difficult to speculate on how performance outcomes might differ with respect to within-team competition versus cooperation, but some field experiments in naturalistic settings could certainly help provide some direction and principles for coaches to follow.

Martens (1975) in his recent analysis of cooperation and competition suggested that discussions labeling either process as "good" or "bad" have not been empirically verified. Therefore these discussions provide us with little direction in dealing with sport teams. Instead, Martens attempts to clarify the confusion previously existent in the literature by clearly defining what competition is and how the process of competition relates to motor performance. Martens prefers to limit his decision to individual competition rather than group competition or cooperation so that the competitive process alone can first be understood. Since Martens provides a fairly comprehensive survey of the elements and processes which may possibly occur during competition, his view of the competitive process will be reviewed here.

Martens suggested that competition is a process composed of various substages. The objective competitive situation, the subjective competitive situation, the response and the consequences of the response are linked events which are influenced by the individual's personality, abilities, motives and attitudes.

The first stage, labeled the *objective competitive situation,* is concerned with defining what constitutes a competitive event. In the past, most researchers have generally accepted a reward definition of competition. Within this definition, competition occurs when the available rewards for success are distributed unequally to contestants dependent on their performances. Usually there can only be one winner. A cooperative situation is viewed as one in which rewards are divided equally among participants. Here everyone can be a winner. Martens suggests a number of limitations inherent in the reward definition approach to competition. It is difficult to define what each individual's goals for reward may be. For example, if a high school runner has the chance to compete against a pro or any superior athlete, her goal may be to keep pace with this runner until the final stretch, knowing full well that she has little hope of winning the race. According to the reward definition of competition, the high school runner failed if she lost the race. According to her own standards she succeeded if she kept pace until the final stretch. The reward definition requires assumptions to be made about how the participant perceives the competitive situation. Instead, Martens has defined an objective competitive situation as one "in which the comparison of an individual's performance is made with some standard in the presence of at least one other person who is aware of the criterion for comparison and can evaluate the comparison process" (1971b). Within this definition the standard may be another person, the athlete's own previous performance, or some idealized level of performance. The evaluator in this situation must be aware of what the comparison standard will be to have a true objective competitive situation. In track and field the athlete may compete against another athlete or her own past performance scores, or the athlete and coach may set some idealized standard to be achieved during the season. Under Martens' definition all of these situations would be classified as competition as long as another person who is aware of the standard is present to evaluate performance.

The next stage to be considered in the competitive process is the *subjective competitive situation*. This stage is concerned with how the person perceives the objective competitive situation. This may of course vary dependent on whether the individual actively seeks out the competition or whether she finds herself confronted with a competitive situation. An individual's competitiveness is thus determined by her tendency to seek out or to avoid competition.

The final two stages of the competitive process are the *response* and *consequences of the response*. A person, once in a competitive situation, may choose to respond or not respond and the consequences may be either positive or negative. The runner mentioned above lost the race against the pro athlete, but the consequences were personally positive if her goal of keeping pace until the final stretch was achieved.

Martens and his associates (Martens, Gill, Simon & Scanlon, 1975) have attempted to investigate more closely the subjective competitive process. Their recent work has been primarily concerned with competitive trait anxiety and how this personality disposition influences the subjective competitive situation. Their goal is to be able to predict varying levels of state- or situation-specific anxiety in people across different competitive situations. A Sport Competition Anxiety Test (SCAT) was developed to assess competitive anxiety (Martens, in press). People who score high on SCAT are those who become the most uptight in competitive situations whereas low SCAT individuals are more relaxed when facing competition. A great deal of work has been done with the SCAT scale to ensure its reliability and validity—important attributes of any psychological test but properties that are oftentimes overlooked. One interesting finding from the above research was the low correlation between individual athlete's ratings of competitive anxiety and the coach's ratings of each athlete's level of anxiety. Usually coaches are quite confident that they can accurately evaluate their own athletes' competitive anxiety levels. If this is so, a high correlation would be expected between individual and coach ratings of anxiety. Such was not the case. A low correlation coefficient ($r = .14$) indicated that coaches were not able to accurately assess their athletes' self-reported anxiety levels. Results also indicated that the SCAT scale was a more accurate predictor of athletes' anxiety state than either a general trait scale or the coaches' ratings. Subsequent findings (Gill, 1976) support the predictor capabilities of SCAT. Thus the scale has provided us with an instrument whereby we can identify which athletes tend to become more anxious when anticipating competition. SCAT is especially important to coaches and physical educators because it was specifically designed to be used in sport settings and is easy to administer to athletes. Research next needs to answer how people who differ in levels of competitive anxiety differ in performance.

MOTIVATION

Individual Motivation

In almost any sport situation it is not difficult to think of numerous examples where the less favored athlete won a victory over the more highly skilled individual. In many cases an upset is attributed to a lack of sufficient motivation on the part of the defeated athlete. Of course the athlete's motivational level will vary depending on many individual factors. As such, the coach will need to employ different methods for motivating athletes, considering such factors as the athlete's age and competitive level. In the following section two concepts that influence an individual's motivational state will be discussed.

LEVEL OF ASPIRATION

Motivation is indeed an important issue when dealing with athletes in sport groups. If athletes are not sufficiently motivated, then performance could be at a lower level than expected. The concept of level of aspiration is concerned with individual motivation for special goals. Kurt Lewin, a prominent social psychologist, was instrumental in developing research on aspiration levels. According to his formulation, a number of factors can determine what goals an individual will set for herself. These include personality disposition, ability and past history of successes and failures to name a few. Success occurs when a person achieves or surpasses her goal whereas failure is nonachievement of a specific goal. Lewin does contend, however, that if the task is too easy or too difficult, then feelings of success and failure will not be experienced. Thus the concept of level of aspiration is only relevant when there is a perceived difficulty range for the task, and when gaining success is of some importance to the individual. But what does success and failure have to do with a person's desire to perform a task? Lewin (1963) cites evidence which suggests that adults usually have little desire to repeat acts at which they are continually successful unless the task distinctly changes, nor do they desire to repeat acts at which they continually fail. Thus, in order to avoid staleness in an athlete, it would seem necessary for the coach to continually help set realistic individual goals. On a track and field team each individual could set a goal that she hopes to achieve during the season. It would be up to the coach to meet with each athlete in order to ensure that these goals are neither too easy nor too difficult. The athlete should have something to continually strive for throughout the season. Welsh (1973) makes the point that "each achieved goal acts as a stimulus to the athlete to go on to the next and so on until the final goal or peak is reached" (p. 60). Thus success can be attained and failure experienced without either necessarily winning or losing to an opponent.

Lewin (1963) gives an example of a discus thrower to indicate how the same achievement can at one time lead to feelings of success and another time lead to feelings of failure. For example, a discus thrower may on a first attempt throw 90 ft. On the second try, 105 ft. is reached and on the third try 120 ft. is attained. However, if on a fourth attempt only 105 ft. is reached, the athlete will most likely experience a sense of failure, even though the same performance led to feelings of success only shortly before. Therefore, level of aspiration is relative rather than absolute and will probably change following success or failure on a particular task. In general it can be said that level of aspiration will be raised following success and lowered after failure. In order to ensure that an athlete's goals are realistic for her particular skill level, there are a number of things the coach could do. It may be useful to graphically plot the performance of each individual athlete after each practice and after each meet. If performance is extremely divergent from the previously set goal, it may be necessary to reassess the goal and make it more realistic for that particular individual. If the goal has been realistic and the athlete, after many weeks of continual practice, attains the goal, then individual success has been achieved. The effort could be made known to other teammates and a new goal should then be set. The coach should keep a careful watch on athletes for whom failure is continual. Lewin suggests that an individual, instead of merely lowering his goal after continued failure, may stop performing altogether. By graphically plotting each individual's performance against her own goal, it should be possible for the coach to intervene and help set a lower goal before the athlete becomes totally discouraged. Peer pressure from the superior athletes on the team may be the cause of unrealistic goals. Therefore the coach must be instrumental in helping set realistic goals that will motivate the athletes to continually strive. By graphically plotting the individual's event scores a coach can get an objective "picture" of each athlete's performance as it progresses and regresses.

ACHIEVEMENT MOTIVATION

A second area of research that is concerned with individual motivation is achievement motivation. Primarily developed for laboratory research by Atkinson

(1957, 1964), achievement motivation is actually an extension of Lewin's level of aspiration. Labeled an expectancy value approach to achievement motivation, Atkinson's contention is that there are two types of individual—those for whom the need for achievement is greater than the fear of failure, and those for whom the fear of failure is greater than the need for achievement. Besides this individual disposition, the environment is also presumed to influence how an individual will respond. Important are both the individual probability of success (dependent on task difficulty) and the incentive value (how much the goal is worth).

In order to measure the personality disposition of achievement motivation, a number of questionnaires and projective tests have been used (see Lynn, 1969; McClelland, Atkinson, Clark & Lowell, 1953; Roberts, 1975). Individuals are then separated into those who have a high motive to achieve success and those who have a high motive or desire to avoid failure. Simply stated, the theory predicts that individuals high in the motive to achieve success prefer competitive situations of intermediate risk when their skill and ability is demonstrated to the utmost. Such individuals therefore prefer to compete against opponents when they have only a 50/50 chance of winning. Individuals high in fear of failure disposition desire to avoid situations where they only have a 50/50 chance of winning and prefer either very easy or very difficult tasks where they can make sure that success is assured or failure is justified.

In general the theory of achievement motivation has accumulated considerable support (see Roberts, 1974, for a review). Although not a great deal of work has been conducted within the motor behavior area, there is some indication that high-need achievement individuals find achievement-oriented motor tasks more attractive than individuals who are high in fear of failure (Roberts, 1972). In a subsequent experiment, Roberts (1974) was interested in whether a competitive element, if introduced, would lead to greater intensity of risk-taking behavior than if subjects performed alone and noncompetitively. Previous research by Ryan and Lakie (1965) had indicated that individuals with a tendency to avoid failure perform better in noncompetitive situations than individuals with a tendency to achieve success. Results indicated that high-need achievers preferred intermediate risk (50/50 chance of winning) to a greater extent than fear-of-failure individuals, who preferred to avoid intermediate risk situations. It was also found that fear-of-failure subjects preferred to engage in very difficult tasks as opposed to extremely easy tasks. The data also indicated that subjects preferred task situations in accordance with their achievement disposition regardless of the social environment (i.e. competition, audience or alone).

It has often been presumed that males have higher achievement needs and take more risks than females, especially in tasks which are male oriented. Today, females are assuming a more equal role in sports so that activities such as track and field may perhaps be considered more neutral than male or female oriented. Roberts (1975) was interested in whether males or females who were physical education students would evidence more achievement-oriented behavior on a motor task considered to be free of sex biases. Results supported the risk-taking theory. Both male and female subjects who had been categorized as motivated to achieve success preferred intermediate task situations to a greater extent than subjects categorized as motivated to avoid failure. The males, however, evidenced these behaviors to a greater extent than the women. There were no actual performance differences between the dispositions or the sexes.

How may these achievement motivation findings be applied to a track and field setting? First of all it should be noted that the probability of success revealed to the subjects in many of the above experiments was manipulated by the experimenter. That is, subjects were told that their probability of achieving success on any particular trial was a certain percentage. Thus if coaches could determine whether their athletes were high in the motive to achieve success or high in the motive to avoid failure, then they could construct situations to correspond to the type of task which would most appeal to the athlete's disposition. For example, if a particular athlete were high in the motive to achieve success, the theory predicts she would be most attracted to intermediate risk situations. Therefore the coach could discuss the opponents before a meet and suggest that the probability of success was only 50/50 or thereabouts. On the other hand, if the athlete were high in motive to avoid failure, it would be better to tell her that she had either a very good chance or a very poor chance of winning. Such an athlete would be more attracted to a very low risk or very high risk situation. Eventually, by achieving a number of goals, this fear-of-failure individual might eventually become more achievement-oriented. These recommendations should be taken cautiously, however, since they have not been tested in actual field situations. What is most certainly needed is more research that can adequately show that persons of particular dispositions are not only more attracted to particular types of tasks, but also perform differently as a function of their expectations for success.

Group Motivation

Zander (1975), a prominent researcher in group dynamics, has suggested a number of ways in which group motivation can be enhanced. His conclusions are based on many laboratory experiments as well as studies conducted in more naturalistic settings. Those findings that seem most relevant for track and field will be mentioned.

Zander extends individual achievement motivation theory to groups and suggests that certain groups may desire to achieve success while others have a desire to avoid group failure. In track and field all events (except relays) are based on individual efforts and abilities and therefore individual achievement motives are probably most important. Nonetheless, Zander does suggest, "A team will be more alert when the desire for group success is stronger than the desire to avoid group failure, instead of the other way around" (p. 29). Although the evidence cited by Zander on the desire for group success and its effect on performance does not deal with actual sport teams, his review of research findings does have possible applications to sport groups. From the evidence cited, he has found support for the notion that group goals which cause the team to stretch hard but that can be attained seem to "stimulate a better group effort than either a very easy or very hard goal" (p. 33). Therefore, throughout the season it would appear best to set goals of moderate difficulty that are within reach of the team. Opposing teams should not be made to appear extremely difficult or extremely easy to beat, since group motivation as a whole may decline. Generally, it has been found that both individuals and groups raise their goals after success and lower their goals after failure. The tendency to raise goals after success is greater, however, than to lower the goals after failure. Especially after failure it is important for the coach to control the team's subsequent efforts and make new goals with the team that are realistic and attainable.

Because the desire to achieve group success seems to be an important determinant of a group's performance as well as an influence on the members' general

Table 3-1: METHODS FOR ENGENDERING GROUP SUCCESS

From Zander (1975, p. 37)	Possible Applications
1. Emphasize the importance of pride in the group, its sources and its consequences for the team. One coach I know makes his seniors responsible for developing these ideas as well as for enthusiasm during practice and games.	Providing a T-shirt for "Most Improved Player" worn on a rotating basis each week insures that even athletes who are not super-stars will gain some recognition. This person could also lead warm-ups.
2. Use various means to underscore how each teammate depends upon the work of each other for the success of their unit.	This could be especially stressed for relay teams.
3. Make sure that each member understands that his contribution to the team is valued.	Attempt to develop the newer athletes as well as refine the old.
4. Emphasize the unity of the group, the score as a product of team effort, and the perception that all members are within the group's boundary.	Team warm-ups or limbering exercises at the beginning of a meet can contribute to such we-feelings.
5. Indicate to members separately how membership helps each individual, so that each will see the group as an attractive entity.	Emphasize the importance of being in good physical condition. Request personal logs of exercise and eating routines to heighten awareness of the necessary aspects of fitness.
6. Take care in the selection of group goals so that these are realistic challenges, not unreasonably hard or easy ends. Set standards of excellence for all skills and activities.	Set definite goals with each individual and at a team meeting determine the group's level of aspiration.
7. Don't be afraid to change goals that are found to be unreasonably difficult. The warmest pride comes from living up to reasonable expectations for that group, not in failing impossibly difficult ends.	Graphically plot the goals and the team's progression towards the goals. If the team has little chance of reaching those goals over the season then it will be necessary to change their aspirations.
8. Once goals have been set, consider what obstacles might prevent fulfillment of these goals and how the obstacles might be overcome by the team.	Lack of depth in skill may prevent the group from attaining the goal. Attempt to develop a well-rounded team in which many rather than few members contribute to the score.
9. Encourage talk in the group about how performance can be improved and how the boring parts of athletics can be made more involving.	Allow team members to contribute ideas and question the training methods employed by the coach.
10. Avoid fear of failure and the tendency to evade challenges that are engendered thereby.	If fear-of-failure individuals are guided into setting realistic instead of extreme goals then success can be achieved and they may in turn be prompted to take a more positive approach to competition.

feelings toward the team, it is important for the coach to foster such feelings among athletes. Based on empirical evidence, Zander (1975) has suggested ten methods for engendering group success. Although some of the methods might seem elementary to experienced coaches, it is hoped that some of the ideas will prove useful in fostering team pride and perhaps subsequent group success. For a list of Zander's methods and possible applications see Table 3-1.

DEMONSTRATION LEARNING

Many previous track and field and coaching method books advocate the use of demonstration to improve athletic performance (e.g., Cratty, 1973; Frost, 1971; Miller, 1974; Singer, 1972; Wakefield, Harkins & Cooper, 1966). Closer inspection of these sources indicate that the authors oftentimes advocate opposite viewpoints on how demonstrations should be effectively used. For example, Miller (1974, p. 63) suggests that awareness of committed errors can be enhanced through demonstration by allowing the athlete to experience both correct and incorrect performances. In contrast, Frost (1971, p. 125) suggests that "imitating wrong and ineffective movements is generally wasteful of efforts." Considering that different viewpoints exist, the following section will briefly review a prominent psychological theory of demonstration learning and present some pertinent research findings. Finally, suggestions will be made on how demonstrations may be effectively used in a track and field setting.

On a theoretical level, there is a need to be concerned about the intervening psychological processes within the athlete that occur between the demonstration and the observer's performance. For example, if while learning a skill, athletes perform better after observing a prestigious athlete or coach perform as opposed to a demonstration by fellow teammates, it may perhaps be assumed that observers learn more because they pay more attention to a coach than their peers. Or, perhaps attention is similar in the two situations but observers for some reason are better able to retain in memory the pertinent performance cues if they watch a prestigious model. Another possibility is that the observer is merely more motivated to perform after observing a prestigious person as opposed to a teammate. All of the above interpretations seem possible, and Bandura (1969), in taking a cognitive approach to observational learning, has therefore suggested that four subprocesses are important determinants of demonstration learning. These processes include attention, retention, motor reproduction and motivation.

Attention

Simply stated, social learning theory (Bandura, 1969) suggests that modeled behavior is stored in the observer's memory in either verbal or imaginal form and it is these representations that subsequently guide the observer's task performance. It is assumed that the degree to which a demonstration will be learned by an observer depends on both attentional and retentional processes. Thus, it is first essential that the observer attend to the demonstration so she can recognize and discriminate the relevant information required for correct performance. Bandura (1969) has postulated a number of variables that are presumed to influence this attentional phase. These include model characteristics such as competence (Baron, 1970), status level (Landers & Landers, 1973), age (Bandura & Kupers, 1964) and social power (Mischel & Grusec, 1966), to name a few. Telling subjects that they will later have to imitate the model's behavior through instruction sets (Yussen, 1974) and observer characteristics such as dependency (Ross, 1966) and self-esteem (Gelfand, 1962) have similarly been shown to influence degree of observational learning, and it is presumed that the attentional phase is influenced. In addition, stimulus input characteristics such as number (Fouts, 1970) and temporal spacing (Landers, 1975) of model demonstrations have also altered level of observational learning.

Since attention is an important component of the demonstration learning process, it has been suggested by Miller (1974, p. 75) that distractions during the demonstration should be kept at a minimum (e.g., whistles, sun, etc.). This does not mean that a rule of total silence should be followed when demonstrations or film loops are shown to athletes. In fact there is some evidence to suggest that limited verbal cues provided throughout the learning sequence may be beneficial, especially in situations where extensive verbal instructions are given initially (Goodenough & Brian, 1929).

Retention

Even though an observer may pay close attention to a modeled demonstration, there is no assurance that the relevant information will be symbolically stored in memory and subsequently be available to guide the performer's actions. Thus retention is an important process in observational learning. Gerst (1971) manipulated the type of coding employed by subjects to determine whether verbal or imaginal coding was better. Results indicated that both types of coding resulted in better performance than performance by control group subjects who were prevented from employing rehearsal strategies. Subsequent studies have also attempted to assess the degree of observational learning when various rehearsal strategies have been compared. Bandura and Jeffery (1973) presented a filmed model demonstrating complex arm movements to college subjects who then rehearsed the movements under one of three conditions. The motor rehearsal condition required subjects to overtly perform the modeled patterns. Symbolic rehearsal subjects repeated aloud the verbal cues which had been assigned to the various movements and a no-rehearsal group performed interpolated activity designed to prevent rehearsal. Contrary to expectation, motor rehearsal did not aid retention on a delayed recall test compared to the no-rehearsal group. Coding operations and rehearsal strategies may be extremely dependent on the type of task which is being learned. It may be that overt physical practice is most beneficial for very complex motor tasks whereas symbolic rehearsal may be more appropriate for tasks that are easily amenable to verbal or imaginal coding.

Motor Reproduction

Since overt performance and practice of complex motor skills may be limited by the physical capacities of an individual, Bandura has suggested motor reproduction as a third process which influences degree of observational learning. According to social learning theory, the observer must attend to the modeled act, symbolically code this act into verbal or imaginal form, and then employ these representations to guide performance. In the case of complex motor skills, attending to and retaining in memory the relevant modeling cues does not provide assurance that the skill can then be efficiently performed. We may watch a superior athlete high jump, attend to her approach pattern, take-off and body control, remember what she did, but still not be able to imitate her performance. Therefore, Bandura suggests graduated modeling procedures for complex skills wherein the elements of the skill may be achieved in a step-wise fashion. Repeating the demonstration more than once (Fouts, 1970) and spacing the demonstrations over the practice period (Landers, 1975; Margolius & Sheffield, 1961) may help in acquiring complex skills. McGuire (1961) found little difference in performance when the behavior to be learned was repeated either two or four times. An earlier study by McTavish (1949) found that for particular films it was more beneficial to demonstrate the skill at least twice initially and then allow the athlete to practice before the skill was demonstrated again.

Motivation

The final subprocess presumed to influence observational learning is the motivational and incentive process. An observer may attend to modeling cues, code and retain the necessary elements and have the necessary ability, but may not be sufficiently motivated to perform the skill. Such abstinence may be the result of insufficient motivation, or of fear of disapproval or punishment. The primary variable which has been manipulated to study motivation in modeling is social reinforcement or the use of praises and incentives.

Flanders (1968) devised a scheme to classify the types of reinforcement that may be delivered to the model, observer or both during the observation of the skill. The observer may be directly reinforced for each response made by the model, receive only vicarious reinforcement (i.e. the model is reinforced or praised for her performance and the observer watches this reinforcement) or neither the observer nor model are reinforced during the demonstrations. Although both vicarious and direct reinforcement increase the level of observational learning (Bandura, Grusec & Menlove, 1967), a number of studies have shown that even when nonreinforced conditions exist, subjects generally perform better than if no model demonstrations had occurred (Landers, 1975; Landers & Landers, 1973). Thus demonstrations certainly enhance performance over levels which would be attained if no demonstrations were provided, especially when initially learning a new skill.

Although Bandura (1969) suggested that model characteristics most probably affect the attentional process during observational learning, it is also possible that observers are more motivated to perform for a high status as opposed to a low status model. A motor performance experiment by Landers and Landers (1973) clearly demonstrates the potency of model characteristics in modifying motor performance. In this study, junior high school females observed either a teacher or peer model demonstrate a novel motor task in either a skilled or unskilled manner. Results indicated that subjects performed well after observing the teacher model perform skillfully but performed poorly after observing unskillful teacher performance. It seems as though subjects attempted to exactly copy the performance of the teacher whether the performance was done well or poorly. Performance after observing a skilled and unskilled peer demonstration was intermediate and in the opposite direction to those obtained for teacher demonstration. Although this experiment certainly demonstrated interesting effects of model status and model ability level on motor performance, it is difficult to discern which of the underlying cognitive processes is being affected by the model status manipulation. An experiment presently in progress by the author suggests that a model status manipulation does not seem to be an attentional variable. It is probably more reasonable to assume that the model's status level affects the observer's motivational level. Such increased motivation may be due to expectations of future rewards or future interactions with the high status model. This experiment also suggests that performance differences after observing a high status as opposed to low status model are relatively short-lived. Once incentives were offered to highly motivate the subjects, the benefits of watching a high status as opposed to a low status model disappeared.

Practical Considerations

Most of the experiments concerned with observational learning have not been conducted by motor skill researchers, and we therefore lack a firm empirical basis for establishing principles of observational learning for simple and complex motor skills. The void in research by physical educators is indeed surprising since demonstrations are an integral part of the teaching process. Nonetheless, some possible applications of the research findings to track and field will be made.

The use of loop films in athletic training is fairly widespread and a question of importance is whether the use of such films is more advantageous than employing live demonstrations or no demonstrations at all. A number of experiments have studied the effects of filmed demonstration on badminton (Gray & Brumbach, 1967), bowling (Lockhart, 1944), golf (Nelson, 1958) and tumbling (Brown & Messersmith, 1948). In general the studies have not had adequate control groups, and the effectiveness of loop films has therefore been difficult to assess from these studies. More recently a laboratory study (Martens, Burwitz & Zuckerman, 1976) compared live demonstrations of a novel task with filmed demonstrations and found no differences in subsequent observer performance. Since both types of demonstrations seemed equally effective it would probably be more efficient, at least in some cases, to employ loop films, since all athletes could benefit from observing a correct model and the film could easily be repeated whenever needed. In addition to presenting a standardized demonstration to the athletes, a loop film could also be used as a motivational technique. For example, it may be beneficial to employ loop films with prestigious athletes demonstrating the various track and field skills.

The benefit of allowing athletes to observe correct demonstrations was alluded to earlier. A recent series of experiments (Martens *et al.*, 1976) compared subjects' performance of a novel motor skill after observing either a correct demonstration, an incorrect demonstration, a learning sequence demonstration in which the model got progressively better over trials, or no demonstration. On the basis of results from a previous animal study (Herbert & Harsh, 1944) it was hypothesized that subjects would obtain a greater amount of information and hence perform better after observing a learning sequence model where perform-ance improved over trials. The results (Exp. 1) did not provide data very supportive of this hypothesis. Certainly further experimentation employing more difficult motor tasks would have to be conducted before a conclusive answer can be provided to this question. Perhaps the information conveyed to a learner would be more beneficial and meaningful if it consisted of a video tape replay of her own performance which the coach and athlete could compare to the correct demonstra-tions previously provided. The coach could then give criticisms for incorrect and praise for correct performance. The video-tape replay could thus serve as a demonstration from which the athlete could gain valuable information about her own performance. This type of information has been labeled knowledge of performance. (See the next section for a more complete description.)

A controlled experiment employing athletes in their natural surroundings could provide insight into the use of demonstrations. The benefits of employing demonstrations as compared to no demonstration has clearly been shown for novel motor tasks (Landers, 1975; Landers & Landers, 1973). Thus for athletes initially learning a novel track and field skill, it is probably better to give demonstrations than to have the athlete attempt to learn through her own trial and error or through observing someone demonstrating incorrect skills.

From the information provided, it will now be the coach's duty to extrapolate and test some of the above-mentioned ideas. It would seem important to keep in mind Bandura's model when using demonstrations so they can be employed to the best advantage. Since attentional and retentional processes are presumed to influ-ence the actual amount learned, it would be important to heighten the variables presumed to influence these stages. To heighten attention it will be necessary to keep distractions at a minimum while demonstrations are shown, and with dif-ficult skills the number of demonstrations and their spacing will also need to be carefully considered. Athletes will also need to rehearse and practice the skills to be learned to adequately maintain them in memory, with the extent and type of rehearsal dependent on the specific skill. Even though adequate provisions have been made to ensure that a skill or technique is well learned, there may still be times when the athlete does not display performance commensurate with the amount she has previously learned. When this occurs it will be necessary to increase motivation, the fourth process in Bandura's model. The use of incentives, social reinforcements, loop films or perhaps the reintroduction of demonstrations which have not been seen for some time may prove useful in making actual performance levels approach their optimum.

PROVIDING COMMENTS TO THE ATHLETE

During practice sessions the coach has the responsibility of helping the athlete improve and perfect her skills. The judicious use of demonstrations is one consideration just discussed that may aid in achieving this goal. A further consideration is the type of verbal comments a coach can make to an athlete to provide her with information concerning performance. First of all, the coach can inform the athlete as to whether the goal was attained or not. In events in which the outcome is difficult to discern such as running events, the coach may provide augmented knowledge of results by informing the athlete of her time. In some events (e.g., high jump) this type of comment will not provide the athlete with a great deal of new information, since she can easily determine whether the bar was cleared or not. Secondly, the coach may provide the athlete with knowledge of performance which is information about the form and style of the movements produced. Within this area there has actually been little research to guide our teaching and coaching. Marteniuk (1976) suggests that the same principles may hold true for both augmented knowledge of results and knowledge of performance, but cautions that the research literature provides little direction. A third type of comment that the coach can provide is encouraging or discouraging remarks about the athlete's performance or the results of her performance. In this section the research which has investigated these types of comments will be reviewed.

Knowledge of Results

In general, the studies which have investigated knowledge of results have been conducted in laboratory settings. In many situations the tasks employed have not allowed the subjects to objectively determine their own performance outcomes. This type of task situation is similar to speed events in track and field where it may be difficult for the athlete to determine exactly how well she has done unless a time is reported. Extensions from laboratory experiments are more difficult to make for tasks where the athlete can objectively determine her own outcomes (e.g., high jump). With these limitations in mind, the experimental evidence will be reviewed.

Our first concern should be whether the coach needs to provide the athlete with knowledge of results (KR) to improve performance. In general, the experimental findings have shown that unless the learner receives KR, performance will not improve (Bilodeau, Bilodeau & Schumsky, 1959; Trowbridge & Carson,

1932). Thus, KR has the function of providing information to the learner which can then be compared with the feedback they themselves received from the movement. Once a consistent and proficient level of performance has been reached, the dependency on KR is reduced. Evidence with novel motor skills indicates that performance can be maintained even when KR is withdrawn (Newell, 1974; Wallace, DeOreo & Roberts, 1976) but there is little evidence to support any improvement in performance in the absence of KR. Therefore the coach may not need to provide continual KR to highly proficient and motivated athletes. Instead, other forms of encouragement could be used.

Although knowledge of results is essential for learning, is it necessary that KR be provided after every trial? Perhaps intermittent use of KR is sufficient to maintain or even improve performance. Bilodeau and Bilodeau (1958a), researchers who have done a considerable amount of work on determining the effects of KR on motor performance, designed a study directed at this frequency of KR question. In this experiment, subjects received quantitative KR after every trial, every third trial, every fourth trial or after every tenth trial. Once all subjects had received 10 KR trials, performance was plotted and compared. No differences were found between the four groups. It should be noted that the group which received KR after every tenth trial had performed 100 trials by the time performance was compared whereas the other groups had received only 10, 20 or 40 practices on the task. Therefore results indicated that performance was dependent, not on the total number of trials, but rather on the total number of trials with KR. These results would seem to suggest that knowledge of results should be provided as frequently as possible when learning a new skill.

In providing KR we also need to be concerned about when in time we provide the learner with this information. Should coaches record the scores attained and then wait until all athletes have finished the event before relaying the scores or should the athlete be provided with performance results immediately? Two time gaps are of importance when considering the timing of KR.

The first time gap involves the lapse between the actual completion of the skill and the moment at which KR is provided. This time is referred to as the KR delay interval. The second lapse is the interval between the presentation of KR and the learner's next attempt at the skill. This interval is referred to as the post-KR delay. Evidence has shown that extremely short (i.e., 1 as opposed to 5, 10 or 20 seconds) post-KR delays can be detrimental to performance (Weinberg, Guy & Tupper, 1964). With very short post-KR delay intervals it is assumed that the learner does not have sufficient time to compare the KR with his own performance and then decide on how to improve the next response. In track and field there is usually a considerable post-KR delay since the athlete must physiologically recover before a second attempt is made. Therefore we will turn our attention to the KR interval which can be more readily altered by the coach or teacher.

To correct inaccurate movements it is necessary that the learner remember information about the movement she completed and then compare this information with the KR which is provided by the coach or teacher. Since it is possible that the learner could forget the movement if the KR delay period is too long, it is necessary to carefully consider this time period so that KR can be as useful as possible. It is also important that distractions be kept to a minimum so the performer can efficiently compare knowledge of performance with the augmented KR provided by the coach or teacher. Research results on the topic of KR delay indicate that the first consideration of remembering knowledge of performance does not appear to be a problem. Delaying KR for as much as an hour for simple movements does not seem to affect learning when compared with KR delay intervals that are only a few seconds long (Bilodeau & Bilodeau, 1958 b). To avoid the possibility of interference from other activities, the best prescription would seem to be the rather immediate provision of KR.

Another question remains as to what type of augmented KR the coach or teacher should employ. An early study by Trowbridge and Carson (1932) provides some insight. In this study four groups of subjects were required to draw a pencil line of a specified length while blindfolded. One group of subjects received qualitative KR in which the experimenter told them they were either correct or incorrect. Subjects in a quantitative KR group were informed that they had overshot or undershot the distance to be learned by so many units. A third group of subjects received irrelevant KR after each trial which provided no information as to how well they had performed and a fourth group of control subjects received no KR whatsoever. Results indicated that subjects who received quantitative KR improved the most and reached the highest level of performance. These findings would seem to suggest that constructive criticism which precisely indicates the type of error made is more beneficial than merely indicating that a movement is correct or incorrect. Next we may ask—how precise should this information be?

The Trowbridge and Carson study just cited would seem to suggest that the more precise the KR the better the performance. Although some studies seem to support this idea (Chansky, 1960; McGuigan, 1959), studies by Bilodeau (1959) and Green, Zimiles and Spragg (1955) provide limitations to the notion since precise KR did not improve performance over more limited types of KR. In fact further experimentation (Bilodeau, 1966; Rogers, 1974; Smoll, 1972) seems to suggest that as KR becomes more precise, performance improves to an optimal level beyond which further precision does not aid. Some evidence even suggests that extremely precise KR may have detrimental effects on performance outcome (Rogers, 1974) as well as detrimental effects on subjects' ability to estimate their own performance (Gill, 1975). It has also been shown that the effects of KR precision vary with age. Newell (1976) has shown that young children have great difficulty using very precise KR. Thus, although providing precise information seems to aid performance, a coach should be careful not to overload the learner with considerable information that cannot be used effectively.

From the experimental evidence reviewed, the benefits of providing the learner with knowledge of results has been shown. Evidence concerning how often KR should be given, when it should be given and the preciseness of the information has been mentioned. It is suggested that the coach try manipulating the types of KR used and then objectively measure whether performance can be improved.

Praise versus Punishment

It is well known that many coaches have a particular style or method of coaching. Coaches such as Bobby Knight or the late Vince Lombardi have been well publicized as providing their athletes with a great deal of negative criticism. Other coaches take a more positive approach and believe positive reinforcement is the best way to motivate athletes to perform maximally. In light of these varying approaches, a question of concern to many teachers and coaches is whether praise or punishment is more beneficial in improving performance.

Social reinforcement (SR) refers to positive or negative evaluation of performance through the use of verbal cues. In laboratory research this reinforcement is not always contingent on the subject's performance (i.e., praise may be given when subjects are doing poorly or reproofs could be administered when subjects are doing well). When SR is contingent, similar to knowledge of results, it can provide the learner with information relative to her performance. In addition, the expression of praise or reproof may also serve as a motivator of performance and if used effectively can even be used to modify performance in a particular direction.

A matter of importance to coaches and teachers is whether social reinforcement can actually modify an athlete's immediate performance. Can a word of praise or encouragement motivate the athlete to perform at maximum or is it better to supply her at times with some disapproval? Also what are the long term effects of only praising an athlete's performance or of continually providing punishments? Experimentally it is of course easier to answer the first question which deals with the immediate effects of social reinforcement on performance.

A number of studies by Martens and his associates have studied the effects of contingent social reinforcement on motor performance. In these experiments if subjects improved their performance over previous trials, they are administered positive SR in the form of praise and smiles. When performance did not improve over previous trials, no reinforcements were administered at all. Subjects in a punishment condition were presented with reproofs and sneers when their performance deteriorated. In a series of experiments which assessed novel motor performance (Martens, 1970; Martens, 1971; Martens, 1972; Roberts & Martens, 1970) there was little evidence of performance changes due to the reinforcement manipulations.

A subsequent study by Harney and Parker (1972) suggested that the above experiments did not administer the reinforcements often enough to produce behavioral changes. Therefore regardless of how the children were performing, the experimenter administered SR on every trial. There were three groups: positive SR, punishment and a conversational control group. Girls performed similarly on the novel motor task under all three conditions whereas boys' performance was detrimentally affected in the conversation control condition.

As opposed to the frequency of SR argument taken by Harney and Parker, Martens (1972) extended an informational viewpoint to account for the lack of significant findings in his previous studies. He suggested that the social reinforcement information provided to subjects in these experiments was actually redundant since subjects could either objectively determine their progress by observing their performance or they were made aware of their progress by the augmented knowledge of results from the experimenter. Therefore Martens, Burwitz and Newell (1972) suggested that during early trials when a subject is originally learning a skill, provided that other forms of performance feedback are readily available (e.g., knowledge of results), social reinforcement will be redundant and thus will not modify performance. On the other hand, once the task is well learned and the subjects are performing at a consistent level, then social reinforcement may provide enhanced motivation that would lead to subsequent performance improvement. Results did not clearly establish performance differences dependent on type of reinforcement nor was there clear support for the notion that reinforcement would prove more beneficial once a task had been well practiced.

A more recent study by Gill and Martens (1975) attempted to determine the informational and motivational effects of knowledge of results and social reinforcement. Novel task performance was monitored during early learning trials as well as during later trials when more consistent performance levels had been reached. Based on Martens' previous notions, the motivational effect of SR was hypothesized to have little effect during initial learning whereas the informational component of both KR and SR was expected to enhance early learning trials. Once the task was well learned, then the subjects would not require a great deal of information about their performance but the motivational effects of SR were expected to enhance performance. Unfortunately the results did not provide clear-cut support for the above hypothesis.

From the literature reviewed there is not a great deal of evidence to suggest that the use of social reinforcers has a tremendous influence on motor performance. All of the above studies were conducted in laboratory settings with novel tasks and subjects may not have been intrinsically interested in their task performance. Also, in all cases the SR was administered by an experimenter previously unknown to the subjects. In a realistic sport setting, a coach who has a great deal of future control over the athletes might be more influential, and social reinforcement would probably have greater effects if dispensed by such a person. It has also been suggested that the use of reinforcers may aid in the establishment of a more positive relationship between the teacher and student or coach and athlete (Martens, 1975) and may help to at least maintain performance at its present level.

Once again, there is a void of empirical research in actual track and field and other sport settings investigating the use of of various reinforcers. For example, providing athletes with frozen oranges or ice-cold popsicles for improved performance during hot practices is most certainly a form of tangible reinforcement. Do such rewards actually have any effect on subsequent performance or does it merely make the continued efforts of a hard practice more enjoyable? If such reinforcers can even serve this latter objective then they are certainly worthwhile, but we should be cautious in concluding that we have increased an athlete's performance because of them. Also we should probably use such reinforcers sparingly since athletes may become extremely dependent on these rewards and come to expect them in return for good performance rather than gaining joy from the activity for its own sake. Another possibility for reinforcers in a track and field setting is to set an example of players who improve the most during the week's training sessions. Whether it be in a track or field event, the coach could keep careful records of weekly scores for each event. Players who improve substantially might be rewarded with a T-shirt, for example, indicating their accomplishment and would be allowed to wear this shirt for a specified time period. Since improving individual skill level is certainly a primary objective, the most improved weekly player would certainly be meeting this goal. Coachs' bulletin boards could also be used to an advantage in this vein. The effects of such incentives will most probably differ depending on the age and competitive level of the athletes involved. It will be up to the coach and teacher to experiment with some of these methods and determine which are best for their athletes.

4 Maurice Sipes

THE
SPRINTS

Author: **Maurice Sipes** has been coaching girls' and women's track and field
in California since 1965, at both the high school and club levels. Frequent
author and lecturer on the women's track and field events, Sipes has coached
hundreds of athletes with a wide range of age and ability.

Unlike some animals whose structural features are adapted to achieving
extremely fast sprinting speeds over short distances, the human being is limited by
a mechanical efficiency that seldom exceeds 25 percent. The other 75 percent is
expended in a variety of ways—overcoming gravitational forces, manipulating
skeletal levers, metabolizing food, etc. The female sprinter is further impeded by
a somewhat lower center of gravity and wider pelvis than is possessed by her male
counterpart. A smaller muscle mass and a generally shorter stride are other factors
which preclude the female sprinter from attaining the times of the male.

A list of the factors associated with successful sprinting would assuredly
include speed of muscular contraction, strength, flexibility, local muscular endurance, looseness and good technique. Objective analysis enables the coach to
assess the motor characteristics of the sprinter, to identify faults in her movements
and, subsequently, to refine those techniques for economy of movement in the
running action.

THE START

Any discussion of sprinting obviously begins with a selection of a particular
type of start to utilize for the event. It has been well documented that the ideal
starting position is the one which permits the greatest amount of force to be
exerted over the longest distance in the desired direction and in the shortest time.
Further, many coaches agree that the crouch start is the most practical of current
starting positions.

The block setting used should provide optimum force and range of motion within the ankle, knee, and hip joints at the initiation of the start. The longitudinal spacing of the blocks has considerable influence on the forces exerted and, thus, on the success of the start.

Crouch starting positions are generally classified into three categories—namely, the bunch, medium, and elongated starts.

In the bunch starting position, the toe of the rear foot is opposite the back of the front heel before the latter is raised. This usually results in a longitudinal spacing of 10-12 in. between the blocks. It is of interest to note that (a) short sprinters tend to use the bunch start, (b) the bunch start usually results in a quick clearance from the blocks and (c) the velocity gained after clearing the blocks from the bunch start is usually less than from other starting positions.

In the medium starting position, the knee of the rear leg, when resting on the track, is opposite the front of the arch of the front foot. The longitudinal spacing between the blocks will be between 14 in. and 21 in.

Research tends to support the use of the medium start as preferred. Studies have indicated that more force is derived from the medium start as compared to the bunch start. Naturally, a longer impulse on the front block is sustained through use of the medium start. Numerous studies point out that use of the bunch start results in a shorter elapsed time to clear the blocks compared to a medium start, but this is questionable as being pertinent to an analysis of the total race.

In the elongated starting position, the knee of the rear leg, when resting on the track surface, is opposite the heel of the front foot. The longitudinal spacing between the blocks will be between 22 in. and 28 in. Tall sprinters tend to gravitate to the elongated position as their choice of sprint start, although this is not a prerequisite to efficient starting.

In all three starting positions, the distance of the front block from the starting line is determined by height and leg length of the sprinter.

"On Your Marks"

A prudent sprinter always checks her blocks for proper placement and executes a number of practice starts prior to the event. Through executing practice starts, the sprinter gains a kinesthetic awareness of the track surface and is thus in a position to make any alterations in her start if the need exists.

Just prior to the command, "On your marks," the sprinter should statically stretch the hamstrings to reduce the possibility of a torn hamstring that might otherwise occur as a result of improper warm-up.

At the command, "On your marks," the sprinter should back into the blocks rather than stepping down into the blocks. Her hands should be placed beyond the starting line and the front foot should be positioned on the front block, followed by placement of the rear foot on the rear block. While starting rules state that the toes must be in contact with the track surface, it is beneficial to have the feet as high on the block as legally permitted. Proper foot placement adds to the horizontal thrust as the sprinter executes the sprint start.

Which foot to have on the front block has been the concern of coaches and athletes for many years. An examination of the literature reveals that the difference in strength levels of the legs is not statistically significant. An important consideration should be the neuro-muscular coordination of the individual. Those who tend to be right side dominant will likely place the left foot in the front block, although this is not always the case. Usually this preference is an individual matter.

In the "On your marks" position, the body weight should rest between the hands and the grounded rear knee. The forearms should be at a 90 deg. angle with the track surface and the thumb and fingers should form an arch, parallel to and directly behind the starting line. The thumbs should be directed towards each other.

The feet and knees should be aligned so that all available forces will be directed in the intended line of motion at the start of the race. Any lateral deviation of the feet or knees is detrimental to the execution of the sprint start. In addition, the athlete's back should be in an essentially straight line.

"Set"

At the command, "Set," the sprinter should inhale, rotate the body forward and elevate the hips in one fluid motion (Figure 4-1). In the set position the shoulders should be slightly forward of the hands and the hips should be higher than the shoulders by about 3 in. The higher position of the hips raises the center of gravity and moves it towards the front of the base of support. This puts the body in a delicate state of static equilibrium—a position which ensures that the moment the hands are lifted from the track, the center of gravity will fall outside the base of support and the forward movement of the body will be underway.

The head, neck and trunk should be maintained in their essentially straight position as the sprinter moves into the "Set" position. This alignment results in the sprinter's gaze being directed at the track surface no more than 1-2 ft. beyond the starting line.

The legs should be flexed with a knee angle of 90 deg. for the front knee, and a more open angle of 115-120 deg. for the rear knee. Research has shown that these are the optimum angles for the imparting of effective force.

While in the "Set" position, the sprinter should concentrate on reacting to any external stimulus, rather than listening for the report of the starting gun. It should be noted that this voluntary decision to initiate a movement when the stimulus occurs is thought to cause a state of readiness to respond to the stimulus. During this foreperiod, there is some amount of preliminary neuromotor response.

"The Gun"

With the advent of electronic devices incorporated into starting blocks, the current vogue seems to be a discussion of *reaction time*. Reaction time is defined as the time which elapses between the external stimulus and the initial response to

Figures 4-1—4-14   **Wyomia Tyus, USA**   **11.07**
                       Barbara Farrell, USA   **22.87**

FIGURE 4-1

FIGURE 4-2

FIGURE 4-3

FIGURE 4-4

FIGURE 4-5

FIGURE 4-6

FIGURE 4-7

FIGURE 4-8

FIGURE 4-9

FIGURE 4-10

FIGURE 4-11

FIGURE 4-12

FIGURE 4-13

FIGURE 4-14

that stimulus. Sprinters require more than 0.1 sec. to react to an external stimulus. It is well to point out that since research has yet to establish an inverse correlation between reaction time and sprinting ability, there is little to be gained from discussing this relationship.

The initial response to the gun is an almost simultaneous lifting of the hands from the track surface. This action causes the center of gravity of the body to fall outside the base of support and thus sets the body rotating forward.

The front foot should begin thrusting simultaneously with the rear foot.* Sophisticated studies show this to be true in the case of outstanding sprinters. It is important for the sprinter to apply a great amount of force against the blocks in the sprint start. This follows from Newton's Third Law of Action and Reaction, which states that for every action there is an equal and opposite reaction.

The rear leg develops a greater peak force than the front leg, but the front leg contributes twice as much to the sprinter's velocity as she leaves the blocks

---

*The following discussion assumes that the sprinter started with the left foot on the front block and the right foot on the rear block.

because of the longer period for which it is in contact with the starting block. As the sprinter continues to exert a strong driving force against the front block, the rear foot is brought forward in a flat trajectory to complete the initial stride efficiently and quickly.

As the left foot is being driven hard against the front block, the left shoulder joint is being flexed, and the right shoulder joint is being extended. This is in keeping with the contralateral principle of movement of the limbs. (It is commonly known that limb movements in walking and running, in the human, are reciprocal. In other words, as the left foot is moving forward, the right arm is moving forward in contralateral synchronization.) The left elbow should be flexed to about 90 deg. and the left arm driven forward and upward during the driving phase out of the blocks. Concurrently, the right arm should be driven backward and upward with a corresponding 90 deg. of flexion at the elbow (Figure 4-2). The flexed elbows function to shorten the turning radius of the upper extremities, and thus permit greater rotary velocities than would otherwise be possible.

The initial stride out of the blocks should be the shortest stride, with the strides becoming progressively longer as the sprinter continues accelerating. A check of this stride pattern may be done on a dirt surface. Each stride may be measured and recorded on graph paper. The strides should show an increase in length of 3-4 in. with each accelerating stride. Should the initial stride be longer than 20 in. beyond the starting line, the mechanics of the sprint start may be suspect, and a cinematographic review of the start would be in order.

If you have access to a high speed camera, you will benefit from viewing films of the sprint start taken from lateral, anterior, and posterior views. Observation should be directed toward the various body segments. The pelvis and trunk should be in a straight line throughout the sprint start to allow force to be exerted most effectively against the blocks and to permit the reaction derived from the blocks to drive the center of gravity most efficiently in the desired direction.

The extensor movements of the hip, knee, and ankle should also be observed. Forceful movement should be performed through a full range of motion of these joints and this can easily be detected from a lateral view of the start. Any extraneous rotations of the spinal column and pelvic girdle in the transverse plane may also be observed. Such extraneous movements can also be detected through non-cinematographic means. If the initial stride is not directly bordering the line of progression, this would indicate spinal rotation and perhaps a weak left arm action.

Finally, the relative location of the center of gravity should be checked. The center of gravity should remain relatively low in relation to the base of support during the sprint start. An elevated center of gravity might be indicative of a premature lifting of the head. A faulty set position might also be at the crux of the problems observed.

ACCELERATION PHASE

The greatest acceleration occurs early in the race. At 20 yd., approximately

95 percent of maximum velocity has been reached. As the sprinter approaches maximum velocity, the strides get progressively longer and the body assumes a more vertical position. The point where maximum velocity is reached (or where acceleration ceases) is usually about 6 sec. beyond the start. The exact point is a function of speed.

Once a sprinter reaches maximum velocity, her rate of deceleration is determined by the level of her muscular endurance. Observations of a 100 m. sprint that lead to the conclusion that some sprinters accelerate in the latter stages of the sprint are actually visual illusions. What is really seen is a greater deceleration by those sprinters who seem to have lost their speed. It is impossible to accelerate once maximum velocity has been reached.

MAXIMUM SPEED

A sprinter moves at maximum speed for only a short distance (15-20 yd.) before the anaerobic energy stores are depleted and deceleration sets in. This is why it is impossible to sprint the entire race at top speed. Superior sprinters will hold the maximum speed for a longer distance, and decelerate less than average sprinters.

SUPPORT AND DRIVING PHASE

In sprinting, the support phase may also be included in the driving phase for purposes of simplicity. Since a long lever develops more speed at the end than does a short lever moving with the same rotary velocity, the length of the leg during the driving phase of sprinting should be as great as possible. This is achieved by proper foot plant and by full extension at the hip, knee, and ankle joints at the end of the driving phase (Figure 4-15).

The track surface is contacted first on the outside edge of the sole, high on the ball of the foot. The foot plant in sprinting should be directly under the line of gravity. Should the foot plant fall beyond the line of gravity, a retarding sensation would be evident. The support phase is brief and at its conclusion a powerful extensor thrust is initiated beginning in the stronger, slower muscles of the lower back and pelvis and moving to the more peripheral, faster and weaker muscles of the leg and foot. This sequential muscular activity provides a summation of forces whose resultant force propels the body into its airborne trajectory.

RECOVERY PHASE

The instant the foot leaves the ground, it undergoes an acceleration, as the leg flexes at the hip, knee, and ankle joints. (Figures 4-16 and 4-17.) It is well-known that shortening the radius of a rotating body increases the velocity of rotation and it is for this reason that the knee is flexed during the recovery phase. With a flexed knee and a high heel lift, the sprinter automatically experiences a

Figures 4-15—4-20   Irena Szewinska, Poland   **11.13**
                                                          22.21
                                                          49.29

FIGURE 4-15

FIGURE 4-16

FIGURE 4-17

FIGURE 4-18

FIGURE 4-19

FIGURE 4-20

desirable knee lift (Figure 4-18). It should not be necessary to shout at the sprinter to lift her knees.

Throughout all phases the arms swing synchronously with their respective contralateral extremities and the trunk rotates away from the support extremity. The arms should be kept close to the longitudinal axis of the body during their forward and backward swings. This reduces the moment of inertia by keeping the mass close to the longitudinal axis of rotation and thus decreases the resistance to rotary motion. Sprinters with heavy legs will find it necessary to abduct the shoulder joints slightly in order to obtain an efficient arm swing.

The elbows should be flexed with a 90 deg. angle between the arm and forearm. This shortens the radius about an axis through the shoulder joint as the arms swing pendulum-like about this axis. The shoulders should not be rotated, but should be kept in constant alignment relative to the head and neck.

The hands and arms influence the movement of the legs and body carriage and seemingly insignificant details of hand and wrist position, elbow angle, and shoulder rotation can set off a chain reaction of form faults. A very slight medial rotation of the wrist is desirable to enhance the arm movement, and the wrist should remain fixed during the rotary motion of the arms. A flippy wrist creates a secondary lever within a primary lever, and does not contribute to the efficiency of the sprint. The thumb should be lightly pressed against the tip of the second or third finger, instead of making a fist, in order to prevent tension in the muscles of the arm. The muscles used to press the thumb against one of these fingers are located in the forearm, while clenching the fist involves muscles of the entire arm and thus causes restrictive arm action. Slightly flexed fingers are natural as the finger flexors are stronger than the finger extensors.

The shoulders should not be elevated during sprinting as this would create tension in the upper body and reduce the effectiveness of the arm swing. The head and neck should be kept in constant alignment with the shoulders, with the eyes directed accordingly. The effects of a poor head position can often be seen at the end of a long sprint, e.g., the throwing back of the head shortens the stride and is thus detrimental to good technique.

FINISHING

Finishing techniques include the lunge, the shrug, and the straight ahead technique. The lunge and the shrug may be difficult to master. Thus the sprinter should carry the sprint straight ahead beyond the finish line to be assured of an effective finish. This precludes an unwanted deceleration which the sprinter might unconsciously initiate prior to the finish of the sprint.

As a point of information, in close finishes, brightly colored clothing is more likely to be picked up by the eye of a finish judge, should there be a mass crossing the finish line. Darker colors tend not be be seen by the human eye when such movement includes a variety of colors.

THE 100 METERS

The strategy for sprinting 100 m. in competition is limited, but there are some keys to performing well over the short distance. Beginning with a proper warm-up and concluding with breaking the plane at the finish line, the sprint involves a number of considerations.

An efficient start and resultant acceleration is crucial to a good sprint. With smooth acceleration to maximum velocity in the vicinity of the 50 m. mark, the sprinter sets the stage for the second half of the race.

As the 50 m. mark is passed, the sprinter should have a kinesthetic awareness of holding that velocity to the 65 m. mark. It is physiologically impossible to hold top speed for more than 15-20 m., thus the sprinter should feel the smoothness which she has developed over the distance.

At 65 m. it is quite likely that the sprinter is beginning to gradually decelerate. She should not fight this, but instead should be confident that her training regimen will result in a minimum of deceleration. Rather than thinking about relaxing, it would be more beneficial for her to concentrate on the preservation of poise for the remainder of the race. Perhaps she can visualize the electronic eye which will capture her form as she crosses the plane of the finish line. Positive thoughts may not enhance her performance, but negative ones will certainly detract from it.

THE 200 METERS

The 200 m. is usually contested from the top of the curve. This gives a long straightaway for finishing the race.

The difference in time between sprinting 200 m. around one curve is approximately 0.2 sec. slower than when executing the same distance on the straightaway, although it may be more for given sprinters. The theory behind this is that as a sprinter runs the curve an acceleration is produced at right angles to the direction she is running. Thus, because of centrifugal force, her speed is reduced.

Short sprinters tend to be better curve runners, as they have a lower center of gravity and thus have fewer absolute problems with centrifugal force in negotiating the curve.

THE 400 METERS

Physiologists have determined that the oxygen requirement for running increases very rapidly as the velocity increases. It has been stated that an even pace is more economical than a variable pace yet a number of designs for running the 400 m. have resulted in outstanding times and successes for given athletes.

It is evident the 400 m. cannot be sprinted at the maximum possible speed throughout the race; thus, racing strategy becomes paramount. Two basic strategies seem to prevail in the 400 m.:

1) The sprinter moves through the first 200 m. very close to her best time for the distance, the objective being an insurmountable lead to offset the resulting deceleration which will be very evident over the last 200 m. of the race.

2) The sprinter runs a more evenly paced race, covering the first 200 m. within 1½ sec. of her best time for the distance, with the last 200 m. 2-3 sec. slower than the first 200 m.

Most 400 m. races are started from a staggered start on the curve, which means that the sprinter has a long straightaway to finish the race. The starting techniques are the same as for the shorter sprints, but the sprinter should note that the blocks should be set at an angle to the inside of the curve so that centrifugal force is not a problem during the initial strides. The left hand in the "On the mark" position will be 3-4 in. behind the starting line as a result of the angled block position.

The middle lanes are advantageous for running the 400 m. as the curve radius is long and the sprinter will have competitors to the outside. Sprinters who draw the inside lanes have shorter radii and thus more acute problems to overcome.

Centrifugal force, which creates a tendency for the body to continue moving in a straight line instead of along a curved path, is a factor in running the 400 m. Centrifugal force is the reaction to an opposite force called centripetal force. To run the curves at high speed, the sprinter must lean toward the inside of the curve, thus keeping the center of gravity to the inside of her base of support.

The right arm should function in a diagonal plane as the sprinter moves through the curves. This means the right arm comes across the anterior surface of the upper body during this phase of the race.

The foot plant in the 400 m. is not as high on the ball of the foot as in shorter dashes. The arm action is less vigorous due to the lesser speed in the 400 m. The rule of thumb is that the faster the speed the more vigorous the arm action and the higher the plant on the ball of the foot.

Overstriding tends to be a problem with some 400 m. sprinters. Overstriding is mechanically inefficient as a tremendous amount of energy is wasted and deceleration is likely to set in at an earlier stage of the race.

It is worth pointing out that should the sprinter execute three consecutive strides on the lane strip, disqualification will result. It is prudent to move through the curves staying close to the stripe on the left side of the lane, but caution should prevail.

The athlete should sprint the straightaways by staying in the middle of the lane. This precludes any chance of bumping or interference by other sprinters in the race.

At the 300 m. mark, the sprinter ascertains her actual position in the race as all lanes have an equal straight run to the finish line. It is imperative to maintain poise during the latter stages of the race. The sprinter who keeps her technique from deteriorating will exhibit creditable finishing characteristics.

TRAINING

Fall-Winter Program

The value of a fall and winter program in the training regimen of the sprinter transcends the importance of the competitive schedule, which comes later in the yearly program. It is of utmost importance to design a program of work which will provide the sprinter with a base for ensuing competitive efforts. (See Table 4-1.)

The program does not need to be overly sophisticated, but it should contain all the ingredients required for proficient performances a number of months after the initiation of the basic background work.

The fall and winter program should stress those objectives which facilitate effective performance. Among the qualities to be developed are strength, skill, speed, endurance, flexibility, and a command of psychological concepts.

Training programs should provide a gradual progression in terms of increased workloads beyond the usual demands of an activity. The overload principle will eventually determine the effectiveness of the training regimen.

During the fall and winter months, the program should allow a great amount of variation as to the environmental setting. Athletes are likely to develop a distaste for training if they are required to use the same workout facility day after day. They should not work on a hard surface, but on a grassy one whenever possible.

Table 4-1: FALL–WINTER REGIMEN

	Monday	Tuesday	Wednesday	Thursday	Friday	Saturday	Sunday
Stress load:	Medium	Light	Hard	Light	Hard	Light	Rest
	Warm-up	Warm-up	Warm-up	Warm-up	Warm-up	Warm-up	
	Flexibility drills daily from Monday through Saturday						
			Skill		Skill		
	Endurance			Endurance			
			Speed		Speed		
	Strength		Strength		Strength		

Warm-up—Half-mile jog or more, followed by static stretching exercises which work both sides of the major muscle joints. Finish by doing easy 60 yd. build-ups.
Flexibility—Continuation of static stretching and dynamic stretching drills.
Skill—Curve techniques
    Form drills:
        starts from curve and straightaway
        stride training (consistency, length, foot plant)
        high knee drills
        quick leg drills
        arm action drills
Speed—Variable distances to 165 yd., progressing to ¾ speed.
Endurance— Overdistance work to 550 yd. at comfortable pace.
Strength—Progressive resistance weight training at the conclusion of work-outs.

Note: Intensity and number are determined by level of fitness of individual athletes.
      Starts should not be executed until after 6 wk. of effort have been put into the fall program.
      Prior to initiation of the fall program, a 2 wk. session of easy stretching and easy 110's will prepare the athlete for the basic program.

Competitive Season

The spring program changes in intensity and complexity. The sprint events are anaerobic in nature and the program should be designed with this in mind. Once again, the key to a good program is a gradual adaptation to stress. Premature exposure to stress may result in debilitating injuries.

Training for the sprint events revolves around three basic programs, although others may be designed and instituted as supplementary to the three basic ideas on sprint training. The three programs are acceleration sprints, hollow sprints, and interval training.

ACCELERATION SPRINTS

Acceleration sprints are designed to develop speed and reduce the possibility of injury to the athlete. The mode of execution is to sequentially jog, stride, and sprint a given distance, and conclude the cycle with a walk of comparable distance. This type of regimen might involve a constant distance of 60 yd. (e.g., the sprinter would jog 60 yds., stride 60 yd. and then sprint 60 yd. This would be followed by a 60 yd. walk for recovery.)

As the athlete becomes more conditioned, the distance may be increased and the intensity may be more demanding. It is not advisable to use distances longer than 120 yd.

HOLLOW SPRINTS

Hollow sprints involve executing two sprints, with an equal distance of jogging dividing the two efforts. These distances may go up to 150 yd. The recovery distance is the same as the work distance.

An example of hollow sprints would be to utilize 60 yd. as the effort distance. The sprinter would move through a flying 60, followed by a 60 yd. jog, then follow with another flying 60. A 60 yd. walk would be the recovery period. Once again the number and intensity are governed by the condition of the sprinter.

INTERVAL SPRINT TRAINING

Interval sprint training is a popular method of training sprinters. The variables involved in interval training are the distance of the runs, the interval of the rest or recovery between runs, the number of repetitions of the run, and the time or intensity of the runs.

Interval sprint training involves running a specific distance at a predetermined speed, resting a specific amount of time after each run, and running a given number of repetitions.

A wide variation in the control of variables is possible in interval training. These variables must be properly controlled for maximum benefit from the training regimen.

During the early stages of training, the rest intervals should be relatively long. As the season progresses, the rest interval may be reduced. Should the intensity be an all-out effort, a full recovery should be used before the next repetition is begun.

In general, distances less than 440 yd. are used, with the ratio of repetition distance and recovery distance being 1:1, with the recovery taking three times the time of the run. The training program must be flexible with the work loads alternating between hard days and easy days. The human body is not designed to withstand a continuous regimen of hard work.

5 Chris Murray

THE MIDDLE AND LONG DISTANCES

Author: **Chris Murray**, one of America's most respected women's middle distance and distance coaches, is women's track and cross country coach at Iowa State University. A member of the National Women's Track and Field Committee and the International Selection Committee, Murray has coached a number of nationally and world-ranked female athletes. His cross country teams have won three national titles; his track teams have finished second once and third twice in the national championships.

This chapter describes the middle distance and distance competitive running events for the female athlete. The middle distance races for young female competitors with limited training and competitive experience include races of 600 yd. up through 1000 yd., while distance races are 1 mile or longer. For the more mature experienced runner, middle distances range from 880 yd. up through 1 mile. Distance races range from 2 miles through 6 miles, and long distance races are 10 miles or longer.

Distance running is considered by many observers as one of the simplest areas of track to coach. This may not be the case. Bud Winter of San Jose College, coach of many world class runners, observed that many coaches train distance runners like sprinters. Coach Winter was simply pointing out that some coaches do not adequately understand the differences between the running events and cannot identify the specific training needs for distance racing.

The purpose of this chapter is to enable the reader to better understand distance running. No attempt will be made to give *"the way"* to coach distance runners. Each coaching situation is unique. The wise coach will use the information learned to develop a training program that best fits the specific needs of the athletes.

THE DISTANCE RUNNER—WHY DOES SHE RUN?

This is a relevant question because of the unique nature of distance running. Most people cannot understand why a distance runner pushes herself day after day, because it appears to be a most ruthless and agonizing sport. Distance runners disagree and defend their chosen love. This infatuation exists because running *is part of the individual*! The distance runner needs to run! Typically, she is a person who is always in a hurry to go somewhere. She craves activity and finds running relaxing and satisfying. The distance runner tends to be a loner who enjoys the solitude that a long run affords. She is goal-oriented and expects to work hard for what she earns. Running provides an avenue for satisfying these needs.

A coach should build on these positive features of running. The daily training sessions and meet competitions need to be challenging and self-rewarding to the runner. By taking the time to make the total running experience stimulating and appealing, the coach will enhance her runners' desires to succeed.

THE DISTANCE RUNNER—A TOTAL INVOLVEMENT

What aspect of distance running is more important—the physical or mental side? There need not be any lengthy debate, as *both* are extremely important! A top distance runner has a slim physique with a low body fat content. Her total body muscular system is strongly developed and able to endure intense work over a long period of time. Her running form is smooth and effortless. Above all, she has an extraordinary high level of endurance that enables her to run great distances at a very fast speed.

The top runner also has the psychological makeup that enables her to take full advantage of her physical potential. She possesses the patience, self-discipline, and determination to endure intense daily workouts over a period of years. Her mental toughness and concentration are the keys to being able to push herself lap after lap in a fiercely competitive race. She has learned to psychologically force her body to continue running when it cries out to quit.

THE COACH—AN EXAMPLE

Coaching distance running requires extreme dedication and a genuine love of running. You should not ask your runners to make a total commitment to running without first being willing to equally share in such a commitment. You must be a strong positive example.

Each coaching situation as well as each runner is unique. A distance runner is so totally wrapped up in running that running becomes a direct reflection of her psychological makeup. The wise coach recognizes this and takes time to learn about each runner and how to best help her reach personal goals and her innate potential.

You must learn to guide your runners and then step back and let them find their own ways. Distance running is a personal challenge and no one except the runner herself can run that race. Finally, a mature coach, just like the athletes, must realize that success in distance running is not measured in the win and loss column, in gold medals won, or in records set.

Few coaches can look forward to coaching a world record holder. However, every coach is capable of helping athletes to run faster and farther. The ultimate satisfaction to a distance coach is a total commitment to the runners and the knowledge that everything possible has been done to help them realize their goals.

SUCCESSFUL DISTANCE RUNNING—PLANNED PREPARATION

A world-class distance runner like United States Olympic 800 m. champion Madeline Manning Jackson appears to run on natural inborn physical ability. This is not the case. Her effortless running style can mask the years of intense training needed to develop this fluency. The complete control that such a top runner exhibits reflects her total preparation from a well-planned, long-range training program.

Some athletes and coaches interpret a long distance training program to mean mileage training, or long continuous runs. This approach builds up an extraordinarily high endurance capacity and also great mental toughness. But does mileage training alone adequately prepare a runner for her competitive races? Most prominent distance running coaches do not think so, and feel that it should be just one part of a much broader and more comprehensive training approach.

Training must take into consideration both the individual runner's personal needs and all of the variables that are involved in successful competitive distance racing. This is where you, the wise coach, must start. Faced with a challenge much like putting a jigsaw puzzle together, your first move is to find all the pieces; in this case, to ascertain what the runners need to develop through their daily training sessions that will make them complete runners.

THE RUNNER'S NEEDS

The distance runner must develop an extremely high level of endurance which will give her the ability to run long distances at a very fast speed. This involves increasing the capacity of the circulo-respiratory system (lungs, heart, and blood vessels) to supply critically needed oxygen to the exercising muscles. This oxygen supply capacity is the key limiting factor in producing the needed amounts of energy to sustain long periods of intensive distance running. This is called *aerobic capacity*. The greater the aerobic capacity, the greater the oxygen supply; and the greater the amount of useable energy, the faster and longer the athlete can run.

The distance runner must learn to judge race pace and to sustain race pace. Race pace refers to the planned speed the runner hopes to run for the entire race or the actual speed that she maintains during a race. Consider the mile race as an example. A runner might set 5 min. 20 sec. (5:20) as her goal for the race. This means that the race pace would be 80 sec. for each 440 yd. If she runs a paced race, her times at the ¼, ½, ¾, and 1 mile marks (called "splits") would be 1:20, 2:40, 4:00 and 5:20. The runner must develop a built-in pace judgment sense and be able to maintain that pace.

The ability to maintain a specific pace is linked with the runner's aerobic capacity and the ability to continue supplying the amount of oxygen needed. If the runner's muscles receive as much oxygen as they use up in energy production, this is called *steady state*. Therefore, the higher the level of steady state, the faster the running pace she can attain and maintain.

Often during a competitive race the runner must run faster than the overall race pace. This can occur in the opening sprint for position, the mid-race accelerations and the finishing kick. Here the energy demands greatly exceed the runner's maximum aerobic energy production and the ability to maintain steady state. The athlete's performance will break down in this situation unless she has an alternate, short-term, high-energy production process that does not require an immediate oxygen supply. This alternative does exist.

Large amounts of energy can be produced by a process called *anaerobic* (without oxygen) energy production for short intense periods of work. But the chemical products used to provide energy anaerobically deplete quickly and waste products accumulate rapidly. The distance runner will be forced to slow down and even stop running if this chemical depletion and waste product accumulation is too great.

Although anaerobic energy production does not require the immediate use of oxygen, it must be utilized later to resynthesize the needed chemicals and oxidize lactic acid. The runner is building up a need for oxygen which is called *oxygen debt*. When the athlete who has been utilizing anaerobic energy finishes running, her oxygen consumption remains at a high level until her oxygen debt is completely paid off. Therefore, it is critical for a distance runner to build up her anaerobic energy production capacity and her ability to tolerate a high level of oxygen debt.

A distance runner needs to develop an efficient, smooth, relaxed running form. Uncoordinated movements increase muscular tension which inhibits maximum running efficiency. Incorrect running form is one of the major contributing factors of muscle stress, strain, and injuries.

The distance runner also needs to develop overall body strength and durability. The continual pounding from running places stress and strain on many body parts. During the later stages of a distance race, runners often experience a weakening (fatigue) in their arms, shoulders and lower back that can cause a "tightening up" and reduction of performance. A runner needs more than just a strong heart and powerful pair of legs. She needs total body strength.

The above needs are all physical in nature. They are important, but if the psychological needs of the runner are not also met, the runner will not realize her full potential. What are the psychological needs of a distance runner?

The runner must develop the right frame of mind for running. She must constantly remind herself of her true potential and must be completely positive about her running. She pushes aside negative thoughts and feelings. The objective is to build a positive self-image and to gain confidence in her running ability.

A second psychological need is to develop the mental capacity to endure several years of intensive daily workouts and highly competitive races. The distance runner must have the determination and self-discipline to reach her goals. She must build up a mental toughness to enable her to push through barriers.

TRAINING SYSTEMS

With the evolution of modern competitive distance running, many training "systems" have developed. They include the continuous running, fartlek training, and interval training systems. These systems have been successfully adopted by both male and female runners of all ability levels. These systems can form the basis for a sound distance running training program. Take the time to examine each system closely to clearly understand all facets and recognize the strengths and limitations of each system. Then, based on your athletes' needs, you can integrate parts of all systems into the total training program.

Continuous Running System

The oldest and best-known training system is the continuous running system. In simplest terms, this system means running long distances at a constant speed, e.g., running 10 miles in 80 min. at a pace of 8 min. per mile. The runner runs such distance workouts daily over a period of weeks. This system is the most effective means of developing a high level of aerobic endurance. The over-all circulo-respiratory system's efficiency and the maximum aerobic capacity is increased significantly, enabling her to run farther and faster in competitive races.

A variation of the continuous running training system is called *Long Slow Distance* or L.S.D. (a term coined by Joe Henderson of *Runner's World*). Here the athlete runs at a moderate speed for a long distance. The runner maintains a pace that she can comfortably handle without experiencing undue post-workout fatigue or painful soreness. Daily L.S.D. workouts over many months progressively increase the runner's aerobic endurance capacity. The moderate running pace of L.S.D. training reduces exhaustion and fatigue, risk of injuries, and loss of motivation because of psychological staleness. For the beginning runner L.S.D. training strengthens tendons, muscles, and joints, giving her a sound base to build upon. The experienced distance runner often uses this training to build up a pre-season base (e.g., summer preparation for cross country competition).

Another variation of continuous running is *marathon training* as made famous by the noted New Zealand coach Arthur Lydiard. Here the athlete runs extremely long distances (10, 15 or even 20 miles per workout) at a medium speed. The running pace is maintained at a level to sufficiently stress the runner's circulo-respiratory system for the entire run. Athletes who marathon train often run over 100 miles per week. Such training builds an extraordinarily high maximum aerobic capacity. The runner develops great physical and mental toughness.

The *continuous stress run* variation of the continuous running training involves having the athlete run very close to her all-out speed for the training run, somewhere between 90 to 95% maximum speed. The distance of such runs is generally 4 to 8 miles. For example, a middle distance runner who can run an all-out 6 mile run in 39:00 (6:30 per mile) might set 41:00 (6:50 per mile) as a target time for a 6 mile stress run workout. The objective of stress run training is to maximally stress the runner aerobically and thereby increase her peak aerobic capacity. The result of such runs is to elevate the oxygen transport capacity of the circulo-respiratory system and, in turn, the level of steady state. This type of training is severe because the runner attempts to push her training run speed to the point where her physiological capacity to maintain aerobic steady state is right at the breakdown point. Therefore, a coach should not overprescribe stress training for even the experienced runner and should never include it for the beginner.

One form of continuous stress running that may be included is the *timed trial*. Here the athlete runs a specified distance that may be shorter or longer than her preferred competitive distance. The run is accurately timed by the coach and intermediate split times, e.g., half way, are taken. You and the runner set a time objective for the run with the time representing an all-out effort, or a set pace for the run. For example, a miler with a best time of 5:26 who has a goal of 5:20 could run a ¾ mile timed trial at an all-out best effort. Or this athlete could set a goal of 4:00 (80 sec. per 440 yd. or 5:20 mile pace). Such a timed trial can be most helpful when a specific meaningful objective is defined and the run accomplishes the set objective. Be careful not to schedule too many timed trial runs.

Fartlek Training System

Fartlek is a Swedish word meaning "speed play" and refers to a system of running between 3 and 10 miles, constantly varying the speed. This system may also be called "free choice variable speed running" system. Each fartlek run is different from any other and each portion of a run varies. Ideally, the athlete tries to get away from the track and find different running areas such as a park, golf course or beach. While running, the athlete varies her pace from fast to slow to fast whenever she wishes and for whatever distance she chooses. For example, an athlete may do her stretching exercises at the track, jog for 15 min. to a large hilly park as a warm-up and then begin a series of 220 to 330 yd. speed runs, slowing to a jog of 100 to 150 yd. between the speed runs. The speed runs are not exact distances but rather odd distances between obvious landmarks like trees or telephone poles. Without stopping, the runner runs five long runs of 660 to ¾ mi, slowing to a 440 yd. jog between the long speed runs. Leaving the park, she runs about 2 miles back to the gymnasium, striding 100 to 150 yd. at 80% effort with a 50 to 60 yd. jog between stride runs. Finishing such a run, the athlete feels exhilarated while realizing that she has completed a demanding workout. This type of training conditions the runner both physiologically and psychologically to adjust to varying running speeds while running continuously for a long distance. At the same time, the runner experiences a mental lift from the complete change in workout format and the free choice of doing what she wants. This is the unique benefit of fartlek training.

Interval Training Program

The interval training program, also called I.T.P., breaks down the total workload for a training session into a series of mini-workloads with a specified rest period (called relief interval) between each mini-workload. Here the distance runner alternately runs a set distance, e.g., 440 yd., rests for a specified relief interval, e.g., 90 sec. and then repeats this run-relief cycle for a set number of times, e.g., 10 times. The name for this system comes from the relief interval portion of the I.T.P. work-relief training cycle.

The I.T.P. system of training incorporates four variables which can be adjusted to meet the intended objective of the workout. This offers far greater variability than the continuous running training system. Let's look at an example. Consider the young distance runner who is striving to run a 5:20 mile. Her coach might assign the following I.T.P. workout: Run 440 yd. for 12 times in 80 sec., each with a 1 min. rest relief interval between each 440 yd. run. This workout is written as follows:

$$12 \times 440 @ 1:20 \ (1:00)$$

Note that the workout includes four variables. To simplify the planning of these workouts, the four variables can be remembered by using the abbreviation DIRT (see Table 5-1).

D = Training DISTANCE in yards, e.g., 440 yd
I = Relief INTERVAL in minutes and seconds, e.g., 1:00
R = Training REPETITION in the number of runs, e.g., 12 times
T = Training TIME in minutes and seconds, e.g., 1:20

Each of the variables can be adjusted and each adjustment will change the total structure of the I.T.P. workout. The four variables are interrelated and a change in one will necessitate changes in other variables. Let's examine the potential modifications for each variable.

The distance variable in an I.T.P. workout ranges between 50 yd. and 2 miles. The distances could be classified as follows:

Short = 50 to 275 yd.
Medium = 275 to 660 yd.
Long = 660 yd. to ¾ mile
Distance = over ¾ mile

The specific choice of the distance of the repetitive run for the distance runner depends on her individual needs and the stated objective of the workout.

The relief interval (rest recovery) variable alters with the fatigue level after each run and the desired level of recovery. The fatigue buildup, i.e., lactic acid accumulation, is directly related to the intensity of the repetitive runs. A distance runner doing repeat 440 yd. runs in 70 sec. each will require a longer relief interval than if she were doing the 440 yd. runs in 90 sec.

The objective of the I.T.P. workout will influence the relief interval. Two examples will illustrate this point. An athlete running all-out maximum 150 yd. repetition sprints must realize a complete recovery from her relief interval before she can sprint her next all-out repetition. Another runner wishes to maintain a light fatigue level (small oxygen debt) from one repetition to the next. This means the relief interval should provide only partial recovery. This could be accomplished by having the runner check her heart rate during the relief interval. When it drops to 120 beats per min., she would start her next repetitive run. (Resting heart rate is usually 40 to 60 beats per min. for a distance runner.)

There are two ways of catagorizing the relief interval:

(a) rest-relief interval = completely stationary or a very easy slow walk
(b) work-relief interval = rapid walking or jogging

Also, there are three commonly used methods of monitoring the relief interval:

(a) timed relief interval, e.g., 1:30
(b) heart rate relief interval, e.g., start again when heart rate drops to 120 beats per min.
(c) distance relief interval, e.g., slow jog for 220 yd.

Regardless of the relief interval used, the success of the I.T.P. training is to prescribe the proper intensity of running followed by the needed relief interval for recovery. An inadequate relief interval will mean accumulation of excessive fatigue products and premature physiological breakdown.

The number of repetition runs that an athlete performs in an I.T.P. workout is related directly to the time for each run and the completeness of the recovery from the relief interval. The physiological stress placed on the runner (a result of the intensity of the run-relief cycle) determines the number of repetitions that she can perform. Conversely, the number of repetitions influences both the time for each repetition and the amount of the relief interval needed.

The time an athlete runs for each repetition indicates the speed of the athlete and the intensity of her running. The faster the times for her repetitions, the faster speed she is running, and the greater stress (fatigue buildup) she places on her body. In referring to the time being fast or slow, it is in reference to the runner's fastest time for that specific distance, not her maximum all-out sprint speed. Note that the time of the runs directly influences the number of repetitions she can attempt and the amount of relief interval she needs.

One added alteration that is sometimes used is called "sets." A set represents one complete DIRT series, e.g., 12 × 440 @ 90 sec (1:00). If you wish to break up a workout into segments, use two or more sets instead of one large set (breaking the total workout into portions). For example, if you use three sets, each set would represent $^1/_3$ of the total workout. Here are three examples of breaking up the workout listed above into more than one set.

(a)   2 sets: 6 × 440 @ 1:30 (1:00)

(b)   Set 1: 6 × 220 @ 0:45 (0:30)
        Set 2: 6 × 440 @ 1:30 (1:00)
        Set 3: 6 × 220 @ 0:45 (0:30)

(c)   Set 1: 4 × 660 @ 2:15 (1:30)
        Set 2: 4 × 440 @ 1:30 (1:00)
        Set 3: 4 × 220 @ 0:45 (0:30)

The four I.T.P. variables give you unlimited latitude in developing interval workouts that fit training objectives and the individual needs of distance runners. Most important, all of the critical physiological elements needed for distance running can be highly developed by carefully planned I.T.P. workouts.

There are so many variations within the interval training program that there needs to be some catagorizing of the workout possibilities, i.e., according to their intensity. The intensity of a workout is directly related to the number of repetitions run, the time for each repetitive run, and the completeness of the relief interval. A workout can have the same intensity whether the choice of distance is short, medium, or long. The chart below shows the range of intensity from maximum to pace.

Intensity	Sets	Repetitions	% of Max. Speed	Relief interval
Maximum	1	1 - 2	95 - 100%	Complete
Stress	1	3 - 5	85 - 95%	Almost complete
Tempo	1 or more	6 - 12	75 - 85%	Near complete
Repetitive	1 or more	13 - 20	65 - 75%	Partial
Slow Endurance	1 or more	21 and over	under 65%	Partial
Pace	1 or more	variable	variable	Adequate

The key physiological elements needed for distance running include (a) aerobic capacity, (b) pace, (c) anaerobic capacity, (d) running efficiency and (e) speed. All of these are important for any competitive runner regardless of her event. But each running event has a different priority level for each element. The following chart shows the priority of these elements for different race events.

Training Element	Sprints	Middle Distances	Distances	Long Distances
Aerobic Capacity	Low	Very high	Top	Top
Pace	Low	High	Top	Top
Anaerobic Capacity	High	Very High	Medium	Low
Running Efficiency	Top	High	Very High	Top
Speed	Top	Medium	Medium/Low	Low

What types of interval training workouts can develop each of these elements? Using the four I.T.P. variables plus that multiple variable of intensity, Table 5-1 gives the characteristic workout factors for each element. It provides the basis for designing individualized interval training workouts. You, the coach, already have your own objectives, the athlete's specific training needs, and the athlete's exist-

Table 5-1:

	D Distance	I Relief Interval	R Repetition	T Time	Intensity
Aerobic Capacity	Any distance of 220 yd. and up.	Such that the heart rate does not drop back too much (partial recovery)	Very High	Good enough to get the heart rate up to 150, but not too fast to create an oxygen debt	Enough to continually work the runner
Pace	Varies according to workout objec-tive. Usually ¼ to ⅓ of race distance	Properly select-ed so runner can complete total workout while retaining pace speed	Varies accord-ing to workout objective	Most often same as runner would run her race—could be a little faster	Hard
Anaerobic Capacity	Needs to be over 250 yd. to get true oxygen debt; Range 300-660 yd. Best from 300-350 yd.	(a) incomplete re-covery so runner starts next repe-tition with small oxygen debt or (b) complete recovery	Varies but may be either 2-4 or 5-8	Must be fast enough to create lactic acid build-up and oxygen debt	Very high to force runner into anaerobic production
Running Efficiency	All distances		All repeats	Any time	All intensity levels
Speed (absolute; all-out maximum)	Distances up to 220 yd.; Best at 50-150 yd.	Complete	Very low	Tops—that is, 100%	Maximum in-tensity

ing condition level as necessary information. The challenge is to utilize a combi-nation of the I.T.P. variables to design a workout that both adequately stresses the athlete and allows enough rest recovery. Since there are thousands of potential I.T.P. workouts that could be designed, they can be both challenging and interest-ing for each athlete.

THE TOTAL PROGRAM

Once you identify the key physiological and psychological elements needed for distance running and the training systems used to develop these areas, you are ready to set up the total program. Such a program should meet two criteria—it is designed specifically for the runners involved and it is a well-planned, long-range approach. To accomplish these criteria the coach must consider the following areas: (a) personal aims, goals and coaching philosophy, (b) the personal needs and goals of individual runners, (c) available facilities, (d) outside factors, and (e) scheduling (training and competitive).

You must know yourself! Why are you coaching? What are your personal aims, goals and coaching philosophy? Is your coaching philosophy compatible with your total outlook? The answers to such questions will provide a direction. How can you guide your athletes without first determining which direction to go?

The physiological and psychological needs of a distance runner have been discussed earlier. In addition to these needs, each distance runner has her own personal goals. A perceptive coach will learn about each runner and build on this understanding. Running is part of a distance runner, not just an activity that she is doing. Effective coaching means that you train the runner as a person, not simply the runner to run.

You need to see what facilities, training areas and equipment are available. Is there an outdoor track and also an indoor track for cold weather? What hours is the track available? Are a weight lifting room, gymnasium, and swimming pool available? What other training areas are available? A distance program should include a wide range of different types of areas that offer variation in surface, e.g., soft dirt, grass, cement; and terrain, e.g., flat, rolling hills, steep hills. Look into the use of nearby parks, golf courses, forest reserves, beaches, and walking trails; map out a wide variety of large running loops with the distances varying between 2 and 15 miles. Location of a "killer hill" and other specialized training aids is also helpful.

Recognize the outside factors that influence the program. These factors involve both activities and people. Some examples of activities include band, choir, student council, part time jobs, cheerleading and other sports such as basketball. The influences these activities can have include competition for facilities, scheduling of competition meets, competition for the runner's time, and sometimes a choice between activities. Do not ignore the existence of these activities, but encourage the interests and hobbies of the runners. A successful distance runner is usually a well-rounded individual. Her boyfriends, parents, other coaches and school personnel can have great influence on the program. Encourage their support and keep them informed about the program.

THE TRAINING/COMPETITION CYCLE

Once you identify the key elements of successful distance running, fit them together to form a total running program, both the preparatory training and competitive races. The training and competition follow a gradual progressive build-up. Both have "on and off" periods. There are two competitive race seasons—cross country and track. In between there is usually no competition. Thus the training program has very intense all-out phases as well as relaxed, non-pressured, easier phases. What exists is a training/competition cycle.

The most appropriate training/competition distance running cycle is a yearly one that corresponds to the school year. The summer vacation is a transitional period to rest from the just completed track season and to start again for the next year's training/competition cycle. The cycle is broken down into phases. Each phase has specific objectives and workouts designed to meet the objectives. The runner progresses through each phase until she reaches the last one when she is fully prepared to perform at her highest level. For example, here is a 10-phase distance running training/competition cycle that could be used in a school situation.

Phase	Activity	Date
1	Active Rest	June to mid-July
2	Base Build-up	Mid-July through August
3	Early Cross Country	September to mid-October
4	Late Cross Country	Mid-October to mid-November
5	Change of Pace	Mid-November through December
6	Second Build-up	January and February
7	Preseason Track	March
8	Early Season Track	Early to mid-April
9	Midseason Track	Late April to Early May
10	Peak of Track	Mid-May to Early June

Phase 1: Active Rest

This period starts right after the last major outdoor track meet and is a time when both the coach and runner get away from running. An "active rest" means that the runner does not completely stop physical activity. Instead she participates in activities other than running such as bike riding, swimming, tennis and basketball. The athlete attempts to get away from running without becoming deconditioned. She should feel completely rested and refreshed after such a period.

Phase 2: Base Build-up

Here the runner begins to train for the new cycle. She builds up a very solid aerobic endurance base by using L.S.D. (long, slow distance) continuous running training. The coach should ease her runners into this initial building phase by starting very moderately and slowly progressing.

For the beginner, this training is light, starting with only 15 min. 4 times per week (every other day). On the off days, the beginner plays 30 min. of basketball or tennis, etc. After 2 weeks, the coach can start the beginners on the regular base build-up workouts with slight modifications.

The returning distance runner starts with 15 min. of continuous moderate activity and gradually increases this each day until she reaches 45 min. at the end of 3 weeks. The majority of these initial workouts are continuous moderate running to keep the heart rate between 140 and 165 beats per min. For variation the runner may split some workouts by running for half of the time and then swimming or bicycling for the rest. Each workout should be preceded by an adequate warm-up.

The last part of this build-up phase includes workouts that are exclusively L.S.D. and fartlek training. Because the runner is running hard and longer, the hard-easy training approach is adopted. Here the runner alternates between one hard day of fast continuous running (30 to 45 min.) and an easier day of moderate L.S.D. running (45 to 60 min.). Again, one day of complete rest is taken each week to allow the runner to start a new week refreshed. Such a workout pattern is individually adjusted for each runner to meet her existing condition level. Remember not to push too hard too fast! The approach is to gradually build up the workload and maintain a consistency of training over an extended period of time.

Often the coach cannot hold scheduled summer workouts. The athletes are on their own. A wise coach does not simply turn her runners loose, but instead gives them proper guidance. An excellent idea is to have a team meeting just prior to the summer vacation for the purpose of completely outlining what the summer program will be and the purpose it serves. Special mention should be made of sensible training habits, e.g., avoiding running in extreme heat. This is especially important for the beginners who will be starting a training program for the first time. The coach should have talk sessions and give them handouts. The topics should include (a) footwear, (b) warm-up, (c) cool-down, (d) diet, (e) injury prevention, and (f) running form. Briefly, what are the points that should be covered under each of these areas?

(a) *Correct footwear* is imperative. If the shoes do not fit properly they will cause considerable discomfort and potentially severe blistering. Blisters often force a runner to cut back her training. Several prominent shoe companies make a wide range of shoes specifically for competitive track and field. These shoes are designed for the event and have features not found in the average athletic shoe. It is worth the investment for a distance runner to buy such shoes. The popular tennis or basketball shoe is not recommended for distance runners.

(b) A *proper warm-up* before each training session is.a must. Such a warm-up will physiologically prepare the runner because it gets all of her systems, e.g., cardiovascular, functioning above the resting level; psychologically prepare the runner for an intense workload and lower the risk of injuries such as muscle strains. The athlete must realize the importance of a proper warm-up and discipline herself to warm-up before every workout and race. Such a warm-up should include:
(i)   5 to 10 min. of very easy jogging
(ii)   Light static stretching of all major muscle groups
(iii) A series of 6 to 8 build-up 100 yd. sprints (first one at 50% and gradually speed up to 95% for the last one)

(c) *An adequate cool-down* is also important. When the runner finishes a workout or race, her body does not immediately return to the resting state. If she has sustained a high level of oxygen debt, the runner's heart rate will remain over 120 beats per min. for some time. An easy cool-down will ease the body back to its resting state and also help metabolize waste products (lactic acid). The cool-down provides a gradual reduction in body temperature after exercise. The cool-down itself is simple—a very slow jog or alternating walk and jog for 5 to 10 min. after the workout or race.

(d) The distance runner cannot neglect her *diet*. The intense daily training greatly increases the runner's caloric needs and depletes nutrients, salts, and fluid. A contributing factor to the rundown condition that many distance runners experience can be a poor diet. The runner should eat three well-balanced, nutritious meals each day. An excellent idea is to incorporate the basic four food groups into her daily meals. They include:

Milk Group—Drink 4 glasses daily. Cheese, ice cream and other milk-made foods can supply part of the milk.

Meat Group—Eat 2 or more servings daily of meat, fish, poultry, eggs, or cheese, with dry beans, peas, nuts or peanut butter as alternates.

Vegetables and Fruits—Use 4 or more servings daily. Include a dark green leafy or deep yellow vegetable or yellow fruit at least 3 to 4 times a week for vitamin A. Include a citrus fruit, tomatoes, or other good source of vitamin C every day.

Breads and Cereals—Eat 4 or more servings daily. Use enriched or whole grain products.

(e) *Injuries* can haunt the distance runner. An unexpected injury, no matter how minor, can hamper and even curtail the runner's training and racing. How can the athlete prevent injuries? The runner should practice good safety habits and guard herself against freak accidents. She should take precautions that will reduce the chances of injuries. For example, she should (i) run on soft surfaces whenever possible, (ii) minimize fast down-hill running, (iii) always warm-up and cool-down, (iv) treat minor problems like blisters immediately.

(f) Correct *running form* is a key facet of distance running. Uncoordinated form will significantly reduce both maximum economy of effort and maximum speed. Many injuries, in part, result from incorrect running mechanics. The coach should view the overall action to see if it is efficient, smooth, and relaxed. The arms and legs should swing rhythmically and smoothly back and forth (Figures 5-1 through 5-7). The entire running action should move along a straight line. If the overall action is poor, the coach should concentrate on the runner's body angle, foot placement, stride length, and arm swing.

The proper body angle is a natural trait. For the distance runner the body posture is erect with a forward lean occuring only when the runner sprints. In foot placement, the landing should be made toward the back of the ball of the foot (Figure 5-3). The body weight then will drop lightly onto the heel for a temporary settling phase before springing back up on the ball and finally raising up onto the toes for the extended pushoff. Note that the foot should point forward, not toe-in or out. The natural stride length is determined by the running speed. A distance runner's stride should be moderate in length. A short, choppy stride is inefficient while overstriding will cause exaggerated bouncing and leg strain. Finally, arm action should be a relaxed, rhythmic swing from the shoulders. A low-swinging arm action seems less tiring and aids in balance.

Figures 5-1—5-7   Francie Larrieu, USA   **4:06.2**
                                                                2:00.2

FIGURE 5-1

FIGURE 5-2

FIGURE 5-3

FIGURE 5-4

FIGURE 5-5

FIGURE 5-6

FIGURE 5-7

For the last three weeks of the build-up phase, the following sample workout pattern could be used:

Day	Beginner	Middle distance	Distance
Monday	5 miles slow	7 miles slow	9 miles slow
Tuesday	5 miles medium	5 miles medium	6 miles medium
Wednesday	Active recovery	5 miles fartlek	6 miles fartlek
Thursday	5 miles slow	7 miles slow	9 miles slow
Friday	5 miles medium	5 miles medium	6 miles medium
Saturday	7 miles slow	8-9 miles slow	10-12 miles slow
Sunday	Active recovery	Active recovery	Active recovery

Phase 3: Early Cross Country

This phase will start in conjunction with the beginning of school in September. If the runners have built up an adequate endurance base during the summer, they are ready to enter a new phase of training that will increase maximum aerobic capacity, elevate their steady state level and develop pace work. A good check to see if they have built up an adequate base is to have the middle distance runners run for 45 min. and the distance runners run for 1 hour. If they can run at a good pace for the entire time period without any undue fatigue, they have succeeded in building up an adequate base.

Training during this phase has a dual purpose. First, it is the second state in the total preparation of the runner for her ultimate race performances in this new cycle (in May and June). Second, it is a preparation for the cross country season. The weekly training pattern now includes not only continuous running workouts, but also interval training (I.T.P.). A greater variety of continuous running workouts is used including long slow runs, medium distance (5-7 miles) faster pace, and fartlek runs. The interval training should be mainly repetitive and of slow endurance intensity. The major emphasis is to increase the runner's maximum aerobic capacity and thereby elevate her level of steady state. The hard-easy approach must be used because the fartlek and I.T.P. workouts are more severe and need to be followed by an ease-off day. Also, the workout patterns for the middle distance and distance runners vary slightly. Although both run cross country, their needs are different. Listed below are samples of weekly training programs for this early cross country phase. When a specific workout is given as an example, it will be for a middle distance runner with 2:25 for 800 m. or a distance runner who could run 5:30 for the mile and 12:00 for the 2 mile run.

Phase 3: Weekly Workout Patterns

Note: A workouts = no competition week
B workouts = competition week
There is a range in the number of repetitions in the sample workouts, e.g., 8-12 × 440. The middle distance runners would do the minimum of 8 repeats and the stronger distance runners would do the maximum of 12 repeats.

Monday	(A) Slow, long intervals, 880 to mile, 80-85%, 4-8 repeats, e.g., 4-6 × ¾ mile @ 4:48 (4:00)
	(B) Continuous run, either fartlek or medium run, e.g., 6-9 miles fartlek
Tuesday	(A) Continuous run, medium or slow, 5-10 miles, e.g., 6-10 miles slow
	(B) Slow, long intervals, 880 to 1 mi., 80-85%, 4-8 repeats, e.g., 3-4 × 1 mile @ 6:30 (4:00) + 1-2 × 880 @ 2:50 (3:00)
Wednesday	(A) Slow, medium intervals, 550 to 880, 75-85%, 6-12 repeats, e.g., 8-12 × 660 @ 2:12 (2:00)
	(B) Continuous run, fast or medium, 5-7 miles, e.g., 5-6 miles fast
Thursday	(A) Continuous run, fast or medium, 5-7 miles, e.g., 5-6 miles fast
	(B) Repetitive short intervals, 110 to 440, 65-75%, 12-20 repeats, e.g., 10-15 × 330 @ 0:55 (1:30) + 6-8 × 165 @ stride (0:30)
Friday	(A) Short, repetitive intervals, 110 to 440, 65-75%, 12-20 repeats, e.g., 10 × 440 @ 1:26 (1:20) + 10 × 220 @ 0:36 (0:45)
	(B) Continuous run, medium speed, plus short strides 55 to 165 yd., e.g., 4-5 mile medium run + 10 × 110 stride (jog 55 yd.)
Saturday	(A) Continuous long slow run, e.g., 8-12 miles slow
	(B) Race
Sunday	(A & B) Active recovery, e.g., 30-45 min. bike ride

An excellent idea during this phase is to have an ease-off week in the middle of the phase where the runners do nothing but non-pressured, easy over distance continuous running. For example, on Monday, Wednesday, and Friday run slowly for 50-60 min., while on Tuesday, Thursday and Saturday run medium fast for 30 min. Have a complete rest on Sunday.

Phase 4: Late Cross Country

As the runner's maximum aerobic capacity increases and the more important cross country meets approach, the workout emphasis shifts. The interval repeats are shorter, e.g., more 220's, 330's and 440's, and the times are faster. The runner now experiences a degree of lactic acid build-up and resulting oxygen debt during the interval workouts. Some pace work training is done to familiarize the runner with her cross country pace. The runners peak very slightly, but the overall objective remains a continued development for the major track meets.

The workouts during the race weeks are reduced on Thursday and Friday. The cross country meets are more important now, e.g., conference championships, and the runners need to be rested for such meets. Before the season's final major meet, the coach should cut back even further. The objective of that week is to sharpen the runners and mentally prepare them.

Phase 4: Weekly Workout Patterns

Note: A workouts = no competition week
       B workouts = competition week
       8-10 repeats means 8 repeats for middle distance and 10 repeats for distance

---

Monday	(A & B) Short, repetitive intervals, 220 to 350 yd., 12-20 repeats, 60-75%, e.g., 8-10 × 440 @ 1:28 (1:30) + 8-10 × 220 @ 0:38 (0:45)
Tuesday	(A & B) Pace intervals of ¼ to ½ race distance, 6-12 repeats, pace, e.g., 6-8 × 880 @ 3:00 (4:00) (if goal for 2 miles = 12:00)
Wednesday	(A & B) Continuous run, fast 4-5 miles or medium 5-6 miles, e.g., medium speed 6-8 miles
Thursday	(A) Short tempo interval, 150 to 330, 65-75%, 15-20 repeats, e.g., 10-12 × 330 @ 1:00 (1:00) + 10-12 × 165 @ 0:27 (1:00)
	(B) Short fast tempo interval, 150 to 330, 75-85%, 10-15 repeats, e.g., 5-8 × 330 @ 0:55 (1:30) + 6-8 × 165 @ 0:25 (1:00)
Friday	(A) Medium length continuous run, e.g., 6-8 mile medium run
	(B) Short continuous run plus short strides, e.g., 3-4 mile medium run, 1 × 220 stride, 8 × 50 stride (50 yd.)
Saturday	(A) Medium tempo intervals, 330 to 660, 6-12 repeats, 75-85%, e.g., 3-4 × 550 @ 1:45 (2:00) + 3-4 × 440 @ 1:20 (2:00) + 3-4 × 330 @ 0:55 (2:00)
Sunday	(A & B) 30 min. active recovery, e.g., bicycle ride 30 min.

The cross country races are the first competitions for this new cycle and the first ever for the beginner. A major goal of daily training is to prepare the runner for competition. Racing is exciting, challenging, and satisfying, but it can also be frightening. A beginner often fears pain, failure, and the unknown as she nears her first competitive race. You, the coach, can do several things to minimize such trauma and fully prepare the runners for competition. First, if you plan the training program properly, there is no need for "psyching-up" the runners. If they are prepared and rested, the runners will eagerly look forward to competition and will be psychologically ready. Always give praise and other psychological rewards to all of the athletes who perform well in races. (A good performance is not necessarily winning—it is relative to the individual's personal ability.) The race schedule should be sensibly selected! Initially there should be a few non-pressured inter-squad races as an initial exposure to competition. The first interscholastic race should be an unimportant dual meet against a team of equal ability. The total number of meets should be kept to a minimum, with one meet per week, ideally. The coach should de-emphasize the early competitions by training through these races (run a full workout the day before the race) and by emphasizing to the runners the greater importance of the later meets.

Finally, do not overreact to a meet performance either by giving excessive praise or severe criticism. If a runner performs well, she should be appropriately congratulated. When she loses, chat with her quietly and both of you can decide how to correct the error to perform better in the next meet. This will give the athlete a much more positive view of competition.

Phase 5: Change of Pace

Following the competitive cross country season, the runner needs a change. There is a natural letdown after the championship meet—win or lose. Although she is physically and psychologically peaked, the runner feels tired from the intense workout schedule.

The purpose for this phase is twofold. First, it gives the athlete a refreshing break from structured workouts and competitive meets. Second, it is a time to continue training at a low-keyed, nonpressured level. Do not supervise workouts, but rather give the runners a few guidelines and turn them loose. The total team should get together once a week for a team workout. Note that following the cross country season some athletes may move into other sports, like basketball. Therefore, these athletes now will be training for their other sport. If the training schedule of this other sport is not too time-consuming and the other coach agrees, these athletes should include a 20-min. continuous free run in their daily schedule. For the athletes training exclusively for competitive running, here is a sample weekly workout pattern for this phase:

Phase 5: Weekly Workout Patterns

Monday	15 min. fartlek plus 45 min. games, e.g., basketball
Tuesday	15 min. continuous run plus strength training*
Wednesday	Warm-up, 10 × 150 strides, 45 min. games, e.g., volleyball
Thursday	15 min. continuous run plus strength training*
Friday	15 min. fartlek plus 45 min. games, e.g., tennis
Saturday	Team Long, Slow Distance run (middle distance runners—4-5 mi.; distance runs—6 mi.
Sunday	Rest

Phase 6: Second Build-up

This phase starts in January and lasts for 9 weeks. The main objective is to further increase the runner's aerobic capacity in preparation for the outdoor track program. A second objective is to develop all-around body strength through a sound strength program. Below are sample hard and ease-off weekly training schedules. Suggested are two hard weeks followed by an ease-off week, and repeating this pattern three times.

Phase 6: Hard Buildup Week

Day	Middle Distance	Distance
Monday	5 miles fast, strength training	7 miles medium, strength training
Tuesday	45 min. fartlek	1 hour fartlek
Wednesday	5 miles fast, strength training	7 miles medium, strength training
Thursday	45 min. fartlek	1 hour fartlek
Friday	5 miles fast, strength training	7 miles medium, strength training
Saturday	8 miles L.S.D.	10 miles L.S.D.
Sunday	Rest or active rest	Rest or active rest

*Purpose of 2 days a week strength training is to ease athlete into a strength program. See Chapter 13 for details.

Phase 6: Ease-Off Buildup Week

Day	Middle Distance & Distance
Monday	15 min. medium run, strength training
Tuesday	15 min. medium run, 30 min. games, e.g., basketball
Wednesday	15 min. medium run, strength training
Thursday	15 min. medium run, 30 min. games, e.g., volleyball
Friday	15 min. medium run, strength training
Saturday	6 mile run, medium
Sunday	Rest

For athletes participating in another sport during this time, encourage them to do a continuous run 20 min. each day and 45 min. on the weekend.

Phase 7: Preseason track

This is a transitional phase to familiarize the runner with the outdoor track workout pattern. It is the first time the runner is on the running track. The workouts are more intense and the runners experience some initial muscle soreness and tightness. The objective here is to ease the runners through the change from an endurance-building phase into the outdoor track workout pattern. The difference between the middle distance and distance runner's workouts become more noticeable now because of the different needs for these race categories. Here is a preseason track workout pattern that may be used for two to three weeks:

Phase 7: Weekly Workout Patterns for Middle Distance Runners

Monday	Short tempo interval (anaerobic) 110-440's, 75-85%, 6-12 repeats, e.g., 8 × 330 @ 0:52 (2:00) on track
Tuesday	Stress interval, 440-880's, 85-95%, 3-5 repeats, e.g., 4 × 660 @ 1:58 (5:00) on grass
Wednesday	Continuous run at medium to fast pace, 5-8 miles, e.g., 6 miles medium
Thursday	Short tempo interval, 110-440's, 75-85%, 6-12 repeats, e.g., 6 × 440 @ 1:14 (2:00) + 6 × 165 @ 0:26 (1:00) on grass
Friday	Pace interval at ¼ to ⅓ race distance, race pace speed, e.g., 2 sets: 8 × 220 @ 0:36 (1:00)
Saturday	Continuous run at medium to fast pace, 5-8 miles; 6 mile medium
Sunday	Rest or active recovery

Phase 7: Weekly Workout Patterns for Distance Runners

Monday	Short repetitive interval, 110-440's, 70-80%, 10-20 repeats. e.g., 15 × 440 @ 1:20 (1:30) on track
Tuesday	Long stress interval, 880-1 mile, 85-95%, 3-5 repeats, e.g., 2 × ¾ mi. @ 4:30 (5:00) + 2 × 880 @ 2:48 (4:00) on grass
Wednesday	Continuous run at medium speed, 6-8 miles. e.g., 8 miles medium speed
Thursday	Tempo interval (anaerobic) 330-660's, 75-85%, 6-12 repeats, e.g., 8 × 660 @ 2:08 (3:00)

Friday	Short pace interval, ⅛ to ¼ race distance, e.g., 2 sets: 8 × 330 @ 1:00 (1:00) on track (for a 5:30 miler)
Saturday	Continuous long, slow run, e.g., 10 miles slow run
Sunday	Rest or active recovery

Phases 8, 9, and 10: Early, Mid, and Late Season

If the outdoor competitive track season is divided up into thirds, each phase represents approximately one third. Here the workouts are designed to prepare the runner for all-out track racing. Each training session is directed at developing a particular element needed for that running event. The specific training is different for middle distance and distance races. Therefore each race category will be discussed separately.

Modern middle distance running was characterized by the women's 880 m. final in the 1976 Olympic Games. This race was won in 1:54.96 with the top four finishers under 1:56. All eight finalists were tightly bunched at the 400 m. mark, at a time of 0:55.3. This tight pack remained through 600 m., when three runners began to fall back. The winner did not assume the lead until the last straightaway, when her greater ability enabled her to pull away to a 5 m. victory.

What did this race show? The first 400 m. is run very fast. Even pace for 1:54.96 would be 0:57.5, whereas the lead group ran it in 0:55.3, which is 2 sec. under even pace. For the next 300 m., the runners push all-out to maintain the earlier race speed. It is an attempt to minimize deceleration. The runner who succeeds is said to have "staying power." For the last 100 m. the runners must utilize their physical reserve to accelerate. Many close races are decided by this late race acceleration which is called the "finishing kick." How does the 800 m. runner develop these qualities? How should she train?

Training is a process of physiological adaptation. If the runner trains daily and if her workouts are nearly equal to the body's normal capacity to handle the workouts, then the body adapts by further increasing its capacity. Now the workouts are increased to match the body's new capacity, which in turn results in an even greater capacity, and so on. This process of increasing the workout intensity to match the increase in the body's capacity is called progressive loading. The middle distance runner uses this principle to effectively increase both aerobic and anaerobic endurance capacity. The build-up period (phases 1 through 6) is used to maximally develop aerobic capacity. The training shifts for the phases 7 through 10 to the final element of anaerobic capacity. This is the key to running the 800 m.! No matter what level of aerobic capacity the runner develops, she cannot rely on it exclusively to run an all-out 800 m. During the middle and particularly the later portion of a race, the runner must use her anaerobic reserve to maintain the running pace (staying power) and to accelerate on the last straightaway.

Two types of workouts develop anaerobic capacity. They are short, fast interval repetition and stress repetition. The object of the short, fast interval training is to run each repetition fast enough to sustain a partial anaerobic oxygen debt and then to have an adequate but not complete recovery interval. The runner runs a sufficient number of repetitions to sufficiently stress the body's anaerobic capacity but not enough to severely overtax the system. Such a workout employs the progressive loading/adaptive principle as each repetition creates an oxygen debt to which the runner's body must adapt. The second type of anaerobic workout is called stress training. Here the athlete runs a limited number of near all-out repetitions. (For example: 3 × 660 @ 95% of maximum speed.) These highly stressful runs place severe demands on the runner's maximum anaerobic capacity and increase her "staying power." Such training closely duplicates actual race conditions. The stress run forces the runner to not only run while incurring a considerable anaerobic oxygen debt, but to tolerate such a stressful situation over distances from 400 m. to 700 m.

Short interval and stress interval workouts are extremely demanding and taxing. Although they are the backbone of the middle distance runner's track workout pattern, there must be a recovery day between such workouts. An excellent recovery day workout is a continuous run which also serves the purpose of maintaining the runner's aerobic capacity. Pace work should also be included in the middle distance runner's workout pattern. Here the pace speed should be the speed that the runner plans to run her first 400 m. For repetitive pace intervals the athlete should run ⅓ to ¼ the race distance. Finally, some all-out speed work helps the runner to build confidence in her final kick. Here is a sample workout pattern for phases 8 and 9:

Phase 8: Early Season Workout Patterns for Middle Distance Runners

Monday	Fast Interval, 220-550's, 75-85%, 6-12 repeats, e.g., 8 × 350 @ 0:57 (2:00) on track
Tuesday	Long stress interval, 660-¾ mile, 85-95%, 2-5 repeats, e.g., 2 × ¾ mile @ 4:25 (5:00) + 1 × 660 @ 1:54 (5:00)
Wednesday	Continuous run and fartlek, e.g., 45 min. ¼ steady run & ¾ fartlek
Thursday	Pace intervals, ¼ to ½ race distance, e.g., 12 × 275 @ 0:43 (1:30)
Friday	Short continuous run and short, fast/medium intervals, e.g., 30 min. run + 20 × 156 @ 0:27 (1:00)
Saturday	Race
Sunday	Rest or short active recovery

Phase 9: Midseason Workout Patterns for Middle Distance Runners

Monday	Fast interval, 220-550's, 80-85%, 5-10 repeats, e.g., 8 × 350 @ 0:55 (1:30)
Tuesday	Stress Interval, 440-660's, 85-95%, 2-5 repeats, e.g., 1 × 660 @ 1:50; 1 × 550 @ 1:30; 1 × 440 @ 1:08; 1 × 220 @ 0:29 (5 minutes)

Wednesday	Short continuous run and short, fast intervals, e.g., 30 min. run + 20 × 165 @ 0:27 (jog 165) on grass
Thursday	Fast pace interval, 250-440's, slightly faster than race pace, e.g., 6 × 440 @ 1:10 (3:00)
Friday	Short continuous run plus very short intervals, e.g., 20 min. run + 12 × 110 stride (55 jog)
Saturday	Race
Sunday	Rest or short active recovery

Phase 10 for the Middle Distance Runner

This is the climax of the training/competition cycle. The "big" track championship meets occur at this time. All training ultimately is directed toward preparation for these meets. The runner usually achieves her seasonal best performances, all-time personal records (PR's). The length of this phase depends on the number of major meets scheduled and the runner's performances in the meets. The most successful runners advance as far as the National Amateur Athletic Union (AAU) Championships and even into the international summer meets. But regardless of the runners' abilities, they can look forward to realizing personal goals and the rewards of hard training.

The training emphasis should be one of peaking and of tuning the runner. Also, it is important that the runner is adequately rested so that she can perform to her maximum capacity. Daily workouts and the overall weekly pattern must reflect this emphasis. Added coaching time needs to be devoted to special areas such as refining the runner's start. The daily workout load should be cut by roughly one third with the emphasis on quality and overall sharpness (fewer repetitions, faster times, shorter distances with longer rest intervals). One day of stress intervals should be retained early in the week. The inclusion of one speed workout is a worthwhile addition. Generally a gradual tapering off should start by Wednesday with Friday being a very light day. A sample weekly workout pattern for phase 10 follows.

Phase 10: Workout Patterns for
Middle Distance Runners

Monday	Short pace interval, 220-300 at pace which runner plans to run her first 400 m. of 800 m. race, e.g., 6 × 250 @ pace (2:00) + 8 × 110 @ 85% (110 jog)
Tuesday	Stress interval, 300-500, 90-95%, 3-4 repeats, e.g., 3 × 440 @ 1:10 (4:00) + 1 × 220 @ 0:29
Wednesday	Continuous run, medium speed 25-45 min., e.g., 30 min continuous run, medium speed + 10 × 50 stride
Thursday	Speed day! Short fast intervals, 110-200, 95-98%, 6-12 repeats, e.g., 6 standing gun starts + 8 × 165 @ 0:23 (1:30) + 10 minute free run
Friday	Loosen up! e.g., 10 min. easy run + 6 × 50 stride, 1 × 220 @ 85%
Saturday	The "BIG" race
Sunday	Jog 10 min.—that's all!

Phase 8 and 9 for Distance Runners

The workout patterns included in this section focus on preparation for the 1500 m. and mile races. These races are the longest track running events in most state high school girls' track. The training now shifts to a wider variety of workouts to develop all of the needs for competitive track races. The 9 month endurance build-up provided the essential aerobic base that the 1500 m./mile runner must have. But the endurance base is only a beginning. The miler now must develop the capacity to run the entire race at a steady, fast pace. Typically the miler must start the race quickly to establish good running position. Then the runner settles into the race pace for the next 600 m. After 800 m., the runner concentrates on maintaining her earlier race pace. She must push herself to prevent deceleration. Finally, over the last 200 m. the runner utilizes her finishing kick.

The workout pattern used to develop the runner's capabilities to run such a race must include maximum capacity aerobic intervals, long stress intervals, pace intervals, anaerobic intervals, and fast continuous runs. The purpose of the maximum capacity aerobic interval workout is to significantly increase the workload intensity that the runner can sustain aerobically. This enables the runner to run a much faster race pace and to maintain this pace without experiencing anaerobic oxygen debt. The aerobic intervals are 330 to 660 yd. in distance, fast enough to elicit a near maximum aerobic output, medium number of repetitions, and adequate but not complete recoveries. A sample aerobic interval workout would be 10×330 @ 0:55 (1:30). The long stress intervals develop the runner's capacity to maintain an intense, stressful running pace for a long interval. Such a workout develops "staying power."

The stress interval workout consists of a limited number of repetitions (2-5), a running pace equal to or slightly faster than race pace, 95% effort, complete interval recovery, and medium distance (550 to 1320) or long distance (1¼ to 2 miles). A sample stress interval workout would be 1×1320, 1×880, 1×660 at 90% maximum speed with 5 min. rest intervals. The pace intervals are designed to familiarize the athlete with running at her planned race pace speed. Typically the repetition distance for intervals is ⅓ to ¼ the race distance. The number of repetitions and rest intervals depends on the athlete's capacity to handle the race pace speed for such interval runs. The miler needs to do some anaerobic workouts because she will undoubtedly experience some periods of oxygen debt during her competitive races. Two types of workouts that can develop anaerobic capacity are the short, fast intervals and fast fartlek training. The miler cannot ignore continuous running simply because her training emphasis has shifted. Such runs are still very important. The runs should use all three forms depending on the workout objective. They are (a) medium fast runs to build up the maximum aerobic capacity; (b) fartlek runs to experience both varying running speeds and anaerobic debt, and (c) longer easier relaxed runs as an "ease off" training day. Sample workout patterns follow.

Phase 8: Workout Patterns for Milers and Distance Runners

Monday	Aerobic intervals, 330-660, 70-80%, 8-16 repeats, e.g., 10× 550 @ 1:45 (1:30)
Tuesday	Medium/long stress intervals, 660-2 miles, 85-95%, 2-5 repeats. e.g., 1 ×1½ miles @ 9:40 (5:00) + 1 × ¾ mile @ 4:24 (5:00) + 1 × 660 @ 1:54
Wednesday	Medium continuous, steady run and fartlek, e.g., 30 min. medium speed steady run + 15 min. fartlek
Thursday	Pace intervals, ⅛ to ¼ race distance at race pace, e.g., 16 × 330 @ race pace (1:20)
Friday	Medium continuous run plus strides, e.g., 5 miles easy run + 8 × 110 strides (jog 55 yd.)
Saturday	Race
Sunday	Active recovery e.g., 30 min. bike ride

Phase 9: Workout Patterns for Milers and Distance Runners

Monday	Medium Stress intervals, 550-¾ mile, 85-95%, 2-5 repeats, e.g., 1 × 880 @ 2:45 (4:00) + 1 × 770 @ 2:22 (4:00) 1 × 660 @ 1:58 (4:00) + 1 × 550 @ 1:32
Tuesday	Medium/fast continuous run, e.g., 7-8 miles medium run
Wednesday	Pace intervals, ¼-⅓ race distance, at race pace, e.g., 12 × 440 @ race pace (1:30)
Thursday	Fast short anaerobic intervals, 220-350, 80-85%, 5-10 repeats, e.g., 8 × 275 @ 0:40 (2:00)
Friday	Short continuous run plus strides, e.g., 3-4 miles easy run plus 8 × 110 strides (55 yd. jog)
Saturday	Race
Sunday	Rest

Phase 10 for the Distance Runner

The training approach for phase 10 is the same for the distance runner as for the middle distance runner. The objective is to peak the runner and be sure that she is adequately rested for the important track meets. Following is a sample workout for this phase.

Phase 10: Workout Patterns for Milers and Distance Runners

Monday	Short pace intervals, 220-440, race pace, e.g., 6 × 440 @ 1:20 (1:00) + 6 × 220 @ 0:40 (0:30)
Tuesday	Medium stress intervals, 550-880, 85-95%, 2-5 repeats, e.g., 2 × 880 @ 2:38 (5:00) + 1 × 550 @ 1:30
Wednesday	Medium continuous run plus strides, e.g., 5 miles medium speed plus 10 × 110 stride (55 yd. jog)

Thursday	Short, fast intervals, 165-250, 85-95%, do ⅔ of normal workload, e.g., 6 × 220 @ 0:30 (3:00)
Friday	Short, easy continuous run e.g., 2 miles easy run
Saturday	Race
Sunday	Rest

RACE STRATEGY

An important responsibility in coaching runners is to teach them correct racing strategy. A race is often won by a lesser runner who wisely makes the correct move at the opportune time. Conversely, the strongest runner in a race sometimes loses because she runs a tactically incorrect race and is unable to utilize her full potential. How does one teach a runner proper strategy?

Unfortunately, all runners cannot become excellent race strategists! Many situations that occur unexpectedly during a race require a split-second instinctive move. But this does not mean that a runner cannot learn to run tactically sound races. The coach should start by clearly explaining and demonstrating the correct and incorrect ways to run and *why* specific tactics are sound or unsound. Next the runner should be exposed to running strategy by running some workout repetitions to experience varied race-type situations and to try specific tactics. The best workout to use for this race-type experience is the stress interval where the runner does a limited number of near all-out repetitions. Whenever possible you and the athlete should observe races together and evaluate the strategy of the participants. Also, following each race, the runner and you should review the race strategy. If some tactical errors were made, both of you examine why the errors were made, how to correct them, and how to avoid them in future races.

Experiment to find out what race strategy best fits the runner's attributes. Every runner has both strengths and weaknesses. Even with extensive training, some weaknesses, e.g., lack of sprint speed, cannot be totally eliminated. Therefore, the general strategy a runner adopts for her racing needs to emphasize her strengths and minimize her weaknesses. Once a runner develops her general competitive strategy, she should plan a specific strategy for each race.

A runner cannot rely exclusively on pre-planned race strategy, however. Unexpected changes just before or during a race can render pre-race strategy inoperative. Such changes could include inclement weather, late new entries or scratches, or a poor race start. Therefore a runner should develop an adjustability that permits her to moderate her strategy to fit the race situation.

The mature runner learns to anticipate most unexpected race problems and to tactically adjust to them. She develops the ability to run very competitively in all types of races. This is what ultimately separates a great runner from a good one—the ability to compete well in all situations. When competitors are evenly matched in talent and preparedness, race strategy is often the difference.

LONG-RANGE PROGRAMS

The ten-phase yearly cycle provides a progressive build-up to prepare the runner for her peak performances at the year-end championship meets. Ultimate success in distance running is dependent on a similarly well-planned, long-term program that prepares the runner to realize her true potential when she reaches physical and psychological maturity. How should a long range program be designed?

The first year should be primarily an introduction to year-round training and competitive racing. The workout load should be built up very gradually. Do not overwork the enthusiastic newcomer. The emphasis should be to develop a sound initial endurance base. This should be a learning time with minimum emphasis on winning or time goals. The most important thing is to get the runner started correctly.

During the second year the runner should start to realize her potential running ability. A distance runner is ready to commit herself to a year-round training program and competitive meet schedule. She needs to set some tangible competitive goals to give specific direction to her training program. Some ideas about long-range training and competitive goals need to be formulated. The workout pattern is now more individualized to incorporate the specific needs of the runner. Special attention is paid to the runner's weaknesses and how to minimize them. The runner is usually very enthusiastic because she recognizes a direction to her training and potential goals that she can achieve.

By the third year the runner is pointing toward specific goals—both short and long-range. The more gifted athletes can start pointing toward major accomplishments such as state championships, records, national meets, and even an international competition like the Olympics. The training program is geared to reaching these challenging goals and becomes much more individualized and long-range. The athlete is not afraid to set very high goals and is willing to train both long and intently to reach them. Even the "plodder" is more ready to follow a specialized long-range workout program to reach her personal ambitions. By this time the runner realizes that there is no easy road to success and that she needs patience and long-term training. You can help the athletes learn this and keep them continually motivated to reach their goals.

THE HURDLES

> *Author:* **Patricia Brown** is girls' track coach at Basin High School, Basin, Wyoming, where she has compiled an enviable coaching record—in 5 years of competing in the Wyoming state meet, her teams have finished first (once), second (twice) and third (twice).

The two recognized hurdle events for women, on the international level, are the 100 m. and 400 m. races. Considering the distance variation and the modification in technique required, most athletes do not attempt to compete in both, but choose to specialize.

100 M HURDLES

Hurdling can best be described as a sprint race over obstacles. Successful hurdlers display as little alteration of sprinting form as possible. Every fourth stride the competitor must step over the barrier with only stride adjustment enough to clear the hurdle efficiently. Good hurdlers display only a 2 sec. increase over their best 100 m. effort when the ten hurdles are added. Good efficiency of motion is beginning to come when this variation is reduced to 4 sec. or less.

The techniques of high hurdling can basically be applied to the women's 100 m. race. Even though the barrier is only 33 in. high, the short stature of most women makes the technique comparison favorable. While the hurdle technique will be broken into segments for analysis, it is important to view the hurdling action as a smooth, coordinated effort which flows in a rhythmic fashion. There is no beginning, middle, or ending; no hesitation or delay.

Start

A sprinter's start must be used. Block spacing, bunched or medium, should be partially determined by personal preference but must be such that the hurdler arrives at the first barrier in the correct stride pattern. When seven strides are used from the start to the first hurdle, the lead leg will be placed on the front block and the take-off foot (trail leg) will be placed on the rear block. For those using eight strides, which may result in a better stride rhythm being established for many girls, the foot placement in the blocks is reversed with the trail leg being placed in the front block. The performance from the gun through the first barrier sets the tone for the entire race, so try to clear the initial hurdle in first place. In addition to the psychological advantage, there are fewer distractions and hazards when leading.

Many novices tend to jump from the blocks and straighten up too suddenly. Make sure the start is the same as a sprinter's for the first three to four strides, stressing forceful arm use and horizontal movement along the track for maximum acceleration.

Because speed is directly related to stride length and frequency, the winning hurdler will display proper sprinting mechanics. For optimum leg speed, a good kick-back (heel lift) should be employed. By thus shortening the lower leg complex, through joint flexion, the inertia around the hip joint is reduced, allowing maximum angular acceleration to develop.

Approach to First Hurdle

Perfecting the approach to the first hurdle requires repeated work at top speed. The length of strides four-five-six may be varied slightly until the approach pattern has been stabilized. Strides one-two-three and strides seven-eight should remain normal.

Visual awareness of the first hurdle should not occur until stride four or five. Then focus on the top rail of the barrier. The arms function identically to those of a sprinter until take-off occurs.

The greater approach speed achieved, the more horizontal take-off thrust may be generated allowing for a lower, flatter flight curve and a resulting quicker hurdle clearance. Ideally the last stride before take-off should be shortened slightly to rotate the trunk forward. Then the drive from the take-off foot will project the body over the hurdle in a more horizontal path. This body lean must be initiated on the ground as the flight curve of the center of gravity will be determined at this stage and cannot be altered in the air.

Take-off

The take-off point will be 5 ft. 9 in.-6 ft. 3 in. from the hurdle depending upon the speed of approach, height of the athlete, length of the lead leg and effectiveness of the lead-leg action. Up to 90% of the clearance action over the barrier is determined at take-off. Body lean must be sufficient to permit clearance with a minimum of upward movement. By lowering the trunk the hurdler can still effectively raise the hips enough for efficient clearance as the center of gravity will remain low.

Leave the ground from the toes of the take-off foot (Figure 6-1). The shoulders, hips, and feet should all be aligned so that they are directly "facing" the

FIGURE 6-1

FIGURE 6-2

FIGURE 6-3

FIGURE 6-4

FIGURE 6-5

FIGURE 6-6

FIGURE 6-7

FIGURE 6-8

FIGURE 6-9

FIGURE 6-10

Figure 6-1—6-10   Annelie Ehrhardt, East Germany   12.59

barrier. The center of gravity must be ahead of the take-off foot as the body leaves the ground. At take-off, lift the lead leg directly forward with the knee raised strongly and well flexed (Figure 6-2). The knee position will be higher than in a normal sprint stride. The speed of lead-leg lift determines the speed of hurdle clearance. Stress strong rapid knee lift. This motion encourages continuation of good sprint action, increases drive through the take-off leg in reaction to the increased speed of the lead leg, results in good separation (splitting) of the legs and increases effective body lean. Strive to move the lead foot so fast it cannot be seen clearly.

As the lead leg begins its lift and extension, the opposite arm will ideally be positioned forward and slightly downward, toward the lead foot and shin, to give continuity and balance to the body motion. This arm action also assists in moving the center of gravity forward and facilitates trunk lean downward. The chest should lower to a position parallel and near the lifting thigh of the lead leg. The trailing arm follows normal sprinting pattern by bending at the elbow and moving back, close to the body, in preparation for its forward stroke at clearance (Figure 6-3).

Clearance and Recovery

By utilizing a fast lead-leg action, a good split between the legs will occur and this, in turn, will make a quick trail leg action possible. Body lean continues in the air with the chin over or ahead of the lead knee, depending on the height of the athlete—tall athletes will display less lean (Figure 6-4). With correct lean at take-off, the body's center of gravity will reach the highest point in its flight curve, 6-12 in. before reaching the hurdle and then pass down over the barrier. Before the hips reach the hurdle, the lead leg will be nearly straight (but not locked) and moving down toward the track (Figure 6-5). Normally the head will face forward at all times. Some men have been experimenting, with mixed results, with dropping the head to look at the knee during the layout phase.

After full extension of the take-off leg, the heel of the take-off foot should be lifted to the hips, as in a normal stride (Figure 6-6). This folding action of the trail leg allows the leg to clear the barrier as an efficient unit. The trail leg begins its forward movement into the next stride at the completion of this folding phase and as, or just after, the hips cross the hurdle (Figure 6-7). When viewed from the side, the thigh of the trail leg would be parallel to the hurdle rail and over or slightly behind it as the hips cross. When the knee of the trail leg crosses the obstacle in advance of the hips, the lead leg action has been slow. A quicker, more forceful drive of the lead leg at take-off is necessary. As the trail leg passes over the hurdle, the inner portion of the thigh will be facing and parallel to the ground. A right angle is formed between the lead and trail legs as the trail leg crosses the hurdle rail. Body lean is maintained through this phase, resulting in the majority of the body weight passing over the hurdle before the trail leg comes through. Cock the foot on the trail leg upward to avoid striking the hurdle with the toes.

As the trail leg passes over the rail, drive the knee strongly upward toward the chest and attempt to stride away from the hurdle (Figure 6-8). When correct trail leg action is implemented, it will be unnecessary to stress lead-leg snap-down. By bringing the trail knee up after hurdle clearance, the equal and opposite occurring reaction forces the lead leg in a downward arc. Landing on the lead leg will occur 3-4 ft. past the barrier with the initial contact occurring on the ball of the foot and the center of gravity being positioned slightly ahead of the contact point (Figure 6-9). During this trail-leg action, the lead arm will begin to recover, with the arm being flexed partially and the hand passing a bit below and outside the pulling trail leg. The trailing arm reaches forward in unison with the trail leg. Premature or violent lead-leg snap-down will force the trunk to rise too quickly. Loss of body lean will cause the trailing leg to drop and possibly strike the hurdle as it attempts to come through.

As the hurdler returns to normal sprinting attitude, the eyes should focus on the upper rail of the next barrier (Figure 6-10).

Between the Hurdles

Three strides must be taken between hurdles. Assuming the athlete lands 3 ft. from the hurdle, has a 5 ft. get-away stride, and takes off for the hext hurdle 6 ft. 6 in. from the barrier, she has a remaining distance of 13 ft. 4 in. to cover in two strides. This can usually be accomplished by a girl of average ability. If she cannot cover the distance in three strides, more strength and technique work must be undertaken.

Finish

Striding off the last hurdle, the athlete will be slowing. She should be aware

Table 6-1: AN EXAMPLE OF STRIDE PATTERN FOR 100 M HURDLING

	Strides	Stride Length	Total Distance
Start and approach to the 1st hurdle	1st stride	1 ft. 8 in.	1 ft. 8 in.
	2nd stride	3 ft. 7 in.	5 ft. 3 in.
	3rd stride	4 ft. 3 in.	9 ft. 6 in.
	4th stride	4 ft. 9 in.	14 ft. 3 in.
	5th stride	5 ft. 3 in.	19 ft. 6 in.
	6th stride	5 ft. 9 in.	25 ft. 3 in.
	7th stride	6 ft. 1 in.	31 ft. 4 in.
	8th stride	5 ft. 3 in.	36 ft. 7 in.
Take-off distance to 1st hurdle		6 ft. 1 in.	42 ft. 8 in.
Landing distance behind 1st hurdle		3 ft. 9 in.	46 ft. 5 in.
Strides between 1st and 2nd hurdle	1st stride	5 ft. 1 in.	51 ft. 5 in.
	2nd stride	6 ft. 7 in.	58 ft. 0 in.
	3rd stride	6 ft. 1 in.	64 ft. 1 in.
Take-off distance to 2nd hurdle		6 ft. 5 in.	70 ft. 6 in.

Table 6-2: SPLIT TIMINGS FOR 100 M HURDLES

Times At Landing of Lead Foot After Each Hurdle Clearance	100 m. Hurdles Time					
	12-12.5 sec.	12.5-13 sec.	13-13.5 sec.	13.5-14 sec.	14-14.5 sec.	14.5-15 sec.
1st Hurdle	2.1	2.1	2.2	2.2	2.3	2.3
2nd Hurdle	3.1	3.2	3.3	3.3	3.5	3.5
3rd Hurdle	4.1	4.2	4.4	4.5	4.7	4.8
4th Hurdle	5.1	5.3	5.5	5.6	5.9	6.0
5th Hurdle	6.1	6.3	6.6	6.8	7.1	7.3
6th Hurdle	7.1	7.4	7.7	7.9	8.3	8.5
7th Hurdle	8.1	8.4	8.8	9.1	8.5	9.8
8th Hurdle	9.1	9.5	9.9	10.2	10.7	11.0
9th Hurdle	10.2	10.6	11.0	11.4	11.9	12.3
10th Hurdle	11.3	11.7	12.1-12.2*	12.6-12.7*	13.1	13.5-13.6*
Finish	12.3	12.8	13.2-13.3*	13.7-13.8*	14.3	14.8-15.0*

*Hurdlers displaying comparatively poor endurance.

of the number of strides to the finish, normally five to six, and maintain aggressive sprinting action right through the tape. (An example stride pattern for the 100 m. hurdles and split times for the same event are shown in Tables 6-1 and 6-2, respectively).

400 M HURDLES

The 400 m. hurdle race is a specialist event requiring concentration on efficient technique and experience to ensure even distribution of effort throughout the entire race. As this race is rather new to the women's events, only limited test information is available concerning time differentials between the flat 400 m. and the 400 m. with hurdles. Available information points to a 4-6 sec. time difference in well-conditioned hurdlers with the first 200 m. being covered 3-5 sec. faster than the second 200 m. With increased participation in this event, these differentials will come down.

The 400 m. hurdle race is probably the most grueling track event for women today. The race requires speed, endurance, relaxation, efficient technique, competitive spirit, a well-established sense of rhythm, and a well-planned stride pattern. Good 400 m. hurdlers follow a race plan suited to their individual stature, stride length, and endurance.

The ability to run the curve and to possibly alternate lead legs is necessary. Ideally the lead leg should be the left, with the opposite arm reaching slightly across the center line of the body, during the hurdling sequence, in order to allow the runner to lean into the curve and use it to her advantage. If a right lead must be used, be sure to carry the trail leg fully over the hurdle, rather than along the side when running the inside lane, to avoid disqualification.

Start and Approach

A sprint start is employed for best results. Acceleration should occur, as in any sprint race, for the first eight to twelve strides. As the desired pace is reached, the athlete must concentrate on establishing the same stride rhythm she requires for smooth clearance of the first two to three hurdles. The following stride series can serve as a guide from the start to the first hurdle:

> 22 strides for a 15 stride pattern
> 22-23 strides for a 16 stride pattern
> 23-24 strides for a 17 stride pattern
> 24-25 strides for an 18 stride pattern
> 25-26 strides for a 19 stride pattern

When an odd number of strides is used to the first hurdle, the lead leg will be placed on the front block. For an even number of strides, the trail leg will be placed in the front block. The correct stride pattern adopted will vary with the natural stride length, e.g., for 17 strides approximately 6 ft. An odd number of strides between barriers will ensure a constant lead leg. When an even number of strides between hurdles is utilized, then the lead leg will alternate.

Take-off, Clearance, Recovery

As the 30 in. barrier is used in the 400 m. event, some modifications of technique should occur to ensure maximum hurdling efficiency. At take-off, the thigh of the lead leg should rise to horizontal and the lower leg should swing forward and upward only the amount required for rail clearance. This requires braking or stopping the forward swing of the lower leg as the heel reaches hurdle height. For tall athletes there will not be a complete extension of the lead leg. If such extension occurs, the hurdler will have difficulty returning to the ground quickly. Shorter athletes will experience more complete extension.

Body lean will be much reduced but must still be present to ensure the center of gravity reaching its zenith prior to passing over the barrier.

The trailing leg will swing through with the knee lowered slightly. As the trail knee clears the barrier, the thigh is lifted to enable the lower leg to reassume the correct sprinting position. Body lean will be more pronounced in the shorter athlete. Do not stress exaggerated chopping down of the lead leg. Be sure the center of gravity moves forward of the lead leg upon contact after the hurdle and a smooth pull through for the get-away stride should follow. A small amount of float may occur while passing over the hurdle, but this may be necessary to maintain the striding rhythm.

Learning to run the curve efficiently in all lanes is necessary and requires great emphasis during training.

Most 400 m. hurdlers will be forced to alter the stride pattern as fatigue increases, usually between hurdles five and six. This technique, called a "change down," should be smooth and must occur gradually over the entire stride pattern, rather than by chopping the last three or four strides before the next barrier. For a smooth change down, work to increase the tempo of the leg action, thereby cutting stride length gradually. If a one-stride change down is used (17 to 18) then the athlete must be proficient with both right and left leads. A two-stride change down is too abrupt for one hurdle flight but may be necessary if the athlete can only lead with one side. If a two stride change down is required, work should be intensive to ensure smooth distribution of change down and to avoid the speed and tempo loss if chopping occurs.

The arm pattern will be the same as for the 100 m., but less exaggerated. Smoothness is vital to efficiency.

Recording touchdown times following each barrier is an efficient, simple way to check pace patterns. Touch-down times for the first five hurdles will range between 4.7-5.1 sec. and will increase to 6.7-7 sec. during the latter portion of the race. Starts will average 6.7-7 sec. from gun to first touchdown (45 m. or 147 ft. 7½ in. plus touchdown distance) and 6.7-7 sec from last touchdown to the finish (40 m. or 131 ft. 2½ in. less touchdown distance).

Finish

The final 40 m. from the last barrier to the finish will reflect the ultimate stamina, running form, and mental toughness of the competitor. Maintaining the established stride pattern will ensure a strong finish. With the oxygen debt now present it will not be possible to increase speed, so consistency will be the key to success.

TEACHING PROGRESSION

1. Divide group according to height into short, medium, and tall clusters and place each group in a separate lane on the track.
2. Start behind a common starting line crossing all three lanes. Have each group sprint down their lane for about 15 strides. Repeat three to four times—stressing top speed. Use a standing start with take-off foot touching line and lead leg taking first stride.
3. Place bamboo sticks (or canes of any lightweight material) across the lanes midway between strides four and five and strides eight and nine. The sticks will be farther apart for the taller groups.
4. Sprint two repetitions over the sticks and shift people who are having problems with three strides. Another lane may have to be established.
5. Place the flat side of a brick under each end of each stick. Continue sprinting over the sticks.
6. Stand bricks on end and top with sticks. Sprint through again several times. Stress aggressive sprinting action.
7. Add a second brick. Continue to sprint through each height increase three to five times. Stress sprint. As the height of the barrier rises, it will be necessary to back up the starting point and the distance between the obstacles. Concentrate on good sprinting action and consistent stride length.
8. As the sticks reach low hurdle height, emphasize good lead-leg action and step down on the ball of the foot, not the heel.
9. Check to be sure arm action remains aggressive and correct.
10. Concentrate on only one portion of the technique required at a time.

Additional Tips:

Hold a rope or place a high jump crossbar about 18 in. above head height at the barrier to encourage the student to lean correctly.

Place a marker in front of the hurdle at the desired take-off point.

As the trail leg passes over the hurdle, allow the knee to turn outward.

Place a marker beyond the hurdle at the desired landing location. Place getaway location of the stride. Hula hoops work well.

Speed along the ground is vital. Spend as little time as possible in the air.

Encourage aggressive attack at the hurdles.

Do not allow the hurdlers to over-stride between the hurdles.

Stress quick lift of the lead leg.

Observe hurdlers from the front, the back, and the side when checking technique.

Make sure feet and toes point directly down the running line.

Observe trail leg action to be sure it passes fully over the hurdle, not alongside.

Never train over a single hurdle.

TRAINING PROGRAMS

Training for both the 100 and 400 m. hurdles must, by necessity, include work in the areas of flexibility (joint mobility), endurance, strength, speed, and technique. Championship hurdling will result when all areas show progressive improvement.

Flexibility

All track and field events require some degree of joint mobility. Hurdling is an event which requires a higher than ordinary degree of flexibility in order to realize an improvement of technique and to avoid injury. Specific areas requiring concentration are the hip joints and the lower back regions.

Mobility may be defined as the range of movement possible in a joint. Before starting on specific mobility work, be sure the athlete has completed an adequate general warm-up involving all parts of the body.

Movement requires the contraction of some muscle groups and the simulteneous relaxation of others. Slight pain may result when stretching beyond accustomed level occurs. The presence of pain acts as a safety value to prevent the tearing of tissue. Stretching should progress gradually to the level where slight pain is present and then be held briefly. Jerky or bouncing-type movements may not allow pain to develop quickly enough to warn the hurdler of tissue injury. All mobility and stretching work should be done slowly and smoothly. Progress to the maximum possible extension and hold. Never bounce to strive for an increase.

The following mobility exercises involve flexion and extension, abduction, and rotation of the hip joint. Flexion occurs when there is a decrease in the angle at a joint. Extension occurs when there is an increase in the angle at a joint. Abduction occurs when the limb moves away from the body, adduction when it returns to the body. Rotation is the turning of a body part on its long axis outward or inward as shown by the position of the toes.

Actions specific to each exercise are keyed as follows in the flexibility diagrams shown:

1) Flexion of hip
2) Extension of hip
3) Abduction of hip
4) Rotation through hip
5) Flexion of spine
6) Extension of spine

FIGURE 6-11 and 6-12: Squat position, feet flat onto the floor. Raise hips,
keeping hands on the floor. (5)

FIGURE 6-13: Stand with legs crossed.
Bend to touch toes. Switch legs and repeat. (5)

FIGURE 6-14: Trail leg along hurdle.
Reach for floor with hands. (1, 3, 4, 5)

FIGURE 6-15: Lead leg on hurdle.
Reach for knee with chin, keeping back
straight. (1, 2, 5)

FIGURE 6-16:   *Standing or lying on side, raise leg and hold. (3)*

FIGURE 6-17:   *On all fours, extend leg upward and behind, then to the side. (2, 3, 6)*

FIGURE 6-18:   *Lying on back, pull knees to chest. (2, 5)*

FIGURE 6-19:   Do V sit ups and bent knee sit ups. (1, 5)

FIGURE 6-20:   Hurdle position on the floor. Move chin towards knee. (1, 3, 4, 5)

FIGURE 6-21:   Standing or sitting on floor, feet astride, hands behind head, bend forward. (1, 3, 5)

FIGURE 6-22:   Lying on back, one leg flat on the floor, raise the other leg straight toward the face. Raise the upper body. (1, 5)

FIGURE 6-23:   Yoga kneeling posi-tion. (1, 5, 6)

FIGURE 6-24:   Sitting, legs straight in front, press chest forward. (1, 5)

FIGURE 6-25:   Lie on back, raise legs back over head. (5)

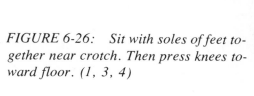

FIGURE 6-26:   Sit with soles of feet to-gether near crotch. Then press knees toward floor. (1, 3, 4)

FIGURE 6-27: Yoga-Snake back extension. (2, 6)

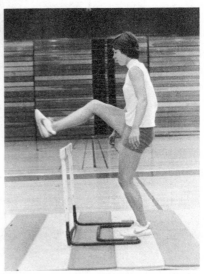

FIGURE 6-28 Lead leg simulation. Lift knee, then extend leg quickly over hurdle. (1, 2, 5)

FIGURE 6:29: Trail leg simulation. Pull leg through, along the hurdle. (1, 3, 4)

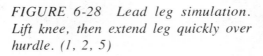

FIGURE 6-30: Sit with soles of feet together. Slide feet out, pull head toward feet. (1, 3, 4, 5)

FIGURE 6-31: Holding a support, swing leg forward and back, keeping the leg straight. (1, 2)

FIGURE 6-32: Holding a support, raise outside leg, with knee flexed and toes turned out. (3, 4)

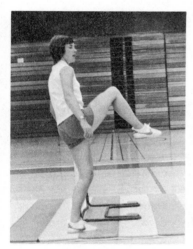

FIGURE 6-33: Holding a support, raise outside leg to front, with knee flexed. Extend straight behind, and abduct with knee flexed. (1, 2, 3, 4)

Mobility work must be a part of the year-round training program. Fifteen to twenty minutes per day is a minimum recommendation. Rapid improvement in suppleness will be evident in most novices. The first few weeks some soreness should be expected, but it will work out as improvement is noted. Stretch every day, especially when sore.

Endurance

Hurdling is basically sprinting, so concentration on good running habits is important. Early season training should include jogging and then speed work at over-distance. All of the running types of training—fartlek, circuit training, interval training—may be utilized. Workouts should be varied to keep the interest of the hurdler high and designed with specific goals in mind. As the competitive season approaches, much of the distance running will be replaced by work over the race distance so that stride rhythms can be finalized. 400 m. hurdlers should spend much of their training time at race pace, using interval work, to stabilize race rhythm and stride patterns.

Strength

Strength improvement will obviously be necessary with most athletes. Weight training should be an integral part of the year-round program. Stress total body conditioning. Many athletes will need intensive work to raise the quality of their upper body strength to an acceptable level. Other ideas on strength include:

Running in sand or water.

Running and jumping drills in a swimming pool.

Variations of hopping, jumping, and striding over a set distance, striving to decrease the number of strides necessary to cover the distance.

Hopping, running, jumping in heavy boots, heavy shoes, or with weights attached.

Depth jumping from boxes or stair steps.

Jumping training circuits, using hopping and jumping over and around obstacles.

Running into a strong wind.

Speed and Technique

Improved speed will begin to come as all of the other areas improve. Technique improves rapidly when the hurdler is physically conditioned to meet the demands she is making of her body. Work over three, five, and seven hurdles for form should be used. Gun starts on through the first three barriers should be done at top speed. It may be necessary to adjust the distance between the hurdles slightly until stride patterns have been well established.

Sample Training Programs

This outline should serve only as a guide. The program used must reflect the hurdlers age, experience, time available, facilities available, and temperament.

All Training Periods

Warm-up
Jog 800 m.
15-20 min. mobility exercises
Warm-down
Jog 800 m.
10-15 min. slow stretching

100 M. Hurdles

Off-Season

Monday and Friday:

> Warm-up
> 2-3 miles cross country at easy pace
> Weight training
> Warm-down

Tuesday and Thursday:

> Warm-up
> 10-15 min. warm-up with sprinters
> 5 × start over three hurdles and walk back
> 4 × 200 m. at 6-8 sec. over best 200 m. time—walk recovery
> 4-6 × 100 m. fast with 200 m. jog recovery
> 5 × start over 3 hurdles
> Warm-down

Wednesday:

> Warm-up
> 20-30 min. fartlek running or
> 3-4 × 400 m. at best 400 m. time plus 15-20 sec.—walk 200 m. after each.
> 3-4 × 60 m. sprints from blocks
> Warm-down

Saturday and Sunday:

> Rest

Pre-Competitive Season

Monday and Friday:

> Warm-up
> 4-6 × start from blocks over 3 hurdles
> 4-6 × start from blocks over 5 hurdles
> 2 × 200 m.—walk 200 m. after each
> Weight training
> Warm-down

Tuesday and Thursday:

> Warm-up
> 4-6 × start over 6 hurdles, walk return
> 2 × 200 m. in best 200 m. time plus 5-6 sec.—walk 5 min. between
> 4-6 × 60 m. sprints from blocks
> 1 × 400 m.
> Warm-down

Wednesday:

> Warm-up
> 4-6 × running start through sets of 5 hurdles down and 5 hurdles back
> (turn-abouts)
> 4-6 × sprint 60 m.
> 3-4 × stride 200 m.
> Warm-down

Competitive Season
Monday:

> Warm-up
> 3 × start over 3 hurdles
> 3 × start over 6 hurdles
> 3-4 × 100 m.—return jog 100 m.
> Weight training
> Warm-down

Tuesday:

> Warm-up
> 2-3 × start over 5 hurdles
> 2 × start over 100 m.
> 3-4 × 150 m.
> 4 × 5-8 hurdles—running start
> Warm-down

Wednesday:

> Warm-up
> 2-3 × start over 3 hurdles
> 2-3 × start over 6 hurdles
> 1 × 300 m.
> 3 × 100 m.
> Warm-down

Thursday:

> Warm-up
> 4-6 × start over 5 hurdles
> 4 × 150 m.
> Warm-down

Friday and Sunday:

> Rest

Saturday:

> Compete

400 M. Hurdles

Off-Season
Monday and Friday:

> Warm-up
> 2-4 miles cross country, easy pace
> 2-3 × 300 m. acceleration sprints
> 2-3 × 150 m. acceleration sprints
> Weight training
> Warm-down

Tuesday and Thursday:

> Warm-up
> 2 × 400 m. at race pace
> 2 × 400 m. with hurdles, work stride rhythm
> 6-8 × 150 m. sprints
> Weight training
> Warm-down

Wednesday:
>Warm-up
>20-30 min. fartlek running
>Weight training
>Warm-down

Pre-competitive Season
Monday:
>Warm-up
>4-6 × start through 5 hurdles
>6-8 × 100 m. around curve from running start
>Jog for 10 min.
>Weight training
>Warm-down

Tuesday:
>Warm-up
>2 × start over 4 hurdles
>2 × start over 6 hurdles
>2 × 600 m. with 8-10 min. rest between
>4 × 100 m. sprints
>Warm-down

Wednesday:
>Warm-up
>2 × 400 m. hurdles with 10 min. recovery
>4 × over 5 hurdles
>4-6 × 200 m. sprints
>Weight training
>Warm-down

Thursday:
>Warm-up
>1 × 800 m.
>2-4 × over first 3 hurdles and last 3 hurdles with run in between
>2-4 × start over 3 hurdles
>4 × 150 m. sprints
>Warm-down

Friday:
>Warm-up
>2 × 400 m. with hurdles
>4 × 150 m. from gun start
>Weight training
>Warm-down

Saturday and Sunday:
>Rest

Competitive Season
Monday:
>Warm-up
>2-3 × start over 5 hurdles
>2 × 300 m.

    2 × 150 m. with hurdles
    Weight training
    Warm-down

Tuesday:

    Warm-up
    2 × 400 m. with hurdles
    1 × over 6 hurdles
    2 × 100 m. sprints
    1 × 600 m., moderate pace
    Warm-down

Wednesday:

    Warm-up
    1 × 800 m. at best time plus 15 sec.
    4 × over 5 hurdles
    2 × 100 m. sprints
    Warm-down

Thursday:

    Warm-up
    2 × 400 m.
    4 × over 3 hurdles
    2 × 100 m. around curve
    Warm down

Friday and Sunday:

    Rest

Saturday:

    Compete

7 Bert Lyle

THE RELAYS

Author: **Bert Lyle** is athletic director and track coach at Texas Women's University in Denton, Texas. His T.W.U. track teams have won the national championships (three times), finished second (once) and third (twice). The performances of his relay teams have been particularly noteworthy. His 1974 440 yd. relay team, for example, set a national collegiate record (46.5 sec.), a U.S.T.F.F. record (45.9 sec.), and won the A.A.U. Championship. Indeed, at some time during the past 7 years, T.W.U. relay teams have held every collegiate record in the book. In addition to his work at T.W.U., Lyle has also served as head coach of the U.S. women's team vs the U.S.S.R. in Moscow, 1974, and as coach of a U.S. junior team in 1976.

THE 4 × 100 M RELAY

The purpose of a relay race is to carry the baton for a specified distance using four runners performing at their maximum pace for a portion of this distance. To facilitate these efforts three relay exchanges must be effectively performed. Since runners constantly work individually upon increasing their racing pace through the development of stride frequency and stride length, the problems in relay running are principally related to baton exchanges.

To be effective these exchanges must be performed at as near top speed as possible. This would seem to be more difficult for women than men since women are decelerating more quickly than men at the end of their 100 m. legs, preventing the exchange from taking place late in the exchange zone when the outgoing runner is near maximum velocity. However, this negative acceleration factor is compensated for since women achieve their maximum velocity earlier than men. A recent study of national class United States women sprinters indicated that while maximum velocity was achieved between 30 and 40 m., near maximum velocity (96.5% of maximum velocity) was attained between 20 and 30 m.[1] The velocity maintained between 100 and 110 m. was only 91 percent of maximum and was just 95 percent of the velocity attained between 20 and 30 m. Since the velocity of the approaching runners was decreasing at the rate of 2 to 3 percent each 10 m. segment after 80 m., the loss of velocity would indicate that the outgoing runner should be running faster than the incoming runner by the middle of the exchange zone if the recipient has utilized the 10 m. international zone for acceleration purposes. Therefore the exchange would be most efficiently handled at the point in the exchange zone approximately 20 m. after the outgoing runner has commenced her run.

Now these assumptions are generalized and would apply only to two runners possessing similar qualities of acceleration, maximum velocity, and negative acceleration. Obviously adjustments must be made with runners of varying characteristics. However, coaches should realize that there is a point at which diminishing returns will result and this should be determined among the relay personnel at each exchange.

SELECTION OF PERSONNEL

(a) The most effective curve runners should be determined early in the development of the relay team. Since only a very limited number of runners can run the curve as fast the straightaway, the runners need to be timed on both the curve and the straightaway to determine who loses the least amount of time on the curve. Merely testing the runners on the curves is not sufficient since your fastest runners will usually have the fastest time around the curve also. The coach is concerned with the loss of the least amount of time between the straight and the curve, and some runners negotiate the curve more naturally than others. This is not to say that curve running technique cannot be developed, merely that two runners must be sought who are more efficient than the others in their performance on the curve.

(b) Two runners must be found who can both give and take the baton. The incoming runner must be able to maintain near maximum velocity through the zone and lay the baton in the target hand with consistency. The outgoing runner must be able to consistently make her getaway at precisely the right moment and to provide a near-stationary target hand for the incoming runner. The steps and speed from the getaway point to the point of reception should be as consistent as possible. Finding runners who can perform both these functions reliably is not an easy task.

(c) The relay alignment following these assumptions would be as follows: #1 a curve runner who can start well, #3 a curve runner who can handle the baton at both exchanges, #2 a straightaway runner who can handle the baton at both exchanges, #4 the straightaway runner left over, *provided* she is a good competitor.

---

[1]Determination of Maximum Speed of Movement Among Female Sprinters, Lyle, Bert E. and Zoe Cornet. Unpublished Institutional Research. 0945. Funded by The Texas Women's University, Denton, Texas, 1976.

Again, relay teams comprising all the desired qualities are hard to find and adjustments must be made. In some areas of the country where wind is a factor, the ability to shift the #2 and #4 runners when one has difficulty running against the wind is very helpful.

STRATEGY

"Take it early and run like hell!" has often been quoted as a good philosophy for the 400 m. relay, and there is considerable truth in these words, especially when applied to the first exchange. This exchange is the most important in a race among good teams for there is "no more tomorrow" if you miss the first pass. If the second runner takes the baton early in the zone this exchange may be completed first whether the team is actually leading or not. This often causes pressure to be put on the other teams watching at the second exchange. Furthermore any runners at the first exchange who are violating a cardinal rule and watching the other team may also feel the pressure and leave too soon. Another reason for making this exchange early in the zone is that the first runner does not have the advantage of a flying start and therefore exerts more energy starting from blocks and running the curve. The early pass helps prevent a greater period of deceleration. Obviously a fast first runner can also create a psychological effect on the second runners which may cause them to leave too soon. A blazing first leg coupled with an early pass is hard to beat.

It is desirable for the second runner to have an explosive acceleration, for this, combined with an early pass, may oftentimes put the relay away. This leg is most often noted by the fans and is usually accompanied by a collective roar as one team pulls ahead of the other. This is discernible to the fans despite the staggered positions of the runners. Our 1976 Junior National team which beat the 400 m. relay teams of the U.S.S.R. and West Germany (best time, an excellent 44.8 sec.) utilized this strategy and forced the Russians into a bad pass at the 2nd exchange. In the race with West Germany the pressure built up at the third exchange and forced the poor pass at this zone. In both cases the outgoing runners left too soon and then were forced to slow down to receive the baton. Consequently, the U.S. anchor runner, who was the slowest of the four runners, had clear sailing home and was able to run with a relaxation that contributed to a fine leg.

The second runner, who lacks explosive acceleration, should at least have sustained velocity in order that the second exchange can be made at near top speed. The second exchange, when made at good speed with a good curve runner, becomes the next most critical phase. The completion of the second exchange is usually a little more than half of the total time of the relay. In other words, a team running a 47.0 sec. should get the baton to the third runner at about 23.7 or 23.8 sec.

The strategy of the third exchange will ordinarily depend on the capability of the anchor runner as well as the ability of the third runner to maintain momentum off the curve and through the zone. If the third runner can maintain this momentum, the exchange can be made either early or late depending on the capabilities of the anchor runner, since well-matched teams may run within .1 or .2 sec. of each other and the deceleration over the last 10 to 15 m. may vary as much as .1 to .2 sec. among runners with varying speed endurance. Therefore the slower runner, or the runner who decelerates more quickly, might be protected slightly by a somewhat later pass if the curve runner is able to run well through the zone. However, most would agree that it is better to have only one period of notable deceleration in a race rather than two or three. Hence assessing the deceleration qualities of the relay personnel and the assignment of legs as well as the evolvement of the specific exchange points becomes of primary consideration.

It might be of importance to remember that all four runners do not run equal legs on a relay. The first runner may run from 90 to 110 m., depending upon where the exchange takes place in the zone. While most would run from 95 to 100 m. to exchange point, the coach should emphasize that all runners in all legs should continue to run completely through the zone. The second and third runners would have relay legs of 130 m. if they commenced their getaway at the beginning of the acceleration zone and ran completely through the following exchange zone. The fourth leg has a run of 120 m. when measured from the beginning of the acceleration zone.

Certain legs can be protected, particularly the second and third, by taking a late pass and then making an early exchange. The baton can be carried only 80-85 m. by a weak runner using such a plan, however one must also remember a minimum of 15-20 m. acceleration distance must be added to this carrying distance. Considerable work must take place in order that the late pass be well timed under the tension of a big meet and the "cover up" does not end disastrously due to a zone infringement.

In conclusion, coaches must also take into account the differences between practices and meets when evaluating speed of runners and establishing getaway marks. Through rather sophisticated tests using photoelectric cells and electronic timers over the years, the author has discovered that *each* runner will run from .6-1.2 sec. slower in practice than under competitive conditions—and the more intense the competition the faster the time. Fortunately for the coach, the take off marks developed in practice will usually stand up in competition if they were established by the incoming runner utilizing maximum effort over the entire leg. Marks established with 40 or 50 m. run-ins do not account for the deceleration that occurs in the 100-130 m. of running required in the actual relay.

Most runners will accelerate faster in a race than in practice due to the adrenalin from the excitement of the competition; however, they will also decelerate more slowly thus equalizing these two variables. Hence the marks developed in practice by the two runners involved in the exchange for the getaway and the reception of the baton will usually stand under competitive conditions unless one runner is an extraordinary competitor. In such a case, allowances must be made for this "adrenalin abundance" during competitive conditions by shortening the take-off marks and perhaps lengthening the marks of the next runner to account for the unusual speed on race day.

MECHANICS OF THE BATON EXCHANGE

The discussion of strategy and selection of personnel was placed first contrary to the usual presentation of mechanics in the initial portion, since the author wished to give considerable weight to these factors. This is not to minimize the necessity for good technique and plan of exchange. Indeed, a successful relay must have excellent mechanics in the zone if good strategy and proper placement of personnel are to provide a successful relay team.

Responsibility of the Outgoing Runner

The outgoing runner should mark the distance from the point of her stance to the take-off marks by measuring or stepping off the distance on the inside lane stripe (the distance when using the outside line stripe will vary due to difference in widths of track lanes). Adhesive tape may be applied to all-weather track surfaces for this purpose. Two tape lines across the lane 36 in. apart will give greater depth perception than merely one tape line and will permit easier judgement of the incoming runner's exact moment of crossing the plane of this mark. These two lines should be placed some 18-20 linear feet behind the position where the receiving runner will assume her stance (18-20 ft. is a good distance to commence practicing. Experience will dictate changes of distances dependent upon the two runners involved).

The outgoing runner may take her stance anywhere within the 10 m. acceleration zone or even within the 20 m. exchange zone if she so desires. Most use the acceleration zone mark as the position for the getaway.

The position of the getaway stance varies. The most popular are (a) the Russian getaway (the outgoing runner takes a position similar to that in the starting blocks and watches the incoming runner by looking through her legs), (b) the English getaway (a three point stance with the left foot forward and the right hand down. The left arm is flexed and raised. The runner looks back to her left at the incoming runner), and (c) the standing start (the body leans forward with the feet separated 30-36 in. and the opposite arm frontward. Some prefer to place the right foot ahead in order to more easily look over the left shoulder at the incoming runner).

The advantage of the seldom-used Russian getaway is a fast start. The disadvantage is a poor position for depth perception and accurate judgement of the incoming runner's progress. The advantages and disadvantages of the frequently used English getaway—used by the Russian Junior team—are similar, although depth perception is improved somewhat. The standing start gives considerable improvement in depth perception and does not appreciably slow the acceleration phase if proper and vigorous arm action is executed and the first step is made with the back foot rather than the foot ahead. Either the English or the standing getaway will serve well if practiced until the performance of the take-off is explosive and consistent.

After taking off, the outgoing runner will arrive at a point 20 m. from her getaway point in 12-14 steps. This point is approximately midway in the exchange zone if the full acceleration zone was used, and is an ideal location for women to plan to make the exchange due to the acceleration-deceleration factors discussed earlier. It is in this area that the outgoing runner prepares to receive the baton.

The extension of the arm for the baton exchange may be signaled in one of two ways. The outgoing runner upon arriving at a predesignated point in the exchange zone may extend her arm rearward or the incoming runner may give a shout of "Hand" or "Drop" when having approached within sufficient distance to make the exchange. An audible signal may prevent the outgoing runner from running more than one or two strides with her arm outstretched backward, obviously not the best posture for maximum velocity; however, runners who work closely and competently together through a season will usually develop the ability to arrive at a certain point for the exchange with great consistency. Either system has worked satisfactorily, but the methods should not be mixed as the tension of the competition is sufficient without compounding the problems of the runners with either/or alternatives. Simplicity in technique is preferred whenever possible.

Responsibilities of the Incoming Runner

The runner with the baton must first and foremost seek to run as fast as possible completely through the zone with a minimum of speed deceleration. She must be in the correct position within the lane, either on the inner border or the outer border, depending upon the leg being run.

If an audible signal is used for the exchange, the incoming runner must issue this command when the outgoing runner is within sufficient distance for the exchange. The responsibility for making the audible command and placing the baton in the target hand is that of the incoming runner.

After handing off, the incoming runner should stay in her lane until all runners have gone by.

Passing the Baton

The baton should be grasped between the thumb and fingers like a hammer, with a grip that is feathery but secure. The passer should be able to strike quickly and accurately with the baton in a light but firm exchange. Two widely used means of accepting the baton are:

(a) The palm down-upsweep technique is presently used by many European teams. The arm is extended backward and downward with the elbow slightly flexed. The hand is placed slightly behind the hip with the palm downward and fingers and thumb spread. The baton is placed in the receiver's hand with a low upward thrust by the incoming runner who must watch the target hand until the baton has been secured. Some teams seek to place the upper part of the passing hand of the incoming runner into that of the receiver's hand in order to attain a safer pass and overcome the problem that an outgoing runner sometimes has when she grasps the baton by the middle instead of one end. During the exchange, the hand of the outgoing runner overlaps the hand of the incoming runner for a moment prior to securing the baton.

(b) The palm up-downsweep method is presently used by most American university track teams. The arm is extended backward but no higher than parallel to the track. Some coaches emphasize an abrupt forward lean as the arm goes back. Others prefer that the running lean of the runner be influenced as little as possible by any abrupt change of posture since this position may need to be held for 2 or 3 strides and a greater loss of speed would result from an exaggerated lean. The thumb is spread from the fingers—it is important to note that the fingers must be in the same plane as the arm and not turned upwards toward the sky for they will deflect the baton as well as receive a painful bruise. When the hand is placed in the correct position, the thumb is almost aimed at the incoming runner and the fingers are pointing away from this line at approximately 45 deg. The incoming runner fully extends the arm holding the baton and places the baton in the receiver's hand with a slight flick of the wrist. It is fortunate that when the tip of the baton is thrust downward to the target from a fully extended arm, the medial rotation of the wrist (inward rolling) and downward movement of the palm cause the baton to be pointed at a slight angle toward the inside rather than straight ahead. This allows it to cross the palm of the receiver and not strike the wrist. Any looping or exaggerated over-arm motion should be avoided. Indeed this extension and flick of the baton into the target hand should be accomplished in a minimum of time and with economy of movement.

If audible signals are used, care must be taken that the incoming runner does not present the baton prior to the giving of the command or simultaneously as the command is given. The command must be issued and the target hand presented prior to the presentation of the baton in order that a safe and efficient pass can be obtained. The passer should look at the target hand until the baton is secured by the recipient. The placement of the baton across the palm should be emphasized. Striking the wrist with the tip of the baton often leads to fumbles and can be avoided if the target hand position of the receiver is correct and the baton is placed across the palm.

The reception of the baton should act as a stimulus similar to that of a hedge-bush switch upon the behind of a three-year old—all hell should break loose. The runners must be trained in practice to continue to develop acceleration and to reach maximum velocity as soon as possible. The benefits of a more explosive acceleration will apply to a sprinter's individual performance as well as the relays. This is an example of the tension that exists between a more relaxed performance as found in a relay, on the one hand, and the reckless explosive qualities also needed for maximum performance, on the other hand. Participation in a relay is often the "back door" by which a sprinter is able to discover within herself in a competitive situation the balance of relaxed effort and intensity which is most satisfactory. Sometimes the watch will indicate results that utterly flabbergast both coach and athlete!

Alternation of Hands

A discussion of the types of exchanges witnessed at track meets could continue ''ad infinitum.'' Sufficient to say that certain principles have been established that seem sound and should be followed until better methods become available. These are:

(a) Athletes should run on the inside border of the track or lane when running the curve in order to run the shortest distance possible.

(b) Most runners obtain their best times when running the curve with the baton in the right hand.

When these two statements are taken together, a concept can be derived which would apply to the methods employed by some very successful relay teams. The first and third runners would carry the baton in their right hand since they are running the curve. Furthermore this facilitates running on the inside of the lanes during the exchange with the second and fourth runners who will be running near the outer border of the lane. However, this is not detrimental since the second and fourth runners are running the straightaway.

This method permits the curve runners to run the curve on the inside of the lane throughout their leg and continue through the exchange as well as carry the baton in the right hand thus allowing the relay the advantage of the shortest distance possible and the use of the preferred hand around the curve. Therefore the first exchange is a right to left exchange; the second exchange is a left to right exchange; and the third exchange is right to left.

This method has another advantage in that the runner receiving the baton is not required to change the baton from hand to hand after the exchange. Such actions occasionally cause fumbles or, more frequently, a slight loss of acceleration due to the concentration of the change rather than on running. In some cases runners may forget to change hands and go into the next exchange with the baton in the wrong hand, or they may remember and attempt to change prior to the zone, causing a loss of speed or even a fumble. The right to left to right to left technique alleviates these problems and further simplifies the exchanges by requiring fewer actions on the part of the runner, thus permitting greater concentration on the act of running itself.

PRACTICING THE EXCHANGE

Practices are very helpful when the first and third exchanges are held at the same zone in order to permit the coach to watch both work simultaneously. In order that baton exchanges receive the practice required, it is suggested that only the first and third exchanges be worked one day with the second exchange being practiced on the following day. Furthermore, only five or six exchanges should be made each practice with only one or two involving the running of the complete leg by the incoming runner in order that good concentration be maintained and that the runners do not become so fatigued from practicing the relay that other drills and workouts are neglected.

Coaches must constantly stress good consistent effort by both runners working at the exchange. Like the jumping events, relay practice is useless when the participants are tired. Some suggestions are provided for points to stress:

(a) The incoming runner must maintain excellent effort throughout the exchange zone, seeking to pass the receiver if possible.

(b) The outgoing runner must develop a fast, explosive, and continuous acceleration through the exchange zone. Guard against slowing down if the recipient is well into the zone and still has not received the baton. Usually, the longer one goes without the baton, the slower one runs.

(c) The coach should make the adjustment of the take-off distances, not the runners. Too often runners will slow down to make the hand off or receive the pass. Practice is the time to stress all out effort even if passes are not completed throughout the session. Only through this type of work can adjustments be made to enable the most efficient exchanges to be performed.

(d) The unforgivable sin is to take off too soon, before the incoming runner has hit the take-off marks. One must have the discipline to wait for the precise moment.

(e) The hips of the outgoing runner should be as square as possible to the direction of movement while waiting at the getaway in order that a straight driving first step can be accomplished.

(f) If using an audible signal for target hand extension, care must be taken not to extend the hand prior to the command as this may throw off the incoming runner. The outgoing runner must continue to accelerate through the zone using both arms for running until the command is given.

(g) In order to insure that the incoming runner is concentrating on the target hand, Dr. Leroy Walker, outstanding North Carolina Central University coach and 1976 Olympic coach, devised the following stratagem: a number was written on the palm of the receiver's target hand and the incoming runner must be able to recognize it or pay a forfeit.

(h) Don't overlook 200 m. runners and even hurdlers and 400 m. runners when selecting the relay. All have great strength, and while they may be beaten in a 100 m. race out of the blocks, three of the legs are run with flying starts and require 120 to 130 m. of effort. Prairie View A&M University under Barbara Jacket and Hoover Wright has developed some fine relay teams while possessing only one outstanding 100 m. sprinter, but the hurdlers, 200 m., and 400 m. runners all developed good speed and excellent speed endurance qualities which enabled them to run some outstanding times.

(i) Ensure that the outgoing runner remains on her side of the lane and does not cut off the incoming runner by crossing the lane. This is often prevalent at the first and third exchange when the outgoing runner will start on the curve and naturally drive to the inside of the lane (cutting off the incoming runner) instead of running in the outer border of the lane.

(j) View the baton-passing practices from various angles of view—side, front, behind. Usually the view from the side is more effective from a distance of

40-50 yd. One of the most helpful coaching positions during practice is mid-way in the exchange zone (or at the position desired for the exchange), one lane outside the lane being practiced. From this position the incoming runner, the take-off marks, and the outgoing runner can be viewed. The precise moment of the getaway can be observed as well as the paths and mechanics of the runners. The pass should take place at the side of the coach and any deviation is noticeable.

(k) One effective means of judging the effectiveness of the exchange is to time the baton from one end of the zone to the other. Develop criteria pertinent to the ability level of the athletes being coached. A 2.1 or 2.2 sec. time is excellent for a national-class women's team.

(l) Another means of judging the exchange is to have a third sprinter run in an adjacent lane beside the incoming runner and continuing through the exchange zone. The relative positions of the outgoing runner and the runner in the adjacent lane will indicate whether speed was lost during the exchange.

THE 4 × 400 M RELAY

The discussion of this relay will be considerably briefer than the previous one for several reasons: first, certain principles which apply to the 400 m. relay also apply to the 1600 m. relay; second, the options of strategy vary so greatly depending upon the individual personnel of the competing teams that no single presentation could cover all the potentialities; and third, the mechanics of the exchange itself are far simpler. As in the discussion of the 4 × 100 m. relay, the discussion of the type of race and strategy will be presented first.

STRATEGY

This relay is actually two races in one. It is an open 400 m. race run in lanes in which one of the primary requirements of the participants is the ability to judge pace. The second part of the race involves the remaining three runners who are in head to head competition with the opposing runners, each involving the runners in three separate duels. Due to the individual character of these latter races, runners generally can run faster in this type of competition than they are able to in the open 400 m. Furthermore, most quartermilers usually run better when they are behind their competitors, but not so far back as to be hopelessly out of the race. The leading runner generally has the continuing burden of pace judgement combined with the tension of worrying about activities of a following and nonvisible field.

For these reasons it is important that teams sometimes plan to have weaker runners in a trailing position rather than a leading position in order that a maximum performance can be obtained. This strategy is particularly effective if the team possesses an outstanding anchor runner who can be kept within striking distance by the preceding runners.

However, one of the most important considerations when selecting the positions for relay personnel is the obtaining of a reliable runner with a fine sense of pace judgement. This runner will prove invaluable as the first runner in the relay. Many times a potentially fine relay team has been placed far behind because the first runner reacted too excitably and ran the first portion of the race in excess of her ability. The faltering finish which results is little different in final outcome to the race of one who has run well within her limits and has too much left at the finish. A consistent pacemaker in the first position will keep the relay team in the race and allow the succeeding runners to duel from a position of contention.

Ideally the second runner should be able to run a competitive race but still be a strong finisher since the second exchange will be the first made from the common exchange area. A good finish will permit a greater acceleration through the zone since the recipient can be moving faster at the exchange and allow the runner to attain a favorable position going into the curve.

If we continue to hypothesize, the third runner should be the fastest duel runner on the team. This position is preferred rather than the anchor position if a suitable fourth runner is available, since the race can oftentimes be put away on this leg. Such a move requires that the fourth runner be capable of a good final portion of the race, in particular the last 100 to 150 m. A halfmiler with good endurance sometimes serves admirably in this capacity. Whoever is selected must be capable of holding the lead from runners who may be faster in the open 400 m. and fight off the challenge or even regain the lead over the last straightaway.

We have spoken of ideal characteristics for a relay team. However, coaches seldom have this opportunity to choose ideal personnel. For that reason a suggestion of a more practical nature is provided for those less fortunate (a group to which all coaches will belong at one time or another). Some coaches have used a technique that matches their team against a team which is considered as good as or slightly better than their own and then matched their personnel accordingly. All other teams are ignored and a match race is run without, of course, the other team knowing. The order of the personnel is dependent upon the characteristics of the team matched. Certainly a good judger of pace must run the first leg, but the order of the succeeding runners depends upon the coach's evaluation of the best times that the runners can obtain in various situations—running behind but not too far behind and being drawn by the leading runner; being within striking distance for a superior anchor runner; building up such a lead that an outstanding anchor is disheartened and cannot meet the challenge; running the best two runners first in order to stay in the race and hoping to get better-than-usual performances from the succeeding runners. Whatever the decision, teams are often surprised by their performances in such a race.

An interesting situation prevailed in the U.S.-U.S.S.R. Junior Meet in 1976. The Russian Junior Team possessed an anchor runner who narrowly missed selection for their Olympic team and ran the open 400 m. 2.5 sec. faster than the best of the U.S. Junior Team. The U.S. team decided to run the consistent judge of pace first, the strong finisher second, the fastest runner third and the runner with the second best 200 m. time on the anchor. The strategy prevailed, and such a good lead was built up after three legs, approximately 30 m., that the Russian anchor runner became discouraged on the final bend, after pulling up within 15 m., and was unable to make a bid due to the strength of the American girl's finish.

Of course races do not always turn out as planned, but the best performances are usually the result of careful preparation. The goal of all track performances is to come as close to attaining one's potential as is possible. When four runners put together a superb collage of their collective efforts, then they cannot be the loser no matter what the final results.

MECHANICS OF THE PASS

A visual pass is safer and in the author's opinion just as fast as a nonvisual exchange in the 4×400 m. relay. Use of the nonvisual pass is usually restricted to teams with excellent personnel. After an effort of 390 m., even world champions are not accelerating over the last 10 m., merely fighting to maintain a controlled deceleration. For that reason an exchange which is as effective and safe as conditions permit should be utilized by all relay teams.

The best exchange is dependent upon the outgoing runner achieving as quick an acceleration as possible in the few steps taken prior to the exchange. Since the deceleration of the incoming runner controls the speed of the outgoing runner's take-off, the outgoing runner should wait until the incoming runner is very close in order to develop acceleration without having to slow down to receive the baton.

For these reasons the following guides are offered as suggestions for 160 m. exchanges:

(a) The outgoing runner should stand in the rear of the exchange zone as close as possible to the incoming runner. The take-off mark will be 6-8 ft. from the position where the outgoing runner stands.

(b) The receiving runner assumes a standing start position as the incoming runner approaches. During the second and third exchanges when the common exchange zone is used by all teams, the receiving runners may be shuffled as the places of the incoming runners are changed. This may necessitate quick and adaptable responses to a changing situation. When the starting stance is taken, the arm opposite the rear foot should be forward with the other arm back in opposition. If the preference is to take the baton with the right hand, then the receiver stands in position with the right foot back and the left foot forward. The head is turned over the right shoulder to judge the approach of the incoming runner. The left arm is back, the right arm is forward. The position is reversed if the exchange is taken with the left hand.

(c) Many coaches use a right to left pass which necessitates a change of the baton from the left to the right hand after its reception. One advantage of this method of reception is that the runner can view the situation between herself and the curb and thus evaluate her opportunities for moving to a more favorable position inside.

(d) Other coaches use a right to right pass. This permits the left arm to be free as the receiver turns her head forward after receiving the baton and serves to protect her in heavy traffic as she drives toward the inside to a favorable position. This seems more natural than the opposite move and permits viewing of the field as quickly as is needed. Furthermore, in the right to right pass the incoming runner is not tracking the outgoing runner but rather sliding to the right of her path since the position of the receiver's arm and body is different from that used in the nonvisual pass. Since a visual pass is used, the arms are fully extended when offering and accepting the baton, thereby eliminating practically all possibility of teammates becoming entangled during the exchange. Of the many accidents which occur in the 4 × 400 m. relay, this is one that is seldom observed.

(e) A brief description of the right to right pass is provided.

(i)   The outgoing runner assumes her starting stance with the left foot forward, right back, and arms in opposition.

(ii) The outgoing runner takes-off when the incoming runner crosses the 6-8 ft. take-off mark, turning her head forward as she begins to run. By turning her head forward she is enabled to drive in a straight line during the early and critical stage of the exchange.

(iii) On the third step (right) the outgoing runner reaches back with her right arm fully extended at chest height. Her head turns simultaneously and her gaze is fixed upon the baton. While the shoulders turn 90 deg. during this backward extension of the arm, the hips are turned minimally. An exaggerated hip turn must be guarded against, as acceleration will be slowed if this occurs.

(iv) The receiver takes the baton on the fourth step (left) from take-off 4-5 yd. into the zone. The hips and shoulders are open naturally allowing the greatest extension of the arm. The palm is turned up, fingers and thumb spread.

(v)   The baton is presented by the incoming runner as if shaking hands with the receiver. The incoming runner looks at the receiver's target hand as the baton is thrust home.

(vi) Upon taking the baton, the outgoing runner immediately turns her head and runs forward looking for running room to the left in order to angle to the curb as quickly as possible. A too sharply angled cut should be avoided since distance is lost when compared to a more gradual angle. In cutting to the inside of the curve, the runner must balance caution with aggressiveness; however, it should be noted that winners seem to possess the latter in greater quantities.

(vii) After handing off, the incoming runner should stop in her lane, look to her left and move off the track when she is able to do so without interfering with another runner.

(f) The incoming runners in the second and third exchanges must learn to drive down the stretch straight toward the outgoing runner waiting at the common exchange zone. To waver or fail to run aggressively can permit other runners to cut off the incoming runner from the outgoing runner and valuable seconds can be lost. This maneuver should be practiced weekly (in flats) by a full track of runners in order that the technique of shuffling the awaiting runners by position will become familiar, and the ability to maneuver toward the desired exchange point will be mastered. A last spark of aggressiveness is required from a dying runner.

(g) An early exchange, 4-5 yd. into the zone, prevents a period of deceleration for each leg. Countless seconds are saved by a fresh runner taking the baton early from a rapidly decelerating teammate at each exchange. The anchor runner will have a little longer to run, but if all works out she will have the honor of breaking the tape.

The above guidelines pertain to the visual pass. If a nonvisual exchange is desired, the technique followed in the 4 × 100 m. relay would apply with the following exceptions:

(i)   All exchanges would be right to left. In order to get the baton in the right hand, the baton would be changed from the left hand to the right hand by the outgoing runner immediately after reception.

(ii) The take-off marks would be moved closer, 6-9 ft. being sufficient.

(iii) The standing start would be used rather than the English getaway, since speed is not that important and the shuffling at the exchange zone might push an awaiting runner off balance.

Teams utilizing the nonvisual pass must have runners who can finish strongly under control. As mentioned before, the visual pass seems safer in this strenuous event.

8   David Rodda

THE LONG JUMP

> *Author:* **David Rodda** is Superintendent of Human Resources, Lakewood, California and head coach of the Lakewood International Women's Track Team. An assistant coach of the U.S. junior women's team (1973), the U.S. women's team at the Pan-American Games (1975) and the U.S. women's team for the outdoor dual meet with the U.S.S.R. (1976), he has coached several international-class athletes of whom Martha Watson, a four-time Olympian in the long jump, is perhaps the best known.

To some individuals, the long jump presents itself as the easiest jumping event to perform and coach. Perhaps the most elementary mistake among the majority is to treat the long jump as a natural activity. If the athlete (a) runs a prescribed distance, (b) maintains near-maximum controlled horizontal speed, (c) converts some of this speed quickly to vertical lift when she reaches the take-off board, and (d) uses effective movements in the air, it is anticipated the landing will be successful, based on what the jumper does in the air.

In simple terms, those individuals who teach these principles are providing the basis for success in the long jump. Even the most proficient of international jumpers thinks in terms of effective controlled speed, plant, lift and landing. But to reach this point of bringing the long jump down to the basics, one must gain substantial mastery of the many factors involved in this extremely technical skill.

To coach or perform in the long jump, the following major components must be taken into consideration when learning the complete skill: approach, take-off, flight and landing. These four components affecting the attainment of maximum distance will be discussed in detail along with teaching aids and a training program, which should benefit both athlete and coach. Outstanding performances in this event, as natural as it appears to be, are achieved by methods which must be taught with extreme care and by months, even years, of dedicated practice.

APPROACH

The experienced long jumper uses an approach of between 100 ft. and 125 ft. She accelerates smoothly from her starting check mark to reach her take-off at near-maximum speed. The jumper must hit the take-off board as fast as possible with control, balance, and accuracy. Accuracy is vital for two reasons. First, the jump is measured from the front edge of the board. If the jumper takes off behind that edge, she loses valuable inches. Second, when the jumper realizes that she won't hit the board, she often tries to adjust the approach. If she tries to chop or reach for the board, she destroys the timing of her take-off, making for a sub-par jump.

Maximum controlled speed is important because the jumper's distance is closely related to the ability to generate and maintain horizontal speed. The approach run is so vital, that to determine the exact distance of the run is a major part of the athlete's early season training.

To find the correct approach distance, the distance necessary to reach full speed comfortably, place a mark at that point. It can be anywhere from 110 ft. to 125 ft. Stand on the take-off board with both feet parallel, start with the take-off foot, and reverse the run-up. The coach watches where the take-off foot lands closest to the original mark. Repeat often. Now practice the run-up numerous times, placing appropriate check marks, and perfect the approach distance and all check marks through trial and error. Remember, check marks and starting point must be altered to suit varying weather conditions. A tailwind and/or fast runway will require moving the check marks away slightly from the take-off board. A head wind and/or slow runway generally require moving check marks and starting point toward the board. *Approach consistency and accuracy are absolutely essential.*

Check Marks

There are differing opinions on the number of marks necessary to accurately help the jumper gauge her approach. The important factor to remember is that check marks are used as orientation points. Whether you use one or two marks, consistency and accuracy are still a necessity if the approach is to be successful. If using two check marks, the first should be on the third stride, and the second no less than eight strides from the take-off. Some jumpers, mainly experienced ones, utilize a three-step walk up to check mark, then attain immediately the running rhythm to the board. Always start with the take-off foot and hit the check marks with the take-off foot; remember to start and accelerate the same way.

Check marks can offer a feeling of security to the jumper, especially if used properly. When eight strides out, and the jumper hits her mark, she has confidence in reaching the board. Check marks also provide another thought process which can take away from the concentration necessary in maintaining controlled acceleration. The coach must maintain a constant watch on the jumper's attitude toward these marks.

Assuming consistency and speed on the runway have been attained and the athlete has determined her check mark, the remaining phase of the approach centers around the last three to five strides prior to reaching the board. Remember that, except for the final stride, each of the approach strides should be longer than the previous strides.

There are numerous terms used in describing the last three to four strides: "coast," "gather," "settle," or "float." It has been proven with experienced jumpers that their actual striving to maintain speed by increasing tempo during the final four or five run-up strides results in greater take-off velocity, which produces longer jumps. Novice jumpers are usually advised to maintain speed and relax the final three to four strides of the approach. This is best described as a relaxation and settling of the body in preparation for take-off. The trunk comes more upright, the hips sink slightly during the next to the last (or "penultimate") stride. The jumper tries during the coast to preserve previously gained run-up momentum in order to carry her through to the take-off board without undue loss of speed.

There is no exact pattern established for stride length over the final steps of the approach prior to take-off. Jumpers who are fast sprinters show less variation in stride length over the final three steps than those of less sprinting ability. Slower jumpers prefer to jump high, thus preparing themselves more for the take-off by gathering. Throughout the approach the jumper maintains controlled sprinting form. The body is in an upright position. She concentrates on maintaining good knee lift, and the arms drive like those of a sprinter (Figure 8-1).

THE TAKE-OFF

The take-off foot is planted, heel leading with an active downward, and apparently backward motion (Figure 8-2). The foot lands about 12 in. ahead of the body's center of gravity (CG), so the force at take-off can be exerted directly beneath and behind the CG. As the foot touches, the lower leg makes an angle of approximately 118-120 deg. to the ground.

The knee bends to a maximum of approximately 145-150 deg. as the CG moves directly over the take-off foot. If the knee bends too little as the take-off foot is planted, the subsequent take-off movements come too late, the jump is too low, there is excessive forward rotation, and the distance jumped is reduced.

After the foot is actively planted, the thigh of the lead leg is swung forward, and lifted fast and powerfully to a position parallel to the ground in front of the body, thus increasing the force of the take-off foot against the board—action-reaction—(Figure 8-3). The arm opposite the lead leg is "punched" forcefully upward, elbow bent to less than 90 deg. and hand reaching chin height, in coordination with the lead leg. The shoulders and trunk are stretched upward, and the head is tilted very slightly backward. These movements at take-off start the CG of the jumper on its forward-upward path while the body is still in contact with the take-off board.

FIGURE 8-1

FIGURE 8-2

FIGURE 8-3

FIGURE 8-4

FIGURE 8-5

FIGURE 8-6

FIGURE 8-7

FIGURE 8-8

FIGURE 8-9

FIGURE 8-10

FIGURE 8-11

FIGURE 8-12

FIGURE 8-13

FIGURE 8-14

FIGURE 8-15

Ideally, the take-off leg extends fully just before the lead leg and ''opposite'' arm lose their forward-upward speed. At take-off, the long jumper's horizontal speed is about double the upward speed. The flight-path of the body's CG is predetermined at take-off, and cannot be altered once contact with the ground has been broken, but the movement of the body around the CG in the air can be controlled. This control is exerted by the motion of the limbs in the air.

FLIGHT

Most jumpers leave the board with forward rotation, which cannot be altered in the air. However, the movement of the jumper's body around her CG, while airborne, can be controlled by limb movements in flight, thus enabling her to achieve an efficient landing position. The motion of the jumper's arms and legs during flight is executed for the purpose of slowing or reversing forward rotation generated at take-off. This in-flight slowing or reversing of forward rotation, produced by arm and leg movements, is merely superimposed upon the original take-off rotation. Once the arm and leg actions cease, the original forward rotation will again reveal itself. The types of mid-air action used by long jumpers are the sail, hang, and hitch-kick, or combinations of these. Each type has many variations. The take-off is identical for all types of mid-air action, and distinguishing characteristics reveal themselves only after contact is broken with the board.

Sail

Jumpers who employ the sail merely bunch up into a "ball" after take-off, attempt to keep the feet and legs up as high and long as possible, and sail through the air in the position in which they hope to land. Because it increases forward rotation, thus turning the feet prematurely downward to the landing pit, the sail is not recommended.

Hang

The hang mid-air action may drastically reduce forward rotation, but cannot reverse it. After the take-off leg leaves the board and the jumper begins to gain height, the nonjumping (lead or free) leg is straightened and swung back and down to join the jumping leg, which is left trailing. Both arms swing back and down together as the lead leg moves downward to meet the take-off leg. After their downward-backward swing, the arms move upward behind the back and are held extended upward-backward above the head at the high point of the jump. Both arms continue forward-overhead at the high point of the jump. They finish either forward in front of the body, or continue swinging forward-downward to a position behind the body before being brought forward to assist the jumper over the fulcrum of the feet in the pit at landing.

Hitch-kick

The most commonly used mid-air action among top-class jumpers is the hitch-kick. It is executed by continuing to run 1½ or 2½ strides in the air after take-off. Most top women jumpers use a 1½ hitch-kick. The hitch-kick action can reverse the forward rotation of the body, which starts at take-off, providing the airborne leg action is from the hips, rather than small running steps from below the knees, which are ineffective. A 1½ strides in the air hitch-kick action from a right-foot take-off is described simply as follows:

As the right foot leaves the board, extended behind the body, the left thigh is in front of the body, parallel to the ground, with knee well-bent (Figure 8-3). The position of the right and left legs changes as the jumper rises toward the top of her flight path. In so doing, the left leg sweeps downward-backward with the knee unbent and leg thus "athletically" straight (Figure 8-5). The equal and opposite reaction to this motion tends to turn the trunk backward. The left leg continues backward behind the body where the lower leg folds up to the thigh with heel rising to the buttock (Figure 8-8).

With lower leg folded tightly to the left thigh, this leg moves forward as a compact unit exactly as in the recovery phase of a running stride, and rises to a point where the thigh is again parallel to the ground (Figure 8-9). At this point, the left thigh joins the right thigh, which is also roughly parallel to the ground (Figure 8-10). When the right foot leaves the take-off board, its heel rises high toward the right buttock, folding the lower leg to the right thigh (Figure 8-5). The right leg then moves forward as in the recovery phase of a running stride to the front where the right thigh is parallel to the ground (Figure 8-7). The right foreleg is extended forward where it is held as high as possible (Figure 8-9), to be joined by the left foreleg before landing (Figure 8-11). Most athletes using the 1½ strides in the air hitch-kick action make the mistake of completing this running-in-the-air motion too soon before landing. When the motion of the legs (and to a lesser extend, the arms) ceases, the original forward rotation generated at take-off will again reveal itself.

The opposite arms follow and counter-balance the opposite legs during the running-in-the-air motion of the hitch-kick. At the instant of take off, the right arm is forward, elbow bent in excess of 90 deg., and hand about chin height, in coordination with the forward opposite left leg (Figure 8-3). As the left leg moves backward-downward (unbent), the right arm also moves downward-backward, with the elbow only slightly bent (Figure 8-5). As the left leg starts forward (bent), the right arm rises backward-upward, overhead, often somewhat laterally to the right side, arm straight, to an overhead position (Figure 8-6). The right arm then moves from overhead in a downward direction in front of the body as the left leg extends in front of the body for landing (Figure 8-9). Ideally, just before landing, the right arm is swept downward-backward behind the body, arm straight (Figure 8-12). As the heels touch the sand, the arms are thrown forward-upward, elbows unbent, to assist pivoting the body over the fulcrum of the heels (Figure 8-14).

The left arm at take-off is behind the body, slightly bent, in coordination with and counterbalancing the right leg. As the right leg moves forward, the left arm rises upward-forward from behind with forearm often going overhead. The left elbow rises only slightly higher than the shoulder. The arm continues forward, unbent, in front of the body. Ideally, just before landing the straight left arm is swept downward-backward, behind the body. Both right and left arms sweep downward-backward together just prior to landing, and sweep forward-upward together as the heels touch the sand.

THE LANDING

It must be remembered that landing depends very much on the previous jumping action, especially during the flight, and is not an isolated movement.

Obviously a good landing position is one which continues the center of gravity's trajectory as far as possible and provides the greatest possible distance between the jumper's heels and her center of gravity, without falling back.

In addition, attention must be drawn to three common landing faults among the young jumpers—legs brought through in knees-bent position, legs brought through too late, and heels placed far apart. The distance lost in keeping the knees bent is obvious. It can be seen by measuring the difference of the distance between straight legs and legs bent about 60 deg. This can be up to 6 in. The late bringing-through of the legs occurs mainly when a poor hang technique is employed in the air and the heels' wide apart position is usually responsible for one breaking the sand surface ahead of the other. Both reduce the jumping distance by several inches.

At landing, regardless of the mid-air action used, both heels touch the sand approximately together. The upper body should be as nearly erect as possible, permitting stretching forward of the legs to achieve maximum distance. The arms should ideally be thrown backward just before landing to counterbalance the forward thrust of the legs and aid in keeping the trunk upright. The legs should be straight in front of the body, extended slightly below horizontal. At the instant the heels touch the sand, the knees bend and the buttocks are brought forward to assist the pivot of the body forward over the heels.

The best landing position is one which extends the flight path of the CG as far as possible, provides the maximum horizontal distance between the jumper's heels and her CG, and yet does not require her trunk to be so erect as to cause her to fall backward. The greater the jumper's horizontal speed, the more upright can be her trunk at landing without danger of falling backward. It is estimated that for every inch the legs are kept from rotating downward (kept up) at landing, a horizontal jumping distance of 1½ in. will be gained.

TRAINING PROGRAM

Training the long jumper depends a great deal on her stage of development. Beginning jumpers must go through a total conditioning program. This general conditioning includes endurance, speed, power and development of all phases of the jump. The experienced jumper spends less time on the general conditioning and more on a specific conditioning program.

In its simplest terms, the training patterns are broken down into segments and within each segment specific objectives are established to prepare the jumper for the next training phase. Naturally, all training programs are dependent on weather and facilities available to the coach and athlete.

FALL/WINTER (MID SEPTEMBER—JANUARY)

Objective: To establish a total foundation program including strength, endurance and limited jump training.

Endurance Running

(Although not that important to a long jumper, endurance running does establish a level of fitness.)

    (a)   Two days a week, 2-3 miles of long, easy cross country runs. Establish an easy pattern of running. This is not a race, yet, as conditioning, improves tempo.

    (b)   Interval workouts, two days a week, distance from 150-300 yd. Coach should establish a schedule of times run for distances of 150, 180, 200, 220, 250, and 300 yd. During early season, times should be realistic, along with the numbered run. Recovery is based on pulse. Check, and when it returns to 110, continue program. Several kinds of series can be set up to add variety to the program. For example:

Tuesday: 2×150, 3×220, 2×150
Thursday: 1×330, 2×250, 3×200

If timed runs are not desired, then establish running patterns where the tempo becomes increasingly faster the shorter the distance. For example:

1×330 (50%), 1×220 (75%), 1×150 (90%)

Strength Training

    (a)   Weights (discussed in detail in Chapter 13). During this period of training, weights should provide for total strength.

    (b)   Natural resistance exercise: Uphill runs, stadium steps running, and bounding on different surfaces (sand, snow and grass). Natural resistance exercise should not be started until after the first month of training when the jumpers have established a good foundation.

    (c)   Body resistance exercises, using the jumper's own weight for resistance. There are a variety of drills to use during this phase of training. This is a good time in the program to introduce the various elements required in the jump.

Drills

    (a)   Single leg hop over distances from 20-60 yd. (Remember to alternate legs.)

    (b)   Double leg hop—distance from 30-70 yd.

    (c)   Double leg hop over low hurdles (more experienced jumpers—distance between hurdle dependent upon size of athlete).

    (d)   Triple jumps from standing position, taking three strides, five strides, seven strides (if available, this is a good drill on packed sand at a beach).

    (e)   Hopping up stairs—single leg, double legs.

    (f)   Hopping down stairs, with support.

(g)   Depth jumping—jumping downward from a height of approximately 3 ft. and exploding upward.

(h)   Short run-up jumps in pit (pop ups). Concentrate on working with the elements of hitch kick or hang, whichever is the coach's preference.

Through the fall and winter conditioning program in the latter months, the speed training gradually increases and there is a decrease in the long distance runs. Also the runs of 150-300 yd. become quality, not quantity.

There should be an evaluation of the athlete's progress at the beginning of December. At this time, the coach has the opportunity to discuss with the athlete the direction she will take during the upcoming spring training schedule. It is imperative to have two-way communication between coach and athlete.

With beginning jumpers, you gain their confidence if they feel they are a part of the planning process. She generally has an indoor season as well as a heavy outdoor season, and early December is an excellent time to evaluate proposed competition based on the general conditioning progress.

SPRING (FEBRUARY—MAY)

Objective: To concentrate on preparation for the total jump, which includes sprint training, approach, take-off and technique.

Strength Training

(a)   Weights—concentration on specific exercises to gain power for the jump.

(b)   Body resistance exercise—continuation of program except in most bounding drills. Increase distance to 100 yd. and decrease the number within a series.

Sprint Training

Through sprint training, the athlete will also maintain a level of endurance, which will contribute to excellence in the long jump approach.
Drills:
(a)   Walking with high knee lift
(b)   Running with high knee lift
(c)   Stationary arm drills (simulating sprinting arm action while in a stationary position)
(d)   Hurdling
(e)   Changes in stride frequency, alternating ten fast strides and ten medium strides over a distance of 100-200 yd.
(f)   Sprints uphill and downhill
Sprinting Workouts:
When not working on the long jump, sprint workouts should be at least twice a week, concentrating on distance from 60-150 yd. Quality and quan-

tity are based on condition of athlete. Recovery should always be complete and the coach should terminate the workout when the athlete starts to lose the relaxed running rhythm.

Long Jump Workouts

Based on specific training schedule of three days a week during February and March. Maximum emphasis should be placed on approach work. The athlete is physically strong, the endurance level is up, and she should handle a good workout load.

(a) Approach workouts should include at least 15 good run-throughs. The coach concentrates on the check marks; the jumper maintains consistency in speed and acceleration to the board. The last three run-throughs the jumper comes through for "effect." This means she plants and provides the coach with an effective lead leg lift. The jump is not for distance. The objective is to minimize deceleration and maximize speed, with power off the board.

(b) Short run-up jumps at least twice a week. It is imperative the jumper and the coach spend the time analyzing this phase of the practice. Always remember to have the jumper be aggressive. Go into these short run-ups with speed and provide for an effective plant. During this phase of the practices, concentrate on mid-air action and the landing. The number of "pop-ups" and distance of the short runs is dependent on the physical ability of the athlete.

SUMMER (MAY—MID-AUGUST)

Objective: To maintain an excellence in the already conditioned athlete. Quality, not quantity, is the key feature, along with a strong emphasis on mental preparation for the upcoming competition.

Strength Training

Decrease to two days a week. Stop weights if body resistance drills seem to be sufficient. Continue drills as a part of the warm-up process. As the athlete moves toward June, do all drills on a flat surface.

Sprint Training

Heavy concentration on quick explosive sprinting. Work on distance from 40-120 yd.

Long Jump Workouts

Continue the same program as that of the Spring. Work on elements of jump which are problems, especially during competition.

Competition

By this time, all key competitions have been planned and the objectives are to prepare mentally for the upcoming meets. During competition the following points should be remembered:

(a) Warm up completely before getting on the runway.

(b) Run-up should be done without sweatsuit if possible.

(c) Concentrate during practice run-ups as if they were the real thing.

(d) Plant for effect on last run-up to get the feel of the board and give exact indication of foot at the board.

(e) Do short pop-ups to get used to the landing area.

(f) Warm up properly before *every* jump. The number in the event determines the time between jumps. *Don't get caught cold prior to jump.*

LATE SUMMER (MID-AUGUST—MID-SEPTEMBER)

The athletes should maintain an active rest that allows for involvement in other sports, which might have been restricted during the training season. Yet, it must be remembered, active rest means involvement in some level of fitness. These activities should be treated as fun, and need not follow a training plan.

THE HIGH JUMP

Author: **Jim Santos,** head track coach at California State University, Hayward, has had extensive experience in the coaching of both men's and women's track and field. He has been coach of Lebanon (Oregon) Union High School teams which established eleven D.G.W.S. national records; of Cal State Hayward teams which finished first (1972) and twice placed second in the A.I.A.W. national championships; and, most recently, of the highly successful men's team at Cal State Hayward.

THE FOSBURY FLOP

The question has been asked repeatedly, "Which style of high jumping is the most efficient, the straddle or the Fosbury Flop?" The Flop is slowly pushing the conventional straddle style into obscurity, even though the straddle is still used with success by many European jumpers. The success and rapid growth of the Flop can be attributed to its ease of acquisition by the beginner, as well as one who is changing from the straddle to the Flop. Other factors which enhance the use of the Flop in high jumping are numerous. Less leg strength is required for the Flop as compared to the straddle. Application of greater take-off force is generated in the Flop as compared to that of the straddle. The use of running speed converted into the takeoff is more efficient. And one of the most important factors when comparing the two styles of jumps is the critical timing during crossbar clearance. Crossbar clearance when using the straddle is most important, and the jumper must have the technique at a level which produces few errors. When using the Flop however, timing on top of the bar is not so precise, and errors can be accounted for and still have a higher performance level for the jumper, provided that the take-off is efficient.

The Flop has been adopted by the American female jumper to such an extent that it is now very rare to see the straddle used by any competitor, whether it be on the national level or in school competition.

The four areas that require consideration in the Flop are:

(a)   the approach
(b)   the plant
(c)   the take-off
(d)   the bar clearance

As a general rule, the jumper should jump off her stronger leg. If the left leg is the stronger leg, that should be the take-off leg, which means that she will approach the bar from the right side (when facing the bar). It must be emphasized that because one leg is stronger than the other, it does not mean that she must *jump* off that leg. It is very common to find athletes who prefer the other leg because it is more comfortable for them physically, and if this is the case, the athlete should be allowed to jump from that leg. It must be remembered that strength can be attained in both legs through weight training, which is much easier to do than to try to work on the opposite leg, which will change the pattern of the entire body when jumping.

Several factors are important when working with the athlete to determine the approach run. It must be remembered that the approach run is vital to the success of the plant and that, without a good approach run, every other phase of the Flop is affected. With a poor approach run, the plant becomes inefficient, which leads to a poor take-off, which in turn reduces the athlete's ability to raise her center of gravity. The approach is the setup for the plant and this is why it is one of the most important elements in the Flop.

The key factors of the approach run in the Flop are speed and the use of a curved approach path. Most jumpers like to use a long run for their approach, as it offers a more relaxed method in which to attain running velocity. The most common of the curved approaches is the J approach, which means that the jumper takes several initial strides in a straight line and then, in the last 3-4 strides, curves into the take-off area of the plant. Siegfried Heinz of West Germany offers a simple but useful method of determining the approach in the Flop.

(a) Determine the take-off point (A) on the jumping surface, and mark it. The take-off varies with the individual's jumping ability, but is usually from 2-3 ft. from the bar and just inside the near standard (Figure 9-1).

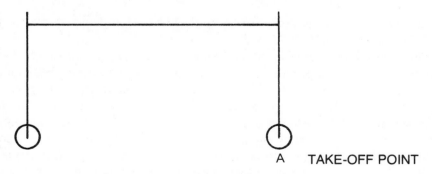

A   TAKE-OFF POINT

FIGURE 9-1

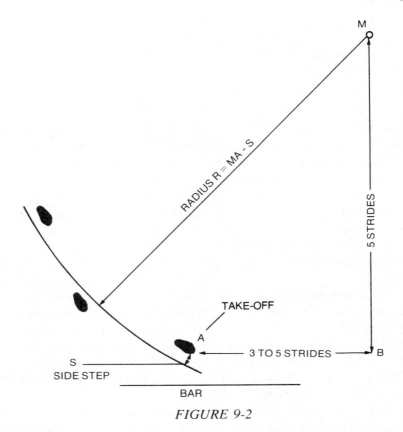

FIGURE 9-2

(b) Establish point M by taking 3 to 5 strides from A parallel to the bar to point B, and 5 strides at a right angle to the line AB to point M (Figure 9-2). For jumpers who like a tight approach curve, the distance from A to B should be 3 strides; for those who like a normal approach curve, this distance should be 3½-4 strides; and for those who like a wide curve, a distance of 4-5 strides should be used.

(c) Place the zero end of the tape measure at M and measure the distance to A. The distance is adjusted to allow for the sidestep S so that the radius R of the curve becomes MA-S.

(d) The last part of the curve is now marked on the jumping surface, using M as the central point and the radius R.

The radius varies between individuals and increases with the run-up speed. In general it is 19-33 ft. for girls and women. The side-step varies from about 6 in. for young girls to as much as 10-14 in. for the more advanced jumper.

For beginners, the number of strides varies from 7-9 strides. For the more advanced jumper, the number of strides will range from 9-13 strides. Keeping in mind that the last 3-4 strides should be on the curve, the first strides should determine how much speed is to be gained by the number of approach strides to the curving point. If the jumper wishes to use a relaxed approach run, but wishes to have good speed coming in for the takeoff, she should use at least nine strides or more. This will allow her to build up speed gradually without rushing into the curve. Remember that the greater the speed into the take-off, the greater the force exerted against the jumping surface, if the plant and take-off are executed properly.

The height achieved by the center of gravity will be determined by the combining of two factors of horizontal speed and its conversion to a vertical speed (or lift) by the take-off mechanism. Speed in the approach is a more important factor than leg spring because, in the Flop, the flexion of the leg is minimal. When looking at many of the outstanding jumpers, it appears that their take-off legs are almost straight on the plant. If the jumpers use a very slow approach, greater leg flexion is required, which in turn means that greater leg strength must be utilized.

The approach factors in the jump are closely related to the take-off factors. It can be stated very simply that the main purpose of the approach is to generate speed for the plant and take-off. Consequently, two problems are created by the jumper's approach speed. They are the checking of horizontal speed and the generation of eccentric thrust. The straddle jumper seeks to solve these problems (a) by having the plant in front of her center of gravity, which requires added strength, and (b) by leaning towards the crossbar in order to insure rotation over the bar.

However, the Flopper uses a curved approach (last 3-4 strides) to more efficiently solve these problems of conversion and rotation. When using the curved approach it is apparent that the jumper is leaning away from the bar on the last 3-4 strides (Figures 9-3 through 9-6). It is this lean that is the key to the Flopper's ability to utilize additional approach speed.

It is interesting to note that when checking linear motion on the plant, the upper body actually increases in speed and will continue in the original direction and rotation will begin. This principle has been experienced by anyone who has been tripped, or who has stepped off a merry-go-round when it was moving. The upper body is thrust ahead of the foot when it contacts the ground. By having a lean away from the bar, the flopper will still take off vertically after planting, without losing much of the horizontal force during conversion.

The key to the plant is simple to coach—the plant stride should be shorter than the next to last or penultimate stride and the plant foot should be parallel, or almost parallel to the crossbar. The angle of the plant foot to the crossbar should vary from 0 deg. to no more than 15 deg.

In Figure 9-2, it will be noted that the plant foot is not in line with the penultimate step, but is off center. This side stepping is important in that it places less stress on the ankle, and also allows for a twisting motion to be set up by the penultimate step. For example, if the left leg is the jumping leg, it will be noted that on the plant, the left knee is pointed in line with the crossbar, or is almost lined up parallel with the crossbar (Figure 9-6). However, the right leg is facing toward the crossbar. This action forces the right hip back slightly, which gives a

FIGURE 9-3

FIGURE 9-4

FIGURE 9-5

FIGURE 9-6

FIGURE 9-7

FIGURE 9-8

FIGURE 9-9

FIGURE 9-10

FIGURE 9-11

FIGURE 9-12

FIGURE 9-13

FIGURE 9-14

twisting effect to the body. On takeoff, the right knee will swing up and across the body almost naturally, without a great deal of emphasis needed by the jumper (Figure 9-8).

The use of a short last step allows the jumper's center of gravity to move over the plant foot at a faster speed, thereby reducing the need for leg flexion and the tremendous amount of leg strength that is needed if a long last step is taken. A biomechanical principle concerned with the development of vertical acceleration comes into play at this point. If the jumper stays on the ground for a long time, the ground reaction is reduced. This can be seen when dropping a tennis ball and a golf ball from the same height and at the same time. The golf ball rises off the hard floor much faster and to a higher height than the tennis ball, because the tennis ball was on the ground for a long time which reduced its vertical acceleration.

During practice sessions, it should be remembered that short and slow approach runs also create problems. There is very little chance to develop sufficient velocity, the centrifugal force and corresponding body lean are limited, which in turn does not give the necessary neuromuscular response that should be practiced for the jump itself. The straightening of the body follows a shorter path at the takeoff and the full exploitation of the eccentric force from the take-off leg is required, as the rotational impulse, created by the straightening of the body, is limited.

Another problem that is created by the short and slow approach is that the jumper subconsciously feels that she will not reach the required horizontal layout in the flight and will put everything into the eccentric takeoff force in order to compensate. This will cause too much lean with the upper body toward the bar, and the jumper will lose the greatest advantage the Flop has to offer.

The take-off is the third factor influencing the raising of the center of gravity. The plant for the take-off must be just inside the standard as mentioned previously, as this will enable the jumper to clear the bar in the middle where it has the greatest sag and allow for a safe landing in the pit. It will also allow the jumper to avoid hitting the bar on the way up, before the complete layout position is achieved.

The short last stride in the Flop promotes the early and rapid drive-through of the arms and the free leg (Figure 9-5). In order to facilitate a quick free leg, and explosive arm action, it must be remembered that the jumper must reduce the radius of both the arms and legs. This means that as she brings her free-swinging leg up, the heel of the leg must almost touch her buttocks, as in the leg action of a sprinter at top speed (Figure 9-7). The arms must be driven up as directly and quickly as possible. One of the problems faced by beginners when they start to use the double arm lift in the Flop, is that they tend to let their arms fall behind their buttocks too far, in preparation for the double arm lift, therefore extending the plant foot, and putting their center of gravity too far behind the take-off foot. In preparation for the double arm lift, the arms should never be straightened, as this tends to slow down the action of the arms (Figure 9-7).

One of the most important factors comes into play as the arms are swinging up, the blocking action of the arms and the free leg (Figures 9-8 through 9-11). The arms should never continue in a pattern over the head and reaching into the pit. It is very common to see beginner, and even world-class jumpers, making this mistake, and it sets up a very poor take-off mechanism. If one or both arms continue over the bar, the hips are forced to move in the opposite direction, which is away from the bar, thereby increasing the amount of eccentric thrust, and reducing vertical lift.

The arms should be brought up high enough so that the upper arm (from elbow to shoulder), is parallel with the ground. This same parallel position applies to the jumper's free leg—the thigh should be brought up so that it too is parallel with the ground (Figure 9-8). When looking at the jumper on film it should appear that she has both upper arms and the thigh of the free leg parallel with each other. When the arms and legs are swung correctly, they create a tremendous ground reaction on take-off, and this is a great aid in lifting the center of gravity of the jumper.

When working out for the actual jump itself, the coach and athlete should devote more time to the approach and take-off than to the bar clearance. Although bar clearance is a necessary factor in the success of the jump, the most important factor is the ability to raise the center of gravity as high as possible. This in turn means that more practice time should be devoted to the approach, plant, and take-off.

Action on top of the bar is the final aspect of the jump that should be considered. Once the athlete is in the air, the path of her center of gravity cannot be altered. This path, termed a parabolic curve, is established by the speed and angle of take-off. Therefore, any movements that the jumper performs in the air will only change the speed of rotation and the position of the body parts in relation to the center of gravity.

Both the curved approach and the driving of the knee of the free leg across the body as the jumper leaves the ground assist in developing rotation about the jumper's vertical axis. Once airborne, the jumper's upper body starts to catch up with the lower body, in which the take-off foot was parallel with the crossbar (Figure 9-8). As she attains height, her back begins to turn toward the bar, so that it is nearly parallel with the bar when going over the top (Figure 9-11).

Having extremities remain close to the axis of rotation will increase the rotational speed of the jumper. If the arms are not bent to at least 90 deg. and if they are extended out in front of the jumper, the upper body rotation will be slowed down.

Once the jumper has her back to the bar, another axis of rotation, the horizontal axis, becomes important. To decrease the time spent on top of the bar, the Flopper increases the speed of the horizontal rotation. Again, a shortened radius increases the speed of rotation. If a jumper's entire body (while on top of the bar) is absolutely parallel with the ground, that is a long radius. In order to shorten that radius, the jumper can do one of two things—she can either sit up by bringing her arms and legs up, which in turn would lower her hips into the bar; or she can arch her back by tucking her heels under the buttocks as far as possible (Figure 9-11). In some cases, dropping the head back might also be of some advantage. By opening the knees, yet keeping the heels together, with the knees flexed and heels below the level of the hips, a further shortening of the jumper's radius is attained.

At the peak of the flight, the jumper should have her hands close by her hips, her knees open, her heels together, and her back parallel or slightly arched (Figure 9-11).

As the jumper clears the bar, her only remaining problem is that of clearing the lower legs over the bar. This can be done by simply straightening the legs as the lower legs pass over the bar, or by using a slight up-lift of the head at the same time the lower legs are also being lifted (Figure 9-13). This lifting of the lower legs is not a slow movement, but is a quick-kicking action as the upper body of the jumper is now on a descending flight into the pit.

TEACHING THE BEGINNING FLOPPER

When teaching the beginner to flop, the first step is to determine which is to be the take-off foot. One method for determining the stronger leg is to set the crossbar at a low height (approximately 2 ft.) and have the athlete simply jump over the bar. Have her run straight at the bar, several times, and observe which foot she prefers to jump from.

After determining the preferred take-off foot, have the jumper move to the side (at about a 30-deg. angle). Those jumpers showing a preference for jumping from the left foot and lifting the right (free) leg must approach the bar from the right side; those who favor jumping from the right foot must approach from the left.

The Approach

Although a measured run-up is not absolutely essential at this stage, it is helpful to have one. To establish the run-up and take-off point for a left-footed jumper, begin by having her stand 18 in. from the right standard, facing the crossbar. Standing at an angle of 30 deg. to the bar, she swings her free leg up, adjusting her position until she can just avoid touching the bar with her free leg.

Turning around, she then runs back five easy paces toward the beginning point of the run-up, starting with the right foot forward. The first stride is short, with strides two, three and four getting progressively longer, so that the fourth stride is the longest. However, the fifth stride should be slightly shorter than the fourth, as the fourth stride will be the penultimate (next-to-last) stride when the direction of the run is reversed and the athlete is approaching the take-off point. The point of the fifth stride is marked with tape on the jumping apron, as it marks the distance (in this case in reverse) from the final check mark to the point of take-off.

After practicing the five-step approach until timing and technique have improved, the approach should be lengthened to include first a seven- and then a nine-step approach, and eventually as many as eleven or thirteen steps. When the run-up is lengthened beyond the five steps, the additional strides in the approach should be in a straight line, with the final three strides employing the curved approach mentioned earlier. It is important to stress to the beginner that her first strides, which are straight, are used to build up speed so that when she hits the curved point in the approach she has sufficient speed for the plant and take-off.

The Arm and Leg Lift

The double arm and free leg lift at take-off must be taught together. Without using the bar or landing pit, have the athlete learn a one-step approach. Standing on the jumping apron with her right foot forward approximately 18-24 in., she steps forward with the left foot while both arms are hanging at her sides, elbows slightly bent. During the step forward, the arms move forward and upward, with an increase in their flexion. By the time she lifts off the ground, the elbows are bent to approximately 90 deg.

When she plants the left foot (heel first, then toe), she lifts the free leg quickly forward and upward, with the knee bent. Her back should be straight and her lift as near to vertical as possible. It is important that she not get her take-off foot too far forward at the plant, as this will cause her to lean back and will reduce the vertical lift.

The next step is to teach a two-step approach. The athlete stands on the jumping apron, this time with the left foot forward. The right foot is brought forward with the length of the stride emphasized, since this step represents the penultimate stride before the plant.

The Rotation

The athlete can begin to learn the rotation from the ground by practicing the take-off (on the apron or on grass), doing a half-turn in the air, and landing on the jumping foot facing backward. The quick lifting of the arms and free leg should still be emphasized. This gives the athlete the feeling of the necessary rotation from the ground without actually having to jump over a crossbar.

After several of these rotational jumps on the ground, the jumper should use the same drill, jumping into a pit, but without a crossbar. As confidence is gained, she can begin to rotate over onto her back as she lands in the pit.

More vigorous movements can then be added by increasing speed, increasing rotation, and landing on her back with her legs up into the air. Then use a crossbar, but at a very low height to begin with.

The action for the jumper is plant, take-off, rotate, and then land on the lower part of the back. As she makes progress, her next step is to increase the height of the bar, increase her approach speed, and land on the middle portion of her back. During her jumps over the bar, the athlete should be reminded to keep her hips up high over the bar during flight.

With the steps measured and the starting and take-off points marked, the athlete can now put together the entire Flop technique. She can spend additional practice time on developing a consistent approach and an efficient take-off. It must be emphasized to the jumper not to let her hips settle when on top of the bar (sitting down on the bar). Keeping her back arched when on top of the bar is important, and if she sits down with her hips, it will simply raise the center of mass in her body and destroy the effects of a good plant and take-off.

The Flop is a rather basic technique, and if the coach becomes too technical too early it will certainly deter from the jumper's progress. Even after just a few short practice sessions, it is evident that most female jumpers can adapt to the Flop technique without the hours that would have normally been spent learning the straddle.

Coaching Points

1. Establish a long run which includes the established number of strides, the arc, the take-off point, and the speed of the approach.
2. Establish a short run of 5-7 strides when working on the plant and take-off.
3. Establish consistency in the approach by working on the first four steps in the approach. These four steps are the most important, since this is where the rhythm of the run is developed.
4. Use good running form throughout the approach.
5. The run should be a gradual acceleration, with stride length increasing throughout.
6. On the ''J'' approach, the jumper should look straight ahead for the first part of the run. Then, as she goes into the arc, she focuses her attention on the top of the crossbar.
7. When changing from the straight-ahead approach to the arc, the jumper should think of a gradual turn, beginning with the outside foot. The arc should be gradual enough so that velocity is maintained through to the plant.
8. On the plant, the jumper must think about quick upward action of the arms and free leg. The biggest problem that jumpers have on the plant when they try to explode from the ground is to take a long last step. The plant is inefficient when the last stride is so long that too much time is spent on the ground at take-off.

TRAINING FOR THE FLOP

When training for the Flop, there are many variables that must be considered. For example, it is important to consider the relationship between the days of practice and the days when competitions occur. Many high schools have as many as two meets per week, which means that during the season the jumper must reduce the number of strength training sessions each week. Then, there are those athletes who compete only on Saturdays, which allows them to train throughout the week.

In-Depth Jumping

Besides the standard strength training exercises recommended for high jumpers (see Chapter 13), in-depth jumping is strongly recommended as an important phase of jump training, since it offers a quick, explosive movement which is important to the training of the jumper's muscle system.

The technique is simple. Jump down from a platform, landing on both feet, with the knees flexed slightly. Explode straight up. Single leg jumps from lower heights should be done in the same way.

Following are a few of the many in-depth jump training possibilities available to the high jumpers:

1. Jump from a box (2-3½ ft. high) onto a resilient mat, and hop over cones or boxes.
2. Hop over hurdles set 2-3 ft. apart.
3. Using only one leg, hop over cones in rapid succession.
4. Jump from a box to the floor, and then quickly up onto another box

In-Depth Jumping Schedule

Off-season: Two days per week.
Pre-season: Two days per week; then one day per week.
In-season: One day per week, early in the season; no in-depth jumping during the week prior to big meets.
Height: Two legs—2½-4 ft.
            One leg —20-24 in.
Number of Jumps: 2 sets of 10 (off-season)
                              2 sets of 15 (early pre-season)
                              2 sets of 20 (late pre-season)
                              2 sets of 15 (in-season)

Do not use in-depth jumping during the two-week period prior to the biggest competitions.

Coaching Points in Training

1. Do not do heavy strength exercises the day prior to major jumping competitions near the end of the season.
2. Do light running and stretching on the day prior to a meet.
3. Lift and do in-depth jumping only after actual jumping practice. Do not lift or do in-depth jumping prior to a jumping session.
4. Jump for height at least once a week in practice.
5. During the season, work toward quick, explosive movements in training.

10 Eleanor Rynda

THE SHOT PUT

Author: **Eleanor Rynda** is head track and cross country coach for both men and women at the University of Minnesota, Duluth. She has conducted numerous track and field clinics and workshops throughout the Midwest; has participated in national track and field coaching schools in the U.S., Canada and Great Britain; and has served in key administrative positions in women's track and field at both regional and national levels.

The words "shift" and "lift" describe the major movements used in performing the shot put, the simplest of the throwing events. The putter stands at the back of the circle with her back to the direction of the put. Movement of the shot is initiated by shifting backward across the circle. The putter reaches the center of the circle in a crouched position ready to lift the shot upward explosively, turning the shoulders to the side and then the front only after the lifting action is well underway. A final impulse is imparted to the implement by striking with the arm, wrist and fingers after the shot has been lifted over the front foot and beyond the toe-board. This sequence of movements produces continuous maximum acceleration to the shot over the greatest range possible.

Progress in the shot put has been great during the past three decades. Olympic champion and former world record holder Parry O'Brien revolutionized shot putting form in 1951 by using a full 180 deg. turn before putting, rather than a turn of only about 90 deg. used by most putters while crossing the circle. The advantage of O'Brien's style was that force could be applied to the shot over a greater distance to produce maximum acceleration of the shot. Many athletes and coaches have refined and improved O'Brien's basic form, but the general pattern of movement remains essentially the same today.

TECHNIQUE

To aid in understanding details of the O'Brien technique of putting the shot, draw an imaginary straight "line of direction" through the center of the circle, bisecting the toe-board, dividing the circle into right and left halves and also draw a "cross line," dividing it into front and rear halves (Figure 10-1).

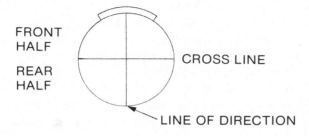

FIGURE 10-1

Step into the rear half of the circle and stand erect with the back to the direction of the put. The right-handed athlete places the right foot on the line of direction with the toes touching the inside rim of the circle.

Hold the shot in the right hand so the weight is supported at the base of the three longest fingers. The weight will tend to lie toward the index finger and thumb. The thumb holds the shot above the palm. The fingers spread around the shot fan-wise (Figure 10-2).

FIGURE 10-2

Holding the shot in this manner, place it against the right side of the neck in the hollow just below the jawbone and above the collar bone so that the body aids in support of its weight. The wrist is well-bent. The right elbow is under the shot and in front of the right shoulder. The shot should be held there with sufficient pressure until the putting motion is started.

Extend the left arm to the front so it points downward toward the ground at an angle of about 45 deg. Keep it relaxed.

Support the weight of the body and the shot on the right leg. Relax the left leg and place it well behind the right leg along the imaginary line of direction. The toes of the left foot lightly touch the ground for balance. The eyes focus a short distance beyond the rim at the back of the circle.

As the left leg is moved backward further, the trunk moves forward over the right knee which bends slightly. The shot is thus moved to a position outside the back rim of the circle (Figure 10-3). If it were to drop, it would land outside the ring. When the trunk is nearly horizontal, the left leg will be fully extended with the left toe touching the ground for balance. Then the straight left leg is lifted upward to near hip height. This places the body in a horizontal position from left toe to left hand, supported in a T position by the right leg (Figure 10-4).

The left leg bends and is brought forward toward the right knee, but not in advance of it. While the left leg moves forward, the right knee bends to lower the entire body into a compact, crouched position (Figure 10-5). These movements overbalance and tip the body weight slightly in the direction of the toe-board. With the bent left knee near the right knee and the body weight starting to move backward, the putter shifts directly backward by a simultaneous extension of the left leg toward the toe-board and a powerful push off the right leg resulting from a vigorous extension of the right knee (Figure 10-6). The right foot scrapes the ground as it is pulled backward quickly to land directly under the body. If the shot were to drop as the right leg lands, it would not hit the knee or foot, but would fall to the ground well beyond the right foot and knee (Figure 10-7).

The right foot lands flat, having just crossed the center of the circle on the line of direction with the foot having been turned to point between 45 and 90 deg. to the left of the line of direction. The instep of the right foot is on the line of direction and the right knee remains bent, supporting the weight of the body and the shot. (Figure 10-7).

The foot of the left leg lands flat on its inside edge. The foot is touching the inside of the toe-board and is parallel to it. The left knee is slightly bent (Figure 10-8). The left foot lands only a fraction of a second after the right foot lands.

The hips have turned slightly to the left as a result of the left foot landing parallel to the toe-board during the shift. The trunk has raised only slightly and the eyes remain focused on the rim at the back of the circle. The shoulders remain square, facing opposite to the direction of the put, and the left arm remains extended to the rear, pointing to the ground at approximately a 45 deg. angle (Figure 10-7). The putter has moved straight across the circle along the line of direction.

Figure 10-3—10-11   Nadyezdha Chizhova, USSR   70′4½″

FIGURE 10-3

FIGURE 10-4

FIGURE 10-5

FIGURE 10-6

FIGURE 10-7

FIGURE 10-8

FIGURE 10-9

FIGURE 10-10

FIGURE 10-11

Having arrived in the front half of the circle in a compact position, the putter lifts upward powerfully by an explosive thrust of the right leg (Figure 10-8). This thrust of the right leg actually begins even before the left leg makes contact with the toe-board. Strong back and trunk muscles are used simultaneously with the thrust of the right leg to aid in lifting the shot over the left leg and beyond the toe-board.

The drive of the right leg lifts the body and shot over the bent left leg before the hips and shoulders turn to the front. As the body weight moves over the left leg, and as the shoulders turn to the front, the left leg extends and the right arm strikes simultaneously with the elbow high, back of the hand to the rear (Figure 10-9). As the left leg straightens, it lifts the putter on the toes. The right arm strikes at great speed at an angle of approximately 40 deg. to the horizontal. A "flick" of the wrist and fingers adds a final impulse to the shot.

As the right arm strikes, the left arm moves back and down with the elbow bent. During the arm strike, the left shoulder should be as high as possible, the right shoulder should be still higher and the right elbow even higher. Both shoulders should be kept moving forward during the arm strike.

After the lift is completed, as the body weight moves forward in the direction of the put, first the right and then the left foot breaks contact with the ground. Most putters have both feet off the ground a fraction of a second before the shot leaves the hand (Figure 10-9).

When the putter lifts fast and powerfully, it is usually necessary to reverse the position of the feet to avoid going out of the front of the circle. After the shot has left the right hand, the left foot is quickly lifted backward toward the center of the circle (Figure 10-10) and the right foot speeds forward, feet passing in mid-air. The body weight settles over a bent right leg just inside the stop-board (Figure 10-11). This is a reverse. It is the result of correct and explosive putting movements.

During the "shift," the shot moves horizontally along the line of direction, and during the "lift" and arm strike it moves upward and then forward beyond the toe-board. The movement of the shot should not deviate to the right or left of the line of direction as it is carried from the back of the circle to the front. Continuity of momentum and maximum acceleration of the implement over the greatest range possible are the prime considerations in shot putting.

DETAILS OF TECHNIQUE AND CORRECTION OF COMMON FAULTS

The distance the shot can ultimately be put depends on the following basic principles of physics:

1. The velocity of the shot at the instant of release.
2. The angle of the release.
3. Various wind and air resistance factors.

Wind and air resistance factors are negligible in putting the shot; therefore the athlete should concentrate on developing the correct technique which, along with a strong body, makes it possible to impart a maximum velocity to the shot at the instant of release and to release it at the correct angle.

The velocity of the shot at release is increased by the glide, as the longer the distance over which force is applied, the greater will be the velocity—that is, provided the speed gained in the glide action is sustained and transferred efficiently to the shot at the correct angle at the moment of release.

The distance over which force may be applied in accelerating the shot from start to delivery is increased even more when the athlete bends the trunk and moves the shot well outside the back rim of the circle before starting the shift. It is possible to increase this distance by well over 12 in. (30 cm.).

The putter should not change the direction of the shot's movement at any time before the release. The shot should remain at the side of the neck and move in a straight line from the back to the front of the circle. Failure to do this results in the shot seeming to become heavier for the athlete, since more force is needed to continuously change direction of an object in motion than if the object is kept moving in a straight line.

While standing at the back of the circle prior to the shift backward, the left arm may be held above the head with the palm to the front. The arm is then brought downward as the trunk bends down into the movements of the shift. This downward action of the arm may have the effect of moving the center of gravity forcefully toward the back of the circle before it is then suddenly shifted toward the front of the circle in the glide. This, in turn, may upset the proper balance of the athlete, causing a falling off to the side. It may be more efficient, depending on the athlete, to start the shift from a more static position with the left arm pointing downward toward the ground at an angle of about 45 deg. as has been described here.

The athlete must avoid raising the trunk upright during the shift across the circle. The trunk remains essentially horizontal through the shift. The back should be kept flat. Coming upright during the shift reduces the distance over which the shot may be lifted during the putting action. The left shoulder must not prematurely rotate to the left during the shift. The shoulders should be kept square until the landing in the front of the circle.

It is important that the right leg is in its final position for the explosive thrust upward at the instant the right foot lands at the center of the circle. If the shot were to be dropped in this position, it should land to the right of the right foot on the line of direction. If the shot is in a position to drop on the right knee, it means the right foot has not been pulled far enough under the body during the shift toward the toe-board. This is a gross error. Any planting of the right leg at the center of the circle that is followed by a lowering of the body before the lifting, extending action of the right leg at the center, is incorrect.

As the right foot grounds at the center of the circle, there should be a rocking motion of the body from the right to the left foot to keep the common center of gravity of the shot and body moving in the direction of the put. Placing too much weight over the right leg as the foot grounds keeps the left leg hanging in the air, causing a late landing of the left foot and producing a pause which greatly reduces continuity of momentum. There should be only enough rocking of the body from right foot to left foot to aid the body to continue moving in the direction of the put; this rocking motion will help in grounding the left foot. If the left foot grounds too soon after or simultaneously with the grounding of the right foot, there will not be any rocking action of the body from right to left foot, thus reducing momentum and decreasing important shot speed developed during the shift.

Poor placement of the left foot at the front of the circle is a common error. If the left foot lands too far to the left of the line of direction, the athlete has stepped "in the bucket," resulting in a premature opening of the hips and a consequent loss of power during the lift and drive by the right leg. If the left foot lands too far to the right of the line of direction, the left hip "blocks" or stops the range of motion of the right leg and again there is considerable loss of driving power resulting in shorter puts. Coaches need to observe the action of the left (kicking) leg at the rear of the circle. Movement of the leg should be straight forward with the knee bent in the "pump" and then straight backward toward the toe-board in the kick. Even the slightest deviation results in a weak position of the left foot at the front of the circle.

Every effort must be made to avoid a pause or dwelling of the body when it lands in the center of the circle. This error is usually the result of the following:

1. Too much height during the shift.
2. Pausing to "cock" (turn) the shoulders to the right as the right foot lands at the end of the shift.
3. Landing on the ball of the right foot at the center of the circle and then settling down on the heel.
4. Sinking down on the right leg as the right foot lands or right after it lands.
5. Late landing of the left foot at the toe-board which is caused by too much weight over the right leg.
6. Weakness of the right leg and/or trunk muscles which delays the immediate lifting action as the right foot lands.

The blocking action by the left leg as it grounds at the front of the circle transfers momentum developed during the shift upward in the body and eventually to the shot. The motion of the body parts below the center of gravity is stopped, and the motion of the body parts above the center of gravity is accelerated. The higher the parts are above the center of gravity, the faster are they accelerated; therefore, it is essential that the left foot should land with the left knee bent slightly only a fraction of a second after the right foot has grounded, while the right leg is beginning its upward thrust.

When the left foot lands parallel to the toe-board, the hips will necessarily have turned as much as 45 deg. to the left during the shift. Even though the hips have turned to the left, the head, shoulders, and extended left arm must be kept pointing directly toward the rear of the circle throughout the shift, the landing in the putting position and until the lift of the shot is well underway.

Turning the hips to the left before lifting the shot often results in a relatively flat throw. Correct placement of the left foot and keeping the shoulders square to the rear of the circle helps correct this error.

Most of the work of delivery is done by the legs and trunk. With the body in the putting position after the landing in the center and the rocking from right to left foot completed, proper timing to lift the shot upward and then forward before the shoulders turn and the arm finally strikes will add even greater speed to the implement. The slower but more powerful muscles and levels of the thighs and trunk are used first to get the shot moving, and then the weaker but faster muscles and joints of the legs, feet, arms and hands add their forces to an already rapidly moving implement.

The shot stays in the neck-jaw position until the shoulders lift and start turning to the left. When the trunk approaches the vertical, and a line joining the shoulders is parallel to the line of direction, the shot leaves the putter's neck while the chest continues turning to the front. After breaking contact with the neck, the shot continues its upward-forward path in the same vertical plane as the line of direction.

The arm strike is consciously delayed until after the body weight has been lifted over the left leg and the chest has almost turned to the front. The right arm strikes after the right foot has just left the ground and the chest has turned well to the front. When the right hand leaves the shoulder, the right elbow is high and the lower arm and right hand are in an almost horizontal position. During the extension of the arm in the striking action, the right hand twists so that the wrist is below the shot. After the extension and reach beyond the toe-board, a final impulse is added by a rapid "flick" of the wrist and fingers beneath and behind the shot.

The reaction of the putter's body to the final "flick" is just sufficient to keep from fouling in a perfect put. The shot should be released at an angle between 37 and 42 deg. to horizontal, usually approximately 40 deg.

During the arm-strike, both shoulders continue to move forward; however, the right shoulder moves ahead of the left as the right arm continues to accelerate the shot beyond the toe-board.

The left arm, which has been kept extended toward the rear of the circle to help prevent early rotation or "opening" of the shoulders, is lifted vertically as the shot is lifted upward in the putting action. After the lift of the shot is well underway, the left elbow bends to almost a right angle at the same time the shoulders turn to the left prior to the arm-strike. With the trunk almost upright and just prior to the arm-strike, the back of the left wrist passes above and in front of the forehead, with the left upper arm almost vertical. With movement in this plane, the left elbow leads the lifting of the right shoulder to a high, "over the top" position, rather than a mere horizontal turning of it to the front. As the right arm strikes, the left arm moves downward and backward closer to the lower ribs.

When the right leg has nearly completed the lift, the trunk is nearly erect, with the shoulders parallel to the line of direction. The lower back arches somewhat, raising the chest. The head tilts backward so the chin points directly upward and the eyes look across the sky. The putter does not watch the shot leave the hand during the release.

In the perfect put, the shot has been accelerated to its maximum and momentum has been transferred to the shot making a reverse usually (and correctly) necessary to prevent fouling over the toe-board. The reverse is not a part of the delivery action but rather a means to avoid fouling.

The toes of the putter's left foot should remain in contact with the ground just until the shot leaves the fingers at the end of the wrist and finger "flick." The right foot is already moving forward and the left foot breaks contact and moves backward, feet passing in mid-air. The full weight of the body settles over a bent right leg just inside the toe-board.

If use of the reverse does not prevent fouling over the toe-board, the following should be considered as a possible cause:

(a)   Not enough final flick with the fingers.
(b)   Permitting the weight of the body to pass prematurely over the left leg by failing to rock from right foot to left foot at the end of the shift.
(c)   Failing to lift sufficiently with the left leg at the same time the right arm strikes.
(d)   The lifting (vertical) component of the delivery action may be too small when compared to the forward (horizontal) component.
(e)   Shifting too far toward the toe-board causing the right foot to land well beyond the center of the circle.
(f)   Coming upright with the trunk during the shift and landing in the putting position with the trunk too upright. This results in too short a range for delivery action, which in turn does not provide enough reaction from the shot to inhibit forward movement.

The shot should land on or near the line of direction extended through and beyond the toe-board. "Hooking" the shot considerably to the left of the line of direction or "slicing" it to any extent to the right of the line of direction indicates the putting force was not exerted directly behind the center of gravity of the shot. Shorter distances result. The cause of "hooking" the shot is usually stepping "in the bucket" (to the left of the line of direction). "Slicing" of the shot is basically caused by failure to lift the shot "over the top" (above the body's center of gravity) before the arm strikes. Not lifting the chin properly as the chest turns to the front will contribute to failure to lift the shot sufficiently.

During the entire movement of putting, the greatest acceleration of the shot comes during the lifting action after landing in the putting position at the center of the circle. The shift adds only approximately seven percent of the total distance in a 60 ft. (18.3 m.) put. Most putters do not expect the shift to add more than 5 ft. (1.5 m.) to their standing put.

VARIATIONS IN SHOT PUTTING TECHNIQUE

The East Germans were the first to use a putting form which eliminated the T position prior to the glide across the circle as is used in the O'Brien technique. They also shortened the glide, grounding the foot of the driving leg slightly less than half-way across the circle in an effort to lengthen the distance over which force is exerted on the shot in the putting action. The value of this latter feature of technique is subject to question because the putter's center of gravity seldom moves forward over the front leg.

A "rotation" technique in moving across the circle before delivering the shot with an orthodox putting action has been successfully used by some putters. They hold the shot in the familiar neck-jaw position, start in the rear of the circle with the back to the direction of the put, use a discus turn (running rotation) across the circle, and deliver the shot in the orthodox way.

It is apparent that the rotation technique is a more complicated style of putting. Whether or not any of these variations are better than the orthodox O'Brien putting technique depends upon the ability of the athlete using them.

SHOT PUT TEACHING SEQUENCE

Preparation of the Teaching Station

1. Draw a 7 ft. circle on the surface for each student, or at least a 7 ft. start and finish point.
2. Draw a center line for line of direction, dividing the circle into right and left halves.
3. Draw a cross line to divide the circle into front and rear halves.
4. Draw footprints in the circle in the exact spots the feet should be positioned at the start and also for the put (Figure 10-12).

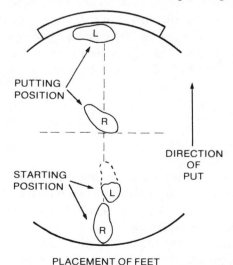

PLACEMENT OF FEET   *FIGURE 10-12*

Standing Put Progression

1. Step into the circle and take the position to put from a stand. Place the feet in the position diagrammed above. Turn the shoulders to face away from the direction of the put. Place the hands on the hips.
2. Bend the right leg, placing the body weight on it, then extend it with a forceful lifting action, driving the right hip through toward the left and turning the hips, then the shoulders to face the direction of the put. The weight shifts to the left toes, the head and chest are high, the back is arched slightly. Practice this lifting, driving action several times. Lift and drive stronger and faster each time, even with a jump off the ground. Observe that this explosive lift has brought the right side and leg through into a natural "reverse."
3. Take the shot in the left hand. Support it with the palm under the shot and hold it against the right shoulder. Repeat the forceful, lifting action in number 2 several times, allowing the shot to be lifted and put out beyond the circle. This drill demonstrates that the legs contribute lift and power to a put and it teaches the student to drive upward and forward by forcefully extending the right leg.
4. Without the shot, place the right hand at the side of the neck as if holding the shot. Reach the left arm straight out in front, relaxed and pointed downward at a 45 deg. angle. Repeat the standing put action several times with emphasis on getting the right elbow high for delivery and in the correct striking angle. Work explosively and reverse.
5. Take the shot in the right hand, wrist bent and elbow beneath, and hold it at the side of the neck. Reach the left arm out in front. Put very easily several times from the standing position. Emphasize lift and drive of the right leg and hip, shoulders square as long as possible, elbow of putting arm high, coming through high on the toes, head and chest high and back arched, delayed arm strike, approximately 40 deg. striking angle. Reverse as the lift becomes stronger and faster with each put. Let it come naturally as the result of a powerful lift and drive with the right leg and hip. Put three to four times with emphasis on each of the above points.

Adding the Glide

(Practice first without the shot.)

1. Take a standing position at the rear of the circle.
2. Bend forward and glide backward several times on the right leg. To help in staying low, clasp both hands beneath the right leg and glide across the circle several times.
3. Glide backward adding a good "pump" and kick with the left leg.
4. Glide backward and attempt to land just over the center line in the front half of the circle. The emphasis is on staying low, the right (driving)

leg scraping the surface, and a good "pump" and kick with the left leg.

5. Glide to the center and turn the right foot to a 45 deg. angle to the line of direction.

6. Glide to the center with emphasis on pulling the driving leg under the body as it lands just over the center line.

7. Glide to the center with emphasis on getting the left leg down quickly into the correct putting position.

8. Glide with a lift and turn of the hips to the front and full putting action of the right arm. Make the shift and lift stronger and faster each time until a reverse is necessary.

9. Take the shot and place it at the side of the neck and work on the glide to the center several times. Emphasis is on each of the above points.

10. Practice the whole putting action with the shot including the reverse. Work basically for form rather than distance.

Young and inexperienced athletes have difficulty in moving from the extreme rear of the circle to the toe-board during the shift. Until they have the strength and coordination to use the full circle, they will benefit from starting with the right foot 6-10 in. (15-25 cm.) inside the rim at the rear of the circle to enable them to shift across the circle and land with the right foot well over the center line and the left foot in contact with the inside edge of the toe-board.

Coaching Points to Check During the Progression

1. Position of the supporting leg on the line at the back of the circle.

2. Slight bend of right knee and toes of left leg touching the ground to aid balance at the back of the circle.

3. Position of the shot at the back of the circle.

4. Left knee is not pulled ahead of right knee in the "pump" at the rear of the circle.

5. Kick with the left leg is straight backward.

6. Trunk and shoulders remain square to the rear during the glide. Watch for early rotation (pulling back) of the left shoulder.

7. Trunk remains horizontal throughout the shift across the circle.

8. Right leg is pulled under the body weight upon landing in the center.

9. Right foot lands flat at the center and turned to between 45 and 90 deg.

10. Left leg lands parallel to the toe-board immediately after the right leg lands in the center. Watch for a hanging delay of the left leg. This stops momentum.

11. Forceful drive upward and then forward with the right leg and hip.

12. A bracing action with the left leg and coming up high on the toes during putting action.

13. High head and chest and arched back during the put.

14. Shot is held firmly at the side of the neck throughout the shift.

15. Arm position during delivery and delay in release of the shot.

16. Quickness of arm-strike and final "flick" with wrist and fingers.
17. Movement straight across the circle.
18. Reverse is not part of the putting action.
19. Gradual acceleration throughout the shift, lift, and delivery.
20. Continuity of movement; put it all together.

TRAINING

The exact training methods used by any one athlete must be planned to best suit that athlete's physiological and psychological makeup. The age and maturity of the athlete should be considered, and allowances must be made for those who may have a heavy work and study program in school. The championship performance must be prepared for and must not be left on the practice field.

Many aspects of technique are very dependent on pure muscular strength. The basic errors of the novice putter can often be traced directly to a lack of muscular strength. An athlete with both strength and skill is a better performer than one with skill alone. Agility, coordination and balance are also important and several studies have indicated that these factors can be improved in conjunction with strength through weight training.

The training program should include exercises for the entire body, but primarily the big-muscle groups. Strength in both the arms and legs is essential. A comprehensive weight training routine prior to and during the season should be followed. Increased strength aids velocity of delivery, ease of handling the implement, prevention of injury, and general improvement in the performance of the athlete.

It is correct to include some throwing practice during the off-season along with weight training. This maintains the neuromuscular pattern of throwing while the new strength is being built.

A good warm-up should precede a training session. Running is to be included. A certain amount of cardiovascular endurance work is necessary because weight training tends to develop larger muscles with more body mass and weight. The putter needs to develop corresponding strength in the heart and lungs. Fatigue breaks down technique and timing. This condition is evident in the athlete who is tremendously strong but who tires quickly. Running a minimum of a mile per day, five days a week at a pace between 8:00 and 9:00 min. per mile will meet minimum fitness standards.

During the preliminary season, the putter may be drilled as a part of the squad, and conditioning exercises can be prescribed for the whole team. This phase of training should include running, general calisthenics, stretching, hopping, bounding, running backward, rope jumping, and leg quickness exercises.

At the beginning of early season, the athletes are grouped according to event. Beginners should devote approximately half of their training time to work in the shot put circle, which includes numerous all-out puts. The less experienced athlete can only improve through actual putting, over and over and over, to learn technique and get the feel of the event. The top performer expects to increase distance by developing more arm, leg, and body strength and increasing foot speed. The novice concentrates on slower, smoother action, while the champion gets more distance with a quicker more explosive action.

Starts and short sprints are high quality work for development of leg speed. Hurdling, jumping, bounding, running up stairs, and sprinting are physically effective and are monotony breakers as well.

Practice as you hope to compete. If you foul in practice, you are a cinch to carry the habit into competition. Do not hurry the reverse.

Most athletes train with weights one day and throw hard the next day. This may be a practical scheme from the standpoint of completing training within a limited time schedule. An athlete must throw near maximum under control in training in order to develop the skill needed in competition. Throwing hard during practice takes a lot of muscular and nervous energy. Hard throwing on alternate days along with weight training on the other days may mean there isn't sufficient recovery time and progress may not be a rapid as it could be with a day of rest between. If done properly, an athlete can do a hard throwing skill practice on the same day as weight training. If this is done, weight training is done after the putting work. Technique is more efficiently practiced when the muscles are loose and fresh. The other days the athlete should jog at least a mile in order to keep physically fit and do stretching exercises and some controlled speed runs over 110 yd. Jogging puts the work on the heart, lungs, and circulatory system and does not tax the muscles that are recuperating from the hard throwing and weight training session.

During two-day meets, the athlete often needs to qualify on one day and throw again the next in finals. This sequence is simulated in practice when the athlete trains hard on Monday and Tuesday and light until the meet on Friday and Saturday. A light-load training session involves out-of-the-circle work. This may include starts, short sprints, running over low hurdles, and some 110 yd. controlled-speed runs with a 110 yd. walk-back.

It is imperative that the athlete remain fresh for competition, so no heavy exercise should be undertaken the two days prior to competition. During the competitive season, the Friday session is light in preparation for a Saturday meet. This allows two days of rest before the meet. Some athletes rest for three days prior to the championship meet at the end of the season.

Off-Season Training

The main objective of training is to increase strength and improve the physical condition of the athlete. The athlete will do weight training for three days during the week of the non-competitive months, usually from September through December. Activities on the other days may include cross country running, fartlek, rope jumping, handball, squash, gymnastics, swimming, medicine ball throws, sprints, and other leg quickness and agility exercises. Putting can be done occasionally to maintain interest and the neuromuscular pattern of throwing while new strength is being built.

Early-Season Training

Weight training will continue 2-3 days per week. If a meet is scheduled, weight training will be cut back so none is done two days before the meet. Also lighten the Thursday workout and do not put on Friday. The Friday session may include form work in the circle without the shot.

Monday	Warm-up with a 1 mile jog, do stretching exercises for 10 min.
	6-8 sprints over 30 yd.
	20-30 puts from a stand working on some particular fundamental, one point at a time.
	6-8 wrist flips with the shot (throwing it up vertically and catching it with the same hand).
	Hard weight training session.
	5 min. of stretching followed by ¼ mile jog.
Tuesday	Warm-up with a 1 mile jog, do stretching exercises for 10 min.
	6-8 sprints over 30 yd.
	10-15 shifts across the circle without the shot, concentrating on foot placement and body position.
	10-15 standing puts.
	10-12 puts with the shift, moderate effort, special attention to reverse.
	3 sets of 5 finger tip pushups.
	4-6 jumps at the long jump area.
	Hopping and bounding 4 times over 20 yd. on each leg.
	Running backward 6-8 times over 20 yd.
	Stretching for 5 min.
Wednesday	Warm-up with a 1 mile jog, do stretching exercises for 10 min.
	6-8 sprints over 30 yd.
	15-20 standing puts, gradually increasing the distance. Concentrate on correct release angle.
	15-20 puts from a shift, gradually increasing the distance.
	6-8 wrist flips with the shot.
	Hard weight training session.
	5 min. of stretching, followed by a ¼ mile jog.
Thursday	Warm-up with a 1 mile jog, stretching exercises for 10 min.
	6-8 sprints over 30 yd.
	10-12 shifts across the circle without the shot.
	10-15 puts with the shift, moderate effort.
	3 sets of 5 finger tip pushups.
	4-6 jumps at the high jump area.
	4-6 runs over 3 low hurdles.
	Running backward 6-8 times over 20 yd.
	5 min. of stretching.

Friday	Warm-up with a 1 mile jog, stretching exercises for 10 min.
	6-8 sprints over 30 yd.
	6-8 puts from a stand, work on lift from the legs and trunk.
	8-10 puts from a shift, gradually increase the effort.
	10-12 puts at full effort.
	6-8 wrist flips with the shot.
	Hard weight training session.
	5 min. of stretching, ¼ mile jog.
Saturday	Warm-up with 1 mile jog, stretching exercises for 10 min.
	6-8 sprints over 30 yd.
	20 standing puts, work on timing for 10, speed for 10.
	8-10 puts from shift, gradually applying more force.
	6 maximum effort puts as if in competition.
	3 sets of 5 finger tip pushups.
	Hopping and bounding 6 times over 30 yd. with each leg.
	Running backwards 6-8 times over 20 yd.
	4-6 controlled speed runs over 110 yd., walk back 110 yd.
	5 min. of stretching.
Sunday	Rest.

In-Season Training

Assuming the athlete will be competing each Saturday, the following plan will therefore provide a vigorous training session on Monday and Wednesday, a moderate session on Tuesday and Thursday, and a light session on Friday. This leaves sufficient semi-rest time before the Saturday competition. Experimentation will determine the type of practice schedule the athlete should adopt.

Monday	Warm-up with a 1 mile jog, stretching exercises for 10 min.
	8 sprints over 40 yd.
	10-12 standing puts, add force to each successive trial.
	5-7 puts with full effort, check the landing of the shot relative to the line of direction.
	6 puts as in competition, measure and record efforts.
	15-20 puts with shift concentrating on some particular fundamental.
	8-10 wrist flips with the shot.
	Hard weight training session, 5 min. stretching, ¼ mile jog.
Tuesday	Warm-up with a 1 mile jog, stretching exercises for 10 min.
	4 sprints over 300 yd, 4 sprints over 60 yd.
	20 min. on some particular fundamental, with or without the shift.
	20 puts from a shift, moderate effort, but measure so the distance may be compared to distance attained with force applied.
	3 sets of 8 finger tip pushups.
	4-6 jumps at the high jump or long jump area.
	Hopping and bounding 6-8 times over 30 yd.
	Running backward 6-8 times over 20 yd.
	5 min. of stretching.

Wednesday   Warm-up with a 1 mile jog, stretching exercises for 10 min.
             8 sprints over 40 yd.
             6-8 standing puts, emphasize speed in delivery.
             8-10 puts with shift, add force to each successive effort, concentrate on
                 smoothness in coordination.
             20 maximum-effort puts, measure best effort, note on which trial it oc-
                 curs.
             8-10 wrist flips with shot.
             Hard weight training session, followed by 5 min. stretching, ¼ mile jog.

Thursday   Warm-up with a 1 mile jog, stretching for 10 min.
             4-6 block starts over 30 yd.
             6-8 standing puts, work on points needed to perfect form.
             10-15 puts with shift, moderate effort, avoid tension.
             3 sets of 8 finger tip pushups.
             6-8 runs over 3 low hurdles.
             Running backward 6-8 times over 20 yd.
             5 min. of stretching.

Friday   Warm-up with 1 mile jog, stretching for 10 min.
             4-6 controlled speed runs over 110 yd., walk back 110 yd.
             Stretching 5 min.

Saturday   Meet.
             Warm-up the same as for daily training sessions. Include 3-4 sprints.
             4-5 puts from a stand.
             6-10 puts using full technique with gradually increasing effort.
             Competition. Note on which effort best mark was made.

Sunday   Rest.

Late-Season Training

Late season refers to the last two or three weeks of the competition period. Competition may be held twice a week or just once in a large meet on Saturday. The championship event closes the season.

Training is geared to perfection of form. The specific problems of the athlete receive the most attention. Special emphasis is on quickness of the shift, smoothness, and good use of wrist and fingers in the final flick at release. One day of hard weight training is sufficient to maintain the strength that has already been developed. Sprinting and flexibility continue to be a part of the program so that quickness and range of movement are maintained. If two meets are scheduled during one week, adjust the program so the day immediately preceding the competition is a rest day. Two or three rest days before the championship meet keep the athlete fresh and eager to compete.

Monday   Warm-up with a 1 mile jog, do stretching for 10 min.
             2 × 20 yd., 2 × 30 yd., 2 × 40 yd., 2 × 50 yd. sprints.
             10 puts from a stand, gradually increasing distance. Work on weak points
                 in technique.

20-25 puts for distance working on smoothness and quickness.
1-leg hops, 6-8 times over 30 yd. with each leg.
Hard weight training.
5 min. of stretching followed by ¼ mile jog.

Tuesday   Warm-up with a 1 mile jog, stretching for 10 min.
4-6 starts from blocks over 30 yd.
15-20 standing puts, gradually increase distance, measure last 2 puts.
10-15 puts with shift. Compare to standing puts for distance.
10-12 wrist flips with shot.
3 sets of 10 finger tip pushups.
4-6 jumps at long jump or high jump area.
6 runs over 3 low hurdles.
Running backward 6 times over 30 yd.
Stretching 5 to 10 min.

Wednesday   Warm-up with a 1 mile jog, stretching for 10 min.
4 × 30 yd., 2 × 40 yd., 1 × 60 yd. sprints.
12-15 puts with shift. Work on quickness.
5-6 puts from stand with heavier shot if available. ¾ effort.
8-10 puts with official shot.
Hopping and bounding 6-8 times over 30 yd.
Weight training at 80% effort.
Stretching for 5-10 min. ¼ mile jog.

Thursday   Warm-up with a 1 mile jog, stretching for 10 min.
4-6 starts from blocks over 20 yd.
10-12 puts from shift. Moderate effort.
4-6 runs over 3 low hurdles.
10-15 consecutive finger tip pushups.
Running backward 4 times over 30 yds.
Stretching 5-10 min.

Friday   Warm-up with ½ mile jog.
4-6 controlled speed runs over 110 yd. with 110 yd. walk.
Stretching 5 min.

Saturday   Meet.
Warm-up the same as for daily training.
3-4 sprints over 25-30 yd.
5-10 standing puts, gradually increase intensity of each put.
5-10 puts from shift with emphasis on staying relaxed, gradually increase
      effort.
Competition.

Sunday   Rest.

11 Olga Connolly

THE DISCUS THROW

Author: **Olga Connolly,** currently Director of Intramural Sports at Loyola Marymount University, Los Angeles, has had an athletic career studded with outstanding achievements. A member of Czechoslovakian national teams in team handball, basketball and track, she emigrated to the U.S. shortly after winning a gold medal in the discus throw at the 1956 Olympic Games. Since then she has won the A.A.U. championship in the discus (five times); set several national records in the same event; represented the U.S. at the Olympic Games (four times); and served as flag bearer for the U.S. team at the Munich Olympic Games. In addition, she has been elected to the U.S. Track and Field Hall of Fame and to the Helms Foundation Hall of Fame.

The discus thrower attempts to smoothly accelerate the discus along the longest possible path of pull. It is achieved by her initial wind-up, by sprint-step progression across the circle from the rear to the front, and by strong muscular unwinding of the legs, the hips, and the trunk-shoulder girdle block, which precede the final whip-like action of the arm and hand. This sequence imparts maximum velocity to the discus and must not be violated.

MODERN TECHNIQUE

With her feet shoulder-width apart and her back to the intended direction of the throw, the thrower settles herself down at the rear of the circle. As she enters the relaxed, but measured, preliminary swing of the arm and shoulders in the direction opposite to the major movement, she bends her knees slightly, then begins to turn on the ball of the left foot. Once her left knee and shoulder point (in a balanced manner) to the direction of throw, she pushes off the left foot in a sprint-like step toward the center of the circle. As the rotational movement continues, both feet are off the ground momentarily; but with a swift, rhythmical progression, the right foot, turned inward, is planted near the center of the circle while the left foot lands close to the front rim. As the trunk, shoulders and arms remain inactive, merely carried along by the legs and hips, this phase of the turn puts the thrower into a strong coiled position, which gets accentuated further by the continuation of the rotation of the feet at the beginning of the final phase of the throw.

Once the discus thrower transfers her weight into the direction of the throw, from the weighted, bent, right knee, onto the weighted, bent, but explosively straightening left knee, she powerfully unwinds her hips, trunk, chest and shoulders into the direction of the throw. The arm whips around and forward with the firm grip of the fingers adding the final rotation to the implement. If the legs and body are in balance, the final impact of the discus release brings the thrower into a natural reverse to prevent fouling.

RULES

The discus is thrown from inside a circle 8 ft. 2½ in. in diameter. A white line is drawn across the center of the circle dividing it into front and rear halves. A 45 deg. sector is marked out on the ground from the center of the circle, and all throws to be valid must fall within the inner edge of the lines forming that sector. The thrower must not touch the top of the circle or the ground outside it with any part of her body. She must not leave the circle until the discus has landed, and after it lands she must leave from the rear half of the circle. The thrower must leave the circle in a balanced posture (must not fall out of the circle).

A throw is measured with a steel tape from the nearer edge of the mark first made in the ground by the discus, to the inner edge of the circle along a line drawn from the mark to the center of the circle. The part of the tape showing the distance thrown must be held at the circle. Distances are measured to the nearest inch below the distance covered, ignoring fractions.

The women's discus weighs 1 kg. (or 2 lb. 3¼ oz.). An official A.A.U. or I.A.A.F. discus is composed of a wooden body with steel center and a smooth steel rim.

TEACHING THE EVENT

There are several principles a beginning discus thrower should understand well enough to be able to explain them to others, and with which she should experiment long enough to be able to use them as "feel" checks for mechanically correct throwing.

(a) *The legs are the prime movers* of the rest of the body, and therefore also of the discus. Continuous, precise footwork determines the length of the path of the discus as well as its gradual acceleration and explosive finish. Throughout the turn, there are extremely important shifts of weight from the right foot to the left, back to the right, and to the left again, which must be controlled by feel. Therefore, the work on discus technique is facilitated by the thrower's knowing the difference in the feel of the weighted foot and leg, the half-weighted foot and leg, and the foot and leg with little or no weight placed on it. The beginning of the development of such awareness is quite simple. The athlete stands comfortably, with feet shoulder-width apart. She lifts up her left foot and rests it at the ankle of her right foot, noticing the feeling of weight in the muscles of the right leg. Then she switches to the left foot, again registering mentally the muscular feeling. Afterwards, she learns to produce various degrees of that feeling in her leg muscles, until she can securely and instantly recognize whether or not she has transferred weight from one foot or leg to the other. By placing her hands on her hips while shifting weight from one leg to the other, the athlete will become aware of the horizontal movement of her body during such a shift. Once these simple concepts are clear, the athlete will be able to easily check the key positions during the turn by knowing the feelings in her leg muscles these positions should produce.

(b) There is an imaginary line that begins at the *left shoulder, passes across the chest, through the right shoulder, and along the throwing arm and hand to the discus*. It is a straight line that *must not be bent or broken*. We can imagine that this line is a wooden stick. We can imagine a second line, or wooden stick, this one passing from the left hip joint through the body into the right hip joint. This is also a straight line. Being aware of the relationship between these lines through the turn facilitates maintenance of the body torque or coil. At the very beginning of the upswing, the hip line and the shoulder-arm line are parallel. But with the completion of the preliminary wind up, these lines form a flat letter X (   ). Throughout the entire turn, this ''X'' must be maintained. It is especially crucial in the power position, at the beginning of the second phase of acceleration. Through the combination of awareness of the crossed hip line and shoulders-chest-arm line, as well as the feel of the muscular tension in the waist produced by the correct body torque, the discus thrower can keep easy check on her maintaining and increasing of the correct torque. Again, through a detailed understanding of these principles, and experimenting with them as to what they feel like, the discus thrower will be able to master more naturally the complex movement in the mid-circle and the power phase of the throw.

(c) The third principle a beginning discus thrower must be clearly aware of, and consciously experiment with, has to do with the position of the discus. If we call the side of the discus that presses against the hand the ''back'' of the discus, and the side which is turned away from the hand the ''face'' of the discus, then we can require that the ''face'' of the discus at all times looks either into the ground or against the body of the thrower. It must never look away from the discus thrower or upward. If, at the moment of release, the ''face'' of the discus is turned upward, then air resistance immediately begins to gnaw on the distance the discus travels. Maintenance of the rule that the discus faces either the ground or the body of the thrower, helps prevent waste of energy during the turn, and waste of power at the release of the implement. This is especially important with the small, aerodynamically unstable, women's discus.

Once these three principles have been thoroughly explained and experimented with, the discus thrower may begin to master the discus technique with confidence.

THE DISCUS HOLD

A good discus thrower has developed an intimate feel for the implement; she is so comfortable in handling the discus that she need not pay special attention to it during the turn. The discus has become *a part of her hand*. This is achieved by constantly handling the discus, even in nonpractice situations. She has to develop the same familiarity with the discus that a good basketball player has developed with the ball.

At first, with the arm hanging loosely along the body, take the discus in the throwing hand (finger tips bent at the first joint, fingers spread evenly across the "back" of the discus) and feel its downward pull. It is like holding a handbag. The discus leans against the fingers and against the thenar part of the palm (the muscle pad at the bottom of the thumb). It does not touch the middle of the palm. The wrist is straight, semi-rigid.

Allow the discus to roll off the fingers, forward, leaving the small finger first, then the fourth, third, and finally the index finger, which should hold it so firmly that one can feel the friction and the rotation of the rim against the skin.

Pick up the discus, but this time, instead of dropping it, flex the legs and, with a long step forward as if bowling, roll the discus out, in front of you, on the grass. A beginning discus thrower should spend a great deal of time rolling the discus on the grass, in a perfectly straight line, increasingly more effortlessly, imparting increasingly more spin to the implement.

From a very low stance, the thrower should learn to scale the discus sideways, low on the grass, the "face" of the discus perfectly downward. One simply cannot think of body torque or footwork while still at the stage of struggling with the discus hold. Remember that the thrower and the discus are not in conflict. The discus thrower is not there to conquer a piece of wood and steel, but rather the thrower and the discus are working together to achieve a distance.

THE POWER POSITION

People used to talk about the standing throw. Some developed techniques in the standing throw that earned them impressive distances. But often these techniques were useless in competition because they could not match a throw with a turn; and the athlete did not succeed in trying to incorporate the standing throw positions into her turn technique. Therefore, we no longer use the standing throw. We begin with rehearsing the second phase of acceleration of the discus, that is, from the power position to the release, and using the movement as it happens in the turn. It can be practiced on the grass along any markings that will enable a check of feet alignment, or in the ring with a chalk line drawn through the center. Referring back to concepts (a), (b) and (c), all three must be meticulously executed during this second phase.

For a right-handed thrower the correct sequence of movements is as follows: stand in the front of the discus circle, with the back to the ultimate direction of throw. While turning the left toe and knee outward, toward the direction of the throw, make a step with the right leg to the center of the circle. At the same time, move the shoulders-chest-arm-discus line backwards, so that this and the hip line form an "X." With the *weight upon the right leg*, bend *both* knees; be like a cat. The head and trunk will remain erect; your left arm loosely bent, reaching forward, aligned with the legs, and aiding the proper balance as well as the body torque. (Experiment with getting to the same position while starting at the center of the circle, and instead of stepping forward with the right leg, step backward with the left.)

Next, without any extension of knees, pivot on the right foot into the direction of throw, and at the same time shift your weight around and forward, onto the left leg.

Keep the discus arm extended at shoulder level (especially important in women's discus). Rotate the hips, trunk, chest, and shoulders around and over the left leg. *Once the left leg is properly weighted*, drive powerfully upward off it. At that moment the hips, chest, shoulders and arms have caught up with the legs (the hip line and the shoulders-chest-arm-discus line are parallel) and your entire torso is thrust forward and upward. The hand still holds onto the discus, releasing it only as it whips around level with the thrower's face.

If this sequence is done with proper timing, the thrower will be driven into a *natural reverse*, that is, a quick replacement of the left footmark with your right footmark; it will also bring the thrower downward onto bent legs and waist.

Some throwers who have relatively long, powerful bodies and shorter legs may not follow through into that kind of reverse. They will recover their stance on an extended left leg. Their right foot will drag on top of its toes as the body unwinds, and will end up next to the left foot. Still other throwers finish their turn by one or more complete rotations about their body axis; but that is good only if the final drive at the moment of discus release was off the left leg. Otherwise this spinning finish may indicate that the thrower failed to properly transfer her weight from the right to the left foot, and therefore, lost last contact with the ground and with it much of the delivery power.

Women, especially, tend to forsake the power drive, and they uncoil their body the moment they feel the pressure of landing in the power position. Once the arm flashes around, the legs can never catch up and a great deal of power is lost.

THE COMPLETE TURN

The thrower positions herself at the middle of the back of the circle, with feet about shoulder-width apart. The right toes touch the rim, the left toes are about 2 in. away from the rim. It is important to keep the head and back straight, the shoulders level, the knees bent, and the body weight somewhat forward but balanced on the balls of the feet. It is good to keep one's eyes at some point on the horizon; it will help to steady the movement.

Start the preliminary wind-up by holding the discus comfortably but firmly, with the discus "face" toward your body. The line, "left shoulder-chest-right shoulder-arm-hand-discus," must be straight and unbent from the very beginning. In the upswing one should therefore use a gentle rotation of that entire line, and a gentle shift of weight; first to the left, then to the right, then to the left again . . . and so on . . . while the arm raises to just below the shoulder level, with the discus "face" down. One or two wind-ups are enough. *Do not use any more than three wind-ups.* The more wind-ups, the more difficult it is to concentrate on the footwork. The purpose of the wind-ups is to catch a good rhythm, and to start building the body torque.

Just as the second (or final) wind-up reaches its extreme point to the right, *lock the entire upper body* into further inactivity which will not allow loosening of the existing coil (Figure 11-1). The mind should be focused on the footwork. (Note: Men often drop the discus to the hip level, but appears that it is better for women to keep the discus arm at just below the shoulder level.)

On bent knees (of course!), shift the weight onto the left foot while pivoting on both feet in the direction of movement (Figure 11-2). Once the weight shift is completed, the left knee pointed to the direction of movement, and the body balanced on the left leg, the *left foot pushes powerfully forward* and *the right leg drives toward the center of the circle*, in a sprinting-step kind of move (Figures 11-3 through 11-5).

(The following exercise will help to develop the feeling for the point at which to push off the left foot: On the grass, either with or without the discus, take up the beginning stance and after one wind-up, begin to turn. When you feel you are in balance, simply sprint out for five or ten yards. If you can run with ease, you are in balance. If you wobble, you are either coming off to early or too late.)

The drive off the left leg brings about the *first phase of the discus acceleration*. The right foot should be brought down swiftly but rhythmically to the center of the circle; and landing, its toe should be *turning inward* to ensure continuity in pivoting action and a smooth transition into the second phase of discus acceleration and continuous pivoting (Figures 11-6 and 11-7). The left foot, turning outward, lands at the front of the circle (Figure 11-8). If the thrower's weight is on the right bent leg in the center of the circle, and the body torque is maintained correctly, the left foot will be placed naturally in a straight line to the direction of the throw. If the right leg is straightened or the body torque is lost, the left will be groping and may land "in the bucket."

A most helpful drill to develop the sense of balanced landing on both feet, with weight on the right bent leg, as well as the continuation of pivoting action, consists of going through that motion over and over again, along a line on the football field, basketball court sidelines, or wherever the thrower happens to be. The more often the thrower rehearses this movement, the more automatic it

Figures 11-1—11-11   Faina Myelnik, USSR   **231'3"**

FIGURE 11-1

FIGURE 11-2

FIGURE 11-3

FIGURE 11-4

FIGURE 11-5

FIGURE 11-6

FIGURE 11-7

FIGURE 11-8

FIGURE 11-9

FIGURE 11-10

FIGURE 11-11

becomes. It is absolutely crucial, however, that rehearsing the movement is done correctly, with conscious realization of its key components. There is nothing worse than rehearsing errors.

Once both feet land in the already familiar power position, the *second phase of acceleration begins* (Figure 11-8). The weight at this point rests on the right leg, knee bent. The upper body is coiled backward, the shoulders-chest-arm-discus line straight, right arm extended and parallel to the ground, left arm semi-flexed in a natural position in front of the body aiding general balance, the "face" of the discus looks down.

The right leg pivots and pushes the body weight over onto the left leg. The hips rotate forward and upward, and the upper body is carried along. As the weight is transferred to the left leg, *it extends explosively*. The thrower brings her hips, chest, shoulders and arms powerfully around and forward. The left arm and shoulder tighten to stop body rotation beyond the center point of the forward lean, thus adding the final acceleration to the right arm which flashes around and past the thrower's face like the tail of a whip (Figure 11-9). The discus is ejected into its orbit, the left arm relaxes, and the movement of the body continues into the reverse (Figures 11-10 and 11-11).

DISCUS FLIGHT

The angle of release and the speed of the rotation of the discus are important ingredients of its ability to cut through the air. The angle of release depends on the leg lift and the chest-arm guidance, as well as the hand position. The overall angles of release should not exceed 40 deg. The stronger the headwind, the flatter the angle of release should be. The ''face'' of the discus should be horizontal. If it is tilted upwards in the slightest way, the air resistance slows it down immediately, and, in fact, continues to tilt it upward until the discus may topple over and come down like a stone. *Flat placing of the discus in the air must be rehearsed continually.* The rolling and scaling drills teach the hand to release the discus properly and with increasingly smoother and more rapid rotation.

A FEW WORDS ABOUT GENERAL CONDITIONING

Power, speed, and *agility* are determining factors in the women's discus throw. Weight-training (see Chapter 13) is a necessary tool for power development, but will not do alone. Below, I therefore present a list of suggestions for activities a discus thrower should build into her training program.

Basketball and *soccer* are the best supplementary sports for track and field athletes. For the discus thrower, basketball improves on her agility, lateral and backward movement, jumping ability, and explosive speed. Soccer develops endurance and nimble footwork.

From among other track and field events, *the hurdles, high jump,* and *triple jump* should be practiced by the throwers. The triple jump, especially, helps build that dynamic kind of leg strength that separates an outstanding thrower from an average one.

Starts followed by *10-to 20-yd. sprints* with explosive acceleration, are other good ways to build strong, quick feet and legs. Fifty yd. dashes have little in common with the thrower's need to build explosive speed and controlled movement within a very small space.

Throwing objects of different shapes and weights, discus style, is an entertaining way to reinforce the basic technique as well as build power.

Running short, steep staircases, steep hills, rope skipping, throwing dumbbells high into the air with utilization of powerful leg drive, and inventing games with medicine balls, all improve the dynamic strength and speed conditioning.

Simple acrobatics is a must for a thrower who wants to become comfortable with the complex discus movement.

Finally, *regular, all-body stretching* is perhaps more important for the discus thrower than for any other track and field athlete. The dynamics of the event call for the instantaneous ability of various muscle groups to tense up or relax in perfect harmony.

TRAINING

While the day-to-day training varies with the thrower's personality, momentary state of conditioning, ability to concentrate, weather conditions, etc., Tables 11-1 and 11-2 can give you an idea of how much it takes to become a steady, 170- to 190-foot discus thrower.

Translation of: "A Year's Training Plan for Discus Throwers" by Peter Tschiene, published in *Die Lehre Der Leichtathletik* April 23 and 30, 1974, Volumes 17 and 18. Translation by G.A. Carr, University of Victoria, B.C.

Table 11-1: A YEAR'S TRAINING PLAN FOR DISCUS THROWERS *(50 meter throwers)*

Aim of Activity	Training Method and Type	Division of a Year's Training into Period and Quantity											
		Preparation Period						Competitive Period				Post-Competitive & Transitional Period	
		Stage 1					Stage 2						
		Nov.	Dec.	Jan. (Indoor Season)	Feb.	Mar.	Apr. (Pre-Competitive Stage)	May June	July	Aug.	Sep.	Oct.	Year's Total
1. Improving overall physical condition	General Developmental exercises for joint & spine mobility (in hours of practice)	10	12	10	6	10	10	6	6 6	6	6	12	100
2. Work on Technique (discus throw)	Standing-throws with competitive weight discus or lighter discus (total no. of throws)	100	100	120	100	120	150	150	100 100	80	80	—	1200
	As above, but from a turn (total no. of throws)	—	50	100	100	150	150	300	300 200	150	150	100	1750
	Practicing the delivery, the turn & separate phases of the throw using discus or substitute (in hours of practice)	—	2	2	2	3	3	3	2 1.5	1	0.5	—	20
3. Specialized forms of strength training	Practicing the delivery with 10-15 kg. (22-33 lb.) weights (total no. of reps in all sets added together)	20	40	50	30	50	40	20	— —	—	—	—	250

Table 11-1 (continued)

		Nov.	Dec.	Jan.	Feb.	Mar.	Apr.	May	June	July	Aug.	Sep.	Oct.	Year's Total
3. (continued)	Throwing from a stand & from a turn (2.5-3.0 kg. (5.5-6.6 lb.) discus for turns & 3-4 kg. (6.6-8.8 lb.) discus or shots for standing throws) (No. of throws)	—	40	40	60	80	40	40	40	20	—	—	—	360
	2-armed throws with shots, medicine balls, etc. (4-5 kg.; 9-11 lb.) over the head, backward, sideways & forward (No. of throws)	80	160	200	80	160	120	100	100	—	—	—	—	1000
	Standing throws using a shot, emphasizing the rotary aspect (No. of throws)	20	40	40	40	80	60	40	40	20	20	—	—	400
	Trunk twisting from standing or sitting. Arms held out using 10-15 kg. (22-23 lb.) weights (total no. of repetitions)	400	500	600	250	400	600	200	150	100	100	—	—	3300
	Deep knee bends & jumping using a barbell, 60-80% of maximum weight (total no. of repetitions)	100	140	160	40	100	160	120	100	80	80	—	—	1020
	Lifting the barbell to chest height also combined with a turn motion to the left 40-60% of maximum weight (total no. of repetitions)	40	80	80	60	120	120	100	60	20	20	—	—	700
4. General strength work	Sit-ups with a twist action on an incline bench, using 5-10 kg. (11-12 lb.) weight. Also leg circling exercises from a hang position for stomach strength (total no. of repetitions)	80	180	160	100	160	160	80	30	30	20	—	—	1000
	Wide-grip snatches with a barbell,	20	35	30	20	30	35	25	25	20	10	—	—	250

Table 11-1 (continued)

		Nov.	Dec.	Jan.	Feb.	Mar.	Apr.	May	June	July	Aug.	Sep.	Oct.	Year's Total
4. (continued)	wide-grip bench-press, 60-80% of maximum weight (figures in tons)													
	Wide arm push-ups each hand on a bench (total no. of reps in all sets added together)	100	100	100	60	80	80	100	80	80	—	—	—	780
	Raising out-stretched arms from lying cross position on back. 10-15 kg. (22-33 lb.) in each hand. Also arm circling with dumbbells (no. of reps per set)	20	40	40	20	40	50	20	—	—	—	—	—	230
5. Development of speed	Running 4 × 30 m. (33 yd.) then steady acceleration sprints 50-80 m. (55-88yds.) sprints from a crouch & a standing start over 20-30 m. (22-33yds.), hurdles, medium height 30-40 m. (33-44 yds.) (numbers indicate total distances in kilometers)	1.5	2	2	2	2	2.5	2.5	3	2	1.5	1.0	—	22
6. Development of spring (leg power)	Long, high, and triple jumps with a run-up, changing jumping leg. (No. of jumps)	100	250	300	150	300	300	350	100	100	100	—	150	2200
7. Development of general endurance & active recovery ability	Easy running	1.5	1.5	1.5	1.5	1.5	1.5	0.5	0.5	0.5	0.5	0.5	2	12.5
	Cross-country skiing					(if available)								
	Games	5	4	4	2	4	2	—	—	1	1	—	—	20
8. Improvement of competitive condition & psychological readiness	Competition	—	—	—	—	1	1	3	3	4	4	2	—	18
	Competition in other throwing disciplines	—	—	—	1	1	—	1	1	2	1	2	—	9

NOTES: An increased amount of strength work with weights (along with regular technique training) should predominate in the training of advanced young throwers (17-18 years) and adults throwing in the range of 45-50 m. (150-165 ft.) The importance of specialized strength training increases with each year. In addition, the methods for specialized strength training will vary. In order to lay the

Table 11-1 (continued)

foundation of a high level of explosive power for discus throwers who are throwing more than 50 meters regularly, highly intensive and effective methods (of power training) must be found. In contrast to the developing young thrower, the top-class thrower will aim for greater intensity rather than sheer volume. For this reason training occurs 2-3 times daily (3-4 days a week, exclusive of "active rest" weeks). Yearly the total of training sessions would range between 220-230 times. For beginners and developing youngsters the absolute yearly volume of work is much less.

Table 11-2: A WEEK'S TRAINING IN PREPARATION FOR COMPETITION

Variation I

Time of Day	Monday	Tuesday	Wednesday	Thursday	Friday	Saturday	Sunday
Morning	Jogging	Warm-up & gymnastics	Warm-up and gymnastics	Jogging	Jogging	Jogging	Jogging
Evening or in relation to demands of competition	1. Special warm-up 2. Discus-throw, exercises with the shot (total 40) 3. Weight training 4. Jumping 5. Warm-down (jogging)	Recovery -rest-	1. General warm-up. 2. Discus throwing. Technique control under competitive conditions. 3. Standing jumps 4. Warm-down (jogging).	1. Special warm-up. 2. Discus throws—flat out 12× 3. Sprints 4. Weight-lifting (80% max, around 4 tons total) 5. Warm-down (jogging)	Recovery -rest-	General warm-up 24 hrs. before competition	Competition

For less advanced throwers there would be no discus throwing on Thursdays.

Maximal poundages and intensity would not be used in weight-training where it occurs at the end of a training session.

Variation II

Mornings	Warm-up—and—Jogging as preferred-						
Evenings or according to demands of competition	1) Competitive throwing (10×) working for technical control (no actual competitors involved) 2. Springing & jumping (20×) 3. Special strength	Weight-training (3 exercises using 90%) Games	1. Special warm-up. 2. Competition 3. Jogging	Recovery -rest-	1. Competitive throwing (10×) working for technical control. 2 throws flat out (no competition) 2. Sprints 3. Jumping 4. Warm-down		Competition

12 Jessica Dragicevic

THE JAVELIN THROW

Author: **Jessica Dragicevic** is women's track coach at the University of Illinois. A national-caliber hurdler and pentathlete in her native Chile, she coached at high school, club, national and international levels before coming to the U.S. in 1974.

Although a tendency exists to differentiate techniques in track and field between women and men, no differences should be made in the javelin throw. All the movements are basically the same, and it is *each* athlete in adapting the technique to her personal characteristics that determines her own specific style.

Four interactive elements determine the technique of the javelin throw. These are: mechanical laws, human physical endowment, javelin design, and event regulations. An individual's performance will depend on the ability to get the best out of each of the above elements combined with serious and dedicated year-round training.

Most of the best throwers in the world are using the "aerodynamic" javelin (AJ), but some athletes still perfer to use the "Finnish" javelin (FJ). The behavior of the two javelins in the air is quite different. The AJ has a high "gliding" capacity that requires a high speed of release and an angle of release of approximately 25 deg. for a better performance. The design of the FJ, on the other hand, requires an angle of release of approximately 40 deg. in detriment to the speed of release and the attainment of the greatest distance. As javelins differ in design and construction, the technique used by a thrower will depend on the implement chosen.

MODERN TECHNIQUE FOR AERODYNAMIC JAVELINS*

To develop a good technique for the javelin throw we need to combine maximum controlled speed with a throwing position which will allow maximum

---

*The following discussion assumes that the thrower is right-handed.

force to be applied to the implement over the greatest possible range of movement, releasing it at an optimum angle of 25-30 deg.

For clarity, the analysis of the technique will be divided into phases, although it is extremely important to remember that the javelin throw is a *whole* that cannot be parceled for good execution. The phases used in the following analysis are:

(a)   Grip.
(b)   Approach (i)   run-up (12 steps).
              (ii)   withdrawal (2 steps).
              (iii)   cross-step (1 step).
              (iv)   sudden-stop or blocking and release (1 step).
(c)   Reverse (1 step).

Grip

For the grip, the javelin must lie diagonally across the palm of the hand with the tail in the direction of the first fingers and thumb, while the last two fingers hold the binding close to the base of the palm in order to keep the hand in position until the release.

Three grips are commonly used; each thrower should decide the one that is best for her. The most popular grip, but one which requires stronger fingers, is the one where the javelin lies between the first and second fingers, both of them gripping behind the binding. This grip allows a better alignment of the javelin with the arm and shoulder, and also allows for greater finger thrust. In the second grip, the javelin is held between the second finger and the thumb, with the first finger curled slightly around the shaft, allowing for better control of direction. The third and least frequently used grip has the first finger and the thumb holding the javelin behind the binding.

The grip should be firm but relaxed, preventing the javelin from slipping out of the hand. It should allow a correct alignment of the javelin with the thrower, the approach, and the direction of the throw. The grip should also allow the athlete to give a rotary movement to the implement at the moment of release.

Approach

The approach is the most fundamental part of the throw. Kinetic energy of a body is its ability to do work because of its motion. The kinetic energy originated through the run-up and cross-step is conserved by transferring it from the motor elements (lower extremities) into the application element (hips) and into the javelin. The "sudden-stop" (landing on the legs ahead of the center of gravity) will result in an increase of speed of the upper body, projecting the javelin at considerable speed.

The approach covers approximately 30-35 yd. from the moment movement starts until the javelin is released, and should be done in as straight a line as possible. The approach can be divided into four stages. These are: run-up, withdrawal, cross-step and sudden-stop. The run-up covers the first 12 steps of the approach, starting with a gradual increase in speed of 6 to 8 steps, and a period of speed maintenance of 4 to 6 steps. The withdrawal of the javelin corresponds to the extension of the throwing arm, and right turn of the shoulder in preparation for the throw, and occurs in the next two steps (13 and 14). The last two steps of the approach are the cross-step, a long step given by the right leg with high knee lift, and the last step, also called "sudden-stop" or "blocking" because the left foot lands well ahead of the center of gravity of the body, producing a backward lean of the body and a stop of the motor elements.

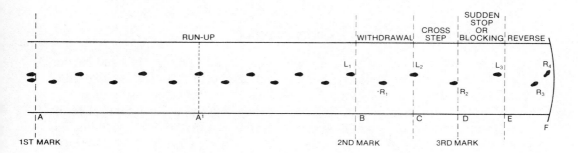

1st mark: the starting point of the approach.

2nd mark: a control mark, the point where the left foot lands and when the withdrawal of the javelin should start.

3rd mark: the place where the right foot lands after the cross-step is completed.

AA'—gradual increase of speed.

A'C—maintenance of speed.

CE—maximum controllable speed.

FIGURE 12-1: THE APPROACH

(i) RUN-UP

The run-up should be fairly long and graduated for development of momentum. This phase covers more or less two-thirds of the complete approach. Its length will depend on the technical ability of the thrower and should be determined by the coach and athlete during practices (not in competition). Generally the run-up consists of 12 steps covering approximately 26-30 yd., counted from the instant movement starts until the thrower approaches the second mark (Figure 12-1) and initiates the withdrawal of the javelin.

The acquisition of speed should be gradual in 6 to 8 steps running low with knees slightly bent. The feet should land flat on the ground with increasing stride length. The throwing arm should be kept over the shoulders, with a slight flexion of the elbow, keeping the javelin high, just above ear level (Figure 12-2). The implement should be aligned in the direction of the run and throw throughout the approach, and kept close to the head. The right shoulder and hand should move back and forth in rhythm with the legs, that is, as the left leg moves forward, the right shoulder and hand should move forward naturally.

The acquisition of speed is the most important aspect of the first 6 to 8 steps of the run-up. Then, in the next 4 to 6 steps the athlete should concentrate on attaining rhythm and optimum controllable speed. While running, the upper body should be kept vertical, with no backward or forward inclination, the feet should land pointing in the direction of the run, and the length of the steps should be even.

(ii) WITHDRAWAL OR TRANSITION PHASE

The withdrawal phase starts upon obtaining the optimum speed and is completed after two steps. Athletes who lose control of their form and their speed of approach by using two steps for the withdrawal will benefit from using up to four steps for this transition period. The turn of the shoulders and withdrawal of the javelin should be done smoothly so as not to alter the rhythm and speed that has been built up during the run-up. The action of withdrawing the javelin starts as soon as the thrower's left foot steps on the second mark (Figure 12-1). The javelin should acquire an angle of projection of 20-25 deg. in relation to the ground, and the center of gravity of the implement should be far behind the body's center of gravity.

In the withdrawal, the shoulders should turn to the side of the throwing arm approximately 90 deg. with respect to the direction of the approach (Figure 12-4). At the same time the javelin should be withdrawn directly backward and downward in a smooth, slow motion. The throwing arm should be positioned straight but not locked, with the palm upward, the wrist rotated inward behind the right hip. The javelin should be in a line with hand, arm and shoulders, with the tip close to eye level (Figure 12-5). The head should be kept facing forward in the direction of the throw and the eyes should be focusing on the throwing area and the imaginary flight path of the implement (Figure 12-6 and 12-7). When the feet land pointing straight ahead toward the throwing section after completion of the withdrawal, the hips should be perpendicular to the direction of the throw.

(iii) CROSS-STEP

The cross-step is an extremely important and decisive phase of the throw, because a long and accelerated step with the right leg will result in a good low position of the motor element (Figure 12-8). The foot should land ahead of the hips, where the center of gravity is located, and well in front of the throwing arm. During this step the arm and javelin should not receive adjustments, the shoulders should stay in their previous position, perpendicular to the scratchline, and the left

Figures 12-2—12-12   Kathy Schmidt, USA   **227′ 5″**

FIGURE 12-2

FIGURE 12-3

FIGURE 12-4

FIGURE 12-5

FIGURE 12-6

FIGURE 12-7

FIGURE 12-8

FIGURE 12-9

FIGURE 12-10

FIGURE 12-11

FIGURE 12-12

arm should be in front of the chest. The cross-position formed by the axes of the hips and shoulders should also be maintained.

The objective of this step is to bring the right leg rapidly forward, passing in front of the left leg with the knee bent at a 90 deg. angle, and the right foot in dorsal flexion and internal rotation. The foot should land pointing in the line of direction of the approach far ahead of the center of gravity of the thrower, which will result in a lowering of the hips and a noticeable backward lean. The speed should not be decreased, because the faster the approach, the farther the foot will land ahead of the center of gravity and the better the resultant position attained for the throw.

The right leg completes its thrust before the left leg lands in the last step of the approach. After the right foot lands, a lowering of the right knee toward the ground should take place, bringing an internal rotation of the foot and an opening of the heel to the right from the imaginary straight line of approach (Figure 12-9).

To complete the analysis of the cross-step, let us consider what its objectives should be in terms of work, impulse, and kinetic energy. Work is the product of the magnitude of a force acting on a body and the distance through which the body moves. Impulse is the integral of a force over the time interval during which the force acts. Therefore, the important aspect of this step is to obtain a position that will allow for greater impulse in the throw resulting from an application of the forces over a longer period of time and over a greater distance (range of motion). At the same time, the accumulation of kinetic energy in the lower extremities through this step is also of great importance, because in the next step (sudden-stop or blocking) that kinetic energy will be transferred to the hips and throwing arm, resulting in a summation of the forces from the lower extremities, hips, and throwing arm which will be transferred to the implement.

(iv) SUDDEN-STOP OR BLOCKING AND RELEASE

This phase is called "blocking" or "sudden-stop" because the "thrower-implement complex" which was carrying a high kinetic energy suffers a sudden halting of the lower extremities. The thrower lands the left leg on the heel well ahead of the center of gravity of the body. This sudden stop of the legs will allow the hips and upper body to continue the forward movement and throwing motion with speed, thus adding momentum to the implement (Figure 12-10).

The landing of the left leg is close in time with the landing of the right foot in the cross-step, but far apart in placement. The left leg is nearly extended but not locked, producing a low and long last step. Although a single step is highly recommended, some athletes need three last steps in order to regain control and momentum after the cross-step. The upper body should still have the backward lean from the cross-step, which will produce a forward drive from the right leg over to the left leg after landing of the left heel. The body weight should now move forward over the left leg which has bent, reducing the resistance offered earlier by the extended leg (Figure 12-10).

The upper body and the arm which has been kept behind will start turning at the same time that the left leg bends at the knee. The hips and trunk should continue their forward movement, producing a forward drag of the right toe on the ground, while the arm is still extended behind the body. The thrower's forward momentum is not destroyed during the "sudden-stop" because the upper body and trunk have completed their turn. The placement of the heel well ahead of the center of gravity, the backward lean, and the arm far back from the hips will offer an excellent positioning of the body so the forces of the legs and trunk can be applied to the arm over a long range of motion, resulting in a powerful pull on the javelin.

The right arm must be extended behind the body while the different parts of the body pull on the javelin. The effect of this will result in an extremely explosive and fast movement, led by the elbow, due to the sequence of action of the legs, hips, trunk, shoulders, arm, and hand (chain reaction), and the summation of each segment's momentum. As the pull starts, the head should be tilted to the left, allowing the implement and arm to come up and over the shoulder (Figure 12-10).

It is of extreme importance to remember that this delayed, powerful, fast action occurs after the weight has been transferred from the right leg to the left leg, the shoulders are facing the throwing area, and the center of gravity of the body is ahead of the vertical. The efficiency and speed of the arm thrust will depend on the body position obtained on earlier steps and the chain reaction of hips, upper body, arm and hand motion.

When the right shoulder is still pulling forward and upward, the elbow is followed by the hand, and moves upward, forward, and along the flight path. The left shoulder should be kept facing forward while the javelin is released as high as possible in relation to the ground at an angle of approximately 25 deg. Keep in mind that acceleration, transfer and addition of momentum through the complete motion is extremely important.

An outward rotation takes place as the elbow rises in the throwing movement. The elbow should be above the level of the hand, the lower arm, and the wrist. The hand under the javelin should whip up and forward along the length of the javelin.

The left arm, which has been bent across the chest throughout the different stages of the throw, should stretch pointing to the throwing area when the shoulders start turning forward. As the shoulders get to the front position, and as the right arm strikes, the left arm should move back and down close to the left side (Figure 12-10).

Reverse

The reverse starts the moment the left foot loses contact with the ground, once the javelin has been released, and comes to an end when complete balance has been regained after several "hops" on the right foot (Figures 12-11 and 12-12).

The reverse is a consequence of the throw and not a part of it, and is done to recover balance of the body after the implement has been released, in order to avoid fouling. The reason for this loss of balance is the progressive accumulation of kinetic energy generated during the approach, and the voluntary and dynamic liberation of the javelin produced by the action of the whole body, causing a forward rotation toward the left. This unstable position will require a reverse to control the forward momentum.

The technique is simply to replace the left leg with the outside of the right foot and leg, which will land toward the inner border of the foul line. The left leg leaves the ground slightly after the right leg swings forward, and then swings back and upward. While the left leg is going through the above moves, the right leg will perform anywhere from one to several hops until complete balance has been regained. The action of the reverse has been considered a follow-through of the throw.

TRAINING FOR THE JAVELIN

Very often, year-round training programs are offered by coaches or top level athletes with the idea of helping other athletes to improve their performances. But these "recipes" cannot be applied to other athletes or will not be of any help if some aspects and principles are not carefully taken into consideration in preparing a program.

To consider individual characteristics is of extreme importance before deciding on the type of training program the thrower needs. Age, sex, length of time the athlete has been involved in the sport and event, technical preparedness of the thrower, length of the season, and competitive schedule are some of the aspects that need to be considered for a well-planned program.

The idea of a year-round training program is not to win, or to break records every week, but to obtain the best performances in the most important meets of the season, usually at the end of it. This means that improvement is gradually developed day by day, from meet to meet. If a curve is drawn based on the results obtained by an athlete at every meet, a curve showing a constant improvement up to the most important competition should be observed (Figure 12-13).

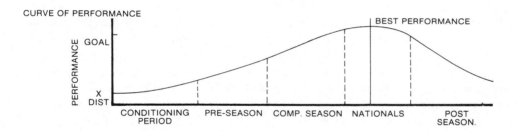

FIGURE 12-13

The curve of performance shows that the goal for the season should be attained at nationals (or at Conference or State meets). Throughout the season the capacities that will help improve the performance should be developed. In the case of the javelin these capacities are: strength, power, speed, endurance, coordination, mobility, agility, flexibility; and all of them specifically used for the javelin throw itself.

The curve of performance should ideally work hand in hand with the building and development of the capacities and the work on technique. This means that the ideal curve of performance will be obtained only if the program emphasizes each one at the right time during the season, and gives parallel attention to the technique throughout the whole year (Figure 12-14).

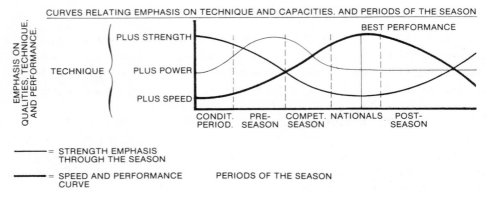

FIGURE 12-14

This curve shows that during the conditioning period major emphasis is given to strength, then power and the least to speed. As the season progresses to the early competitive season, power becomes the most important aspect, while strength diminishes and speed increases. Getting closer to important meets, speed takes priority, while emphasis on strength keeps on decreasing. This does not mean that while the athlete works on speed, power or strength are forgotten. During the whole year all three aspects are considered although the emphasis on each one of them varies. Something similar occurs while working on technique. During the conditioning period the emphasis is given to throws done using a correct technique but with heavier implements such as medicine balls (4 to 6 lb.), or simulating the throwing movement with weights or with the resistance of a partner (work based on strength). For the pre-season, or early competitive season exercises, movements using the correct technique will be done by using implements slightly heavier than the actual javelin, or rocks. These movements or throws should be done from a standing position, or using a sequence of one step, three steps, short run-ups, or complete easy approaches. Several complete throws should also be part of the program. Finally during the competitive season, most of the throws will be at full speed, trying to correct minor mistakes on technique but using complete approaches as the one used in competition.

Qualities such as agility, mobility, flexibility should be built during the general conditioning period, but as the season progresses those qualities will be available to the highest degree and will be applied to the actual throw.

Summarizing what has been discussed, a program should be developed based on the following principles:

1. Technique should be emphasized all year round.
2. In order to obtain maximum results, variations in quality and quantity of weight training should exist, depending on the period of the season.
3. Efficiency and economy in the actual throw will be attained only if loads and specific exercises are done by the muscles in such a way that their

actions correspond to the ones used in the throw (direction, intensity, speed). This principle of specificity is of utmost importance and should be kept in mind every day throughout the year. Specificity refers to the conduct of muscles when trained for determined qualities. This means that a muscle will acquire speed if the major emphasis of training has been given to speed, while strength will be obtained if heavy weights have been used in practices.

A PROGRAM

A program for an athlete should be both long and short term. Long term considerations include the future goals of the athlete, based on aspirations and possibilities, e.g., perform at college level, get to AAU nationals, become an international or Olympic athlete. This long term usually focuses on important meets over at least 3 years.

On a shorter basis, there is a yearly program. It covers only one complete season, but all the meets the athlete will attend are to be taken into consideration. This year-round program should be built on the basis of one curve (top performance will be attained at the most important outdoor meet), or two curves (good performances are expected twice a year in different periods). Usually this double curve includes a good early performance but a better one at the end of the season, after a short period of tapering-off after the peak of the first curve.

A still shorter term in a year-round program considers monthly, weekly and daily workouts. Monthly workouts will be based mainly on the period of the season (conditioning, pre-season, competitive period, and post-season or active rest) and the qualities to be developed and/or emphasized during each one of these. Weekly workouts will be based on the monthly workouts, but will emphasize the weakest abilities of the athlete. Daily workouts will vary in relation to weather, athlete's work load and activities during the day, time of the day, or place where the practice will be held, and are based on the objectives for the week.

A year-round program can be divided into four periods.

(a) Conditioning
(b) Pre-season
(c) Competitive season
(d) Post-season or active rest

Conditioning

During the conditioning period the emphasis should be on building or developing qualities such as strength, flexibility, mobility, agility, coordination, endurance. This conditioning should be 70% general ("building" condition), and

30% specific ("developing" skill or technique) in relation to the throw. Technique is developed doing exercises imitating throws, or standing throws, and even complete throws once a week. Throws with heavy medicine balls are excellent too.

General conditioning should emphasize the use of weights, medicine balls, and rope climbing, in order to strengthen all the muscles to be used later. Calisthenics plus sports such as baseketball, volleyball, gymnastics, and apparatus, will develop agility, mobility and flexibility, plus reaction, power and good mental preparedness. Highly recommended are weight training, exercising with small medicine balls, and throwing with implements heavier than the javelin (small metal bars, 2-3 lb. shots, heavy javelins filled with sand). Extremely valuable is the use of rubber ropes that offer a good resistance while imitating the throwing movement. Wood chopping with an axe of 2 to 4 lb., using an overhead movement from full height is also beneficial. The movements done for the development of specific throwing muscles will be imitating the actual throwing motion, but a certain resistance will be offered. These movements are performed faster, with longer periods of rest and lower resistance than the ones used for strength building. This will result in the development of explosive power which is extremely important in the javelin throw.

This preparatory period is the prerequisite of success, therefore general health condition and function capabilities should be developed. At least 5 practices a week, or 1½ to 2 hours are recommended, and the most important places for practice are the weight room (3 times a week), gym (twice a week), and out in the field once a week whenever the weather permits. Workouts including running are necessary. Distances should not exceed 250 to 300 m. (275-330 yds.) on each repetition. The endurance needed is not to be able to keep a fast rhythm for a long period of time, but to perform short, specific efforts over and over at high intensity.

Pre-season

The pre-season will be characterized mainly by power training, emphasizing speed, power, and the coordination of all the skills. Power will be developed, not only by exercising and calisthenics, but by throwing objects slightly heavier than the javelin at a fast speed. Valuable activities for these months include sprints, long and high jumps, hurdles, throws with shots of 1-2 lb., exercise and throws with smaller medicine balls (with a partner or against the wall), and exercises for flexibility and mobility with and without implements and/or partners on different positions (standing, sitting, kneeling). Technique during this period will be practiced from standing positions, with one step, three steps, easy run-ups and some easy throws with complete approach at least three times a week.

This stage, in comparison to the previous stage, should emphasize conditioning at higher intensity and quantity (training six times a week). It is more specific, therefore power, explosive power, is the most important value. About 50% will be general and 50% specific to the throwing action. Technique should become more important, and about 40 to 45% of the load should be allowed for its improvement.

Competitive Period

After 6-7 months of looking forward to competition, a change in the program must occur. A more specialized workout should be included; conditioning should be very specific and should decrease to 30 or 40% depending on the level of the athlete. The emphasis on technique will increase up to 50 or 70%. Intensity and low quantity will be important during these competitive months of four training days a week.

The coordination of everything that has been built up and emphasized previously will now be of greatest importance. Early and easy competition at the beginning will give experience and will help to solve technical problems under pressure of competition. Speed, control and concentration are the essentials for the period. At the end of the competitive season the attitude should be, "It is time for a great performance, and I can do it." Confidence and performance are the terms to summarize the efforts of the whole year.

The maintenance of the athletic condition and the best performances of the year are supposed to occur during this time. Practices should be of high quality. Weight training should be kept for specific movements, with low weights, but emphasizing speed. Technique should include complete approaches and high quality throws, as if in competition. Speed work on the track is important. Runs of 40 to 80 m., with and without the javelin, and starts from the crouch position should be included daily. Warm-ups should include a great number of exercises for the back, abdomen, legs, arms and shoulders, looking for power, flexibility and mobility.

Active Rest or Post-Season

Post-season or active rest is a period that starts as soon as the last competition is over, usually 15 days to one month long. The value of this month is to keep in shape, relax mentally and physically, and obtain a right attitude for preparation for the season to come. Activities should be easy; other sports such as basketball, volleyball and swimming are helpful and fun. Athletes enjoy being out from the field, developing new goals, ambitions, enthusiasm, and a strong will to come back to the javelin throw as soon as practices start again.

TEACHING THE TECHNIQUE OF THE JAVELIN THROW

The main objective of developing techniques in athletic events is to improve performance. From a pedagogical point of view, the teaching of such techniques should progressively develop a complex gesture, specific in its form and rhythm, and free of errors. Freedom of errors in acquiring a technique is of the utmost importance because errors in an acquired technique become habitual and are extremely difficult to get rid of. Since it is as easy to learn a correct movement as it is to learn an incorrect one, proper instruction from the beginning should be emphasized.

If enthusiastic and motivated athletes are desired, dynamism in teaching is extremely important. The teaching-learning experience should develop interest as well as correct form. The progression followed in teaching-learning should be generalized without emphasizing the correction of details which would result in unnecessary lengthening of the early stages in learning a technique.

Teaching-learning should follow a gradual progression, starting with the throwing pattern in inverse order. Thus the first phase of the throwing pattern to be taught should be the last movement (release). Once the general picture of the release is obtained, the last five steps (the withdrawal, the cross-step and the sudden-stop) should be practiced. Finally, after these steps have been mechanized, the preparation stage or run-up should be taught.

Throughout, it must be emphasized that learning should go from the parts to the whole, and within each part from the general to the specific movements. At the same time it should never be forgotten that the act of throwing is as natural as running or jumping. Therefore we may start teaching the javelin throw by simply encouraging a child to throw stones overhead at targets located at different distances and heights. In this way the future athlete will learn to throw with natural movements rather than awkward ones resulting from self-consciousness.

But the javelin is not a stone, therefore the next step should be to allow the thrower to familiarize herself with the implement and learn how to hold it. The athlete should try different grips and observe the results after several partial throws, deciding on one or another by experience and not merely on whether it feels comfortable after holding it just once.

Teaching of the proper technique for the javelin throw will be described in a sequence of steps that may facilitate the learning process.

1. With the palm of the hand facing up, the binding of the javelin should lie diagonally across the palm. The tip of the javelin should be in the direction of the heel of the hand and the tail in the direction of the first finger. At least two fingers should be gripping behind the binding, depending on the grip chosen (thumb and first finger; thumb and second finger; or first and second fingers). The last two fingers, curled and naturally separated, should be holding the binding.

2. The athlete stands facing in the direction of the throw with both feet pointing forward and spread one step apart, the left foot in front. The shoulders and hips should be parallel to the foul line and the head facing forward. The throwing arm is bent, hand up over the right shoulder with the elbow leading. The javelin is held at ear level and the left arm across the chest.

3. From position 2, extend the right arm forward and downward, smoothly at first, then with an explosive movement, release the

javelin so that it lands about 4 or 5 m. ahead, in front of the thrower. The left arm extends forward in the direction of the throw and then proceeds to open to the left side.

4. The athlete stands as in position 2, with the upper body and shoulders turned to the right, approximately 90 deg. from the direction of approach, forming a "cross" with the hips. The javelin is withdrawn by extending the right arm back and down without locking the elbow, keeping it at shoulder level and parallel to the direction of the throw. The tip of the implement is close to the head, at eye level, still pointing forward in line with the hand, arm, and shoulders. After the turn and the withdrawal are learned separately, the athlete coordinates both movements. She should keep in mind the important fact that the withdrawal is initiated by turning the shoulders and trunk 90 deg. to the right and not by extending the throwing arm to the side.

5. The withdrawal movement should be first tried while walking, then jogging, and finally running. After walking 4 or 5 steps with the throwing arm bent over the shoulder, the upper body turns 90 deg. to the right and at the same time the arm extends straight back and down. Then the athlete starts jogging in that position for 2 or 3 strides. Still jogging, she goes back to the starting position with the upper body facing forward, the arm bent, the elbow leading the action, and the javelin over the shoulder at ear level. Repeat this exercise several times while increasing the tempo from walking to jogging to running, but always try to coordinate speed with rhythm while the javelin is withdrawn and then returned to its initial position.

6. After the javelin has been withdrawn as in 4, turn the shoulders to the left towards the throwing area. As this movement is completed, the throwing arm bends, bringing the elbow forward and up into a leading position. Continue the movement and, using an overhand throw, try to hit a target (circle in the ground, for example) 8-10 m. (25-35 ft.) away. Repeat this exercise as many times as possible, concentrating on the alignment of the javelin and body, and especially on avoiding sidearm throws. Remember that the pull on the javelin must be applied through the length of the shaft and straight forward.

7. Repeat step 6 with a backward lean at the moment of the withdrawal. Both feet should be pointing forward with the weight of the body over the right leg and with the knee bent. The left leg should be extended and supported on the heel without locking the knee. The shoulders and throwing arm should be placed behind the center of gravity of the body, parallel to the direction of the throw, with the head facing the throwing area.

8. From the position in Step 6, transfer the weight of the body forward off the right leg by extending it, and pushing up and forward while the trunk and shoulders start turning to the left. In order to help the thrower

to be aware that the pull of the javelin should not start until the shoulders are forward over the hips and left leg, a partner may help by holding the tail of the javelin until the thrower has completed the turn. Repeat this exercise several times; try it without a partner while actually throwing the javelin.

9. After practicing the withdrawal of the implement, making sure to keep the required backward lean, the low position, and the center of gravity of the body ahead of the shoulders, try two fast steps while maintaining the hips as low as possible. These two steps should be long but quick steps with the right foot landing on its heel followed rapidly by the landing of the left foot on its heel as far in front of the right foot as possible. The long step with the right leg (corresponding to the cross-step) should be taken with the knee high but keeping the hips low and maintaining the backward lean of the body. The step with the left leg should be faster and even lower than the preceding one, emphasizing the landing on the heel. The thrower should keep her hips as low as possible while taking these two steps and at the same time complete the throw of the javelin as outlined in step 8. At first, a marked hesitation in the throwing action will occur just before the release; however after several practices the pause between the stop and the throw will be minimized.

10. The athlete jogs a few easy steps, withdraws the implement, takes two fast steps, and stops the movement completely, keeping a pronounced backward lean. For the last four steps the legs should land far apart and the hips kept low. The feet should land well ahead of the center of gravity. After several trials the ''dead'' points will be reduced, and finally disappear. The body will be driven forward by the action of the right leg, as the left foot approaches the ground. In this way the momentum of the run will be conserved so that it may be utilized in the throw. As the throw nears completion, the right heel should open to the right, and the toe should drag on the ground.

11. The javelin thrower walks 12 steps using a position similar to 1, keeping the javelin moving naturally back and forth in rhythm with the legs. Then she proceeds through the next two steps corresponding to the action of withdrawal, and finally, completes the throw in the two subsequent steps corresponding to the cross-step and sudden-stop. The athlete repeats this exercise several times, changing from a walk to a jog to a running pattern.

As a general recommendation the athlete should learn one stage of the throwing technique and then proceed to the next one. After learning the second stage go back and coordinate it with the first one in succession. Only then should the third stage of the learning process be attempted and, after it is mastered, likewise coordinated with the following stages until stages 1, 2, and 3 are mastered. This method should then continue until all stages required to learn the technique have been mastered and the complete throwing movement can be reproduced. With respect to the speed of motion, the athlete should learn a movement while standing or moving very slowly, then try it walking, jogging, and finally at the actual speed of the throw. However, do not spend too much time in slow motion, because the actual throw is performed at considerable speed. Too often, speed will be lost for accuracy, or accuracy will suffer because of speed. It is for this reason that during the teaching-learning process, the interaction between speed and accuracy should be given special attention with a gradual progression in both speed and accuracy.

13 John Jessee

WEIGHT TRAINING

Author: **John Jessee** is a well-known authority on all aspects of weight training. A former decathlete, wrestler and football player, he has been active in the promotion of weight training programs for clubs and schools for over 25 years and has written more than 80 articles on strength development, injury prevention and weight training.

The basic objective of weight training for strength and power development for athletic participants is not to become the strongest athletes in their specific events, but (a) to develop a relatively balanced strength development throughout the entire body and (b) to improve the qualities of athletic fitness—power, flexibility, endurance, coordination and skill.

No one has yet been able to categorically demonstrate that a certain level of strength is required for superiority in any specific athletic event. All that can be said is that "everything being equal, the strongest person has the advantage."

Valik (1966) has commented that "emphasis should be placed on the harmonious development of the musculature. Most children 12 to 13 years of age when they first enter athletics exhibit a high degree of muscular imbalance. It stands as an insurmountable hurdle on the road to mastery if not corrected and allowed to persist. The main problem in strength preparation of young sportsmen in the first two or three years of training is improvement in the development of those groups of muscles which remain behind."

Valik's statement has been substantiated by numerous studies of posture among American children and college students during the past 70 years. It has been shown that 90% of children and adolescents demonstrate one or more posture faults. These faults are closely associated with muscular imbalance.

Muscular imbalance interferes with the range of joint motion, neuromuscular coordination and skill and has become recognized as a major cause of muscular strains and overuse syndromes. In addition, through fatigue of weaker muscles on one side of a joint there can be interference with the maximum expression of cardiovascular efficiency. A distance runner with weak dorsal and upper back muscles, who allows her upper body to sag forward toward the end of the race, interferes with the efficiency of the prime breathing muscle (diaphragm) when oxygen uptake is most needed.

There can never be complete muscle or strength balance in the human body. The goal is to reduce the ratio of imbalance between the muscular strength on either side of a joint.

STRENGTH DEVELOPMENT

(a) Tension in the muscle created by resistance is the basic stimulus for strength development.

(b) The dominating principle is "overload." Muscles must be compelled to carry out work beyond that which can be performed comfortably, easily and without strain.

(c) The second principle is "progression." The amount of resistance (load) used in an exercise must be increased whenever the athlete becomes able to complete a required number of repetitions with less than all-out effort.

(d) The third principle is the "rate of progression." The body adapts slowly. When the exerciser completes a certain number of repetitions with a given load without strain, she should use the same load for 2 weeks before increasing resistance.

(e) The fourth principle requires that maximum tension be maintained throughout the entire exercise. The greatest tension a muscle can produce is at a slow rate of contraction. This requires that resistance movements used for strength development be done in a smooth and even manner at a slow speed.

(f) The muscle produces its greatest tension when it is on stretch. Each movement should begin from a position in which the joint is fully extended or flexed, and end with a full contraction or extension.

(g) An important point in strength development exercises is the will to perform a maximum (all-out) effort. Deep concentration on the muscles being exercised improves the number and frequency of nervous stimuli going to the muscles, important for developing maximum tension contraction.

POWER DEVELOPMENT

Power, which is force (strength) multiplied by velocity (speed), may be thought of as the ability to apply maximum force in the shortest time.

Power divides into two broad components: force against light external resistance (speed dominated), or force against heavy external resistance (strength dominated). There are three broad areas of training that contribute toward the development of either type of power—strength, speed and skill.

The athlete in training for power must concentrate on improving the mental, emotional and neurological processes involved in increasing the efficiency of the central nervous system (CNS). Speed is the collaborative effort of muscles and nerves, both dependent on the ability of the CNS to coordinate their efforts.

(a)   Muscle fibers demonstrate a broad range of contractile speed. Rapid movements result in the recruitment of the faster fibers.

(b)   Achieving fast and powerful muscular contractions requires the muscle fibers surrounding both sides of joints involved in a specific movement to work as closely together as possible in a highly synchronized, alternating manner (coordination).

(c)   The athlete must learn to consciously relax all muscles not involved or opposed to the desired movement.

(d)   In the use of weight training exercises to develop the speed phase of power, the athlete must cultivate a high degree of concentration in order to produce vigorous and rapid nervous impulses to the muscle fibers.

(e)   There must be a lessening of all mental or emotional inhibitions against the expression of maximum speed or all-out effort.

The development of the velocity (speed) component of power is generally combined with skill training by coaches. Doherty (1971) has divided power training into two phases: related power and specific imitative power.

He defines related power as the development of those muscles and movements that relate to the event for which training is done, and notes a tendency to use submaximum resistances and high velocities. Training of related power tends to use only phases or parts of event movements, seldom the entire action.

According to Doherty, imitative power training is one step beyond related power training in that it involves lighter loads and greater velocities of training movements. It also simulates more closely the actual event skill, whether of the entire skill or of specific phases of that skill such as the Finnish javelin throwers using the full run-and-throw with iron balls weighing 2-3 times as much as the javelin.

SAFETY FACTORS

The great majority of athletic injuries occurring in weight training involve muscle strains to the back, wrists and shoulders. Most of the muscle strains can be prevented by adherence to a few simple rules.

Medical Examination

Weight training, like any physical activity, imposes stresses on the musculoskeletal structure of the body. A prospective female athlete should not engage in weight training without first undergoing a complete medical examination. In addition to the traditional examination there should be analysis of the posture, including X-rays of the spine, pelvis, legs, ankles and feet by a combined orthopedic-podiatric team. Posture deviations are a primary source of injuries as they lead to poor mechanics of running and body movement, interfere with coordination, and limit the range of motion of the joints.

Many persons are born with hidden congenital anomalies, particularly in the spinal joints, hip joints and feet. Imposing added stresses to these joints may lead to serious consequences. In addition, adolescent athletes are faced with the problem of ossification of the epiphyses (growing plates) at the ends of the large bones of the body and around the edges of the spinal vertebrae. The medical literature is full of references to Scheurman's disease of the spine and Osgood-Schlatter's disease of the knee joint, due to stresses resulting from athletic activity which imposes added stresses on these joints.

Warm-Up

The female athlete should always warm-up prior to weight training. This first includes some static stretching movements for the shoulder girdle, lower back, hip flexors and hamstrings. Because weight training exercises are localized, the remainder of the warm-up should be carried out during the strength training exercise schedule. Prior to performing a strength exercise for a particular body part, perform one set of 20 repetitions with the barbell handle or very light dumbbells only, using the same movement as used in the strength-training exerise.

Minor Illness

Weight training should not be done if the athlete is suffering from a fever or cold.

Lifting Form

Master complicated exercises with a light weight before attempting to perform them with a heavy weight. Forcefully control all movements done with weights. Be sure the hands are properly spaced on the bar, or the load will be unbalanced. In lifting heavy weights from the floor, keep the bar close to the body, ensure the back is straight, with head up. Keep the feet flat on the floor, shoulder-width apart.

Equipment and Exercise Area

Avoid the use of weak benches, seats that teeter or boxes that are too flimsy for the support of weights or the body. Ensure that the plates and collars on the bar are securely fastened. The workout area should not be cluttered with loose pieces of equipment which the athlete might trip over while lifting.

Clothing

Wear warm clothing unless the exercise area is heated or during an unusually warm day. High-topped tennis shoes provide good traction and ankle support.

Olympic Lifting and Overhead Movements

Olympic lifting movements should not be used as training movements to develop strength. The skills involved in Olympic lifting have no relation to any other athletic skill except the forward change of the interior lineman in American football. The time spent in learning the skills of Olympic lifting could be much better used in training for strength and the various types of power. If these skills are not learned, the lifting of heavy weights in Olympic type movements with poor form can subject the athlete to serious injuries.

The weakest portion of the body in today's youth is the lower back. The spine is a single weight-bearing column completely supported by muscles. Lifting heavy weights overhead without first developing strong spinal muscles can accentuate a spinal curvature of the lower back (lordosis), and can cause lesions in the intervertebral discs of the spine. For this reason, no female athlete should lift more than 50 percent of her body weight to an overhead standing position until she has spent at least 1 year on exercises specifically designed to strengthen the muscles of the back.

Squats

Sports' medical and training authorities are against the use of the full squat in weight training sessions because of the danger of stretching the ligaments of the knee, making it prone to injury. The athlete should never go below parallel (legs bent to a 90 deg. angle) in the squat.

Squats should be performed with the knees and the toes pointing in the same direction. If the feet are turned outward, the knees should be turned outward.

Females tend to let their thighs sag inwards at the knee joint as they lower themselves in the squat. This places tremendous stress on the medial collateral ligament, causing it to stretch. This is primarily due to a lack of strength in the quadriceps muscle of the thighs. The female athlete should ensure that she can perform squats with an established amount of resistance without bending the thighs and knee joints inward, before adding resistance.

Personal Viewpoint

Remember always you are only competing against yourself in improving your strength. The strength displayed by your teammate will not improve your strength, but may subconsciously encourage you to use weights beyond your capacity to handle safely. The largest single cause of injuries among athletes using weights is exceeding the capacity of the individual to handle a specified resistance.

PRACTICAL CONSIDERATIONS AND PROCEDURES

Weight training consists of isotonic muscular contractions broken down into concentric (shortening) and eccentric (lengthening) movements. The weight trainer can receive the benefits of both types of strengthening movements if she performs all strength development movements at a slow, controlled pace (count of 4), slowly raising the weight (count of 2) and slowly lowering the weight (count of 2).

(a). Concentric strength development requires use of maximum or near maximum weights (85 to 95%) with low repetitions (3 to 6) and a number of sets based on the number of repetitions (3 sets times 6 reps, 5 or 6 sets times 3 reps, etc.).

(b). Eccentric strength development requires use of maximum and over maximum weights with low repetitions (3 to 6) at a very slow, controlled pace (10 to 12 sec.) with deep concentration on the muscles being exercised and a specified number of repetitions and sets, using maximum weight with the most repetitions (100%—6 repetitions) and over maximum weights with the least repetitions (120% load—3 repetitions). True eccentric strength training requires the assistance of two partners to place the weights in the starting position of the exercise.

(c) Strength-dominated related power development requires use of light to medium weight loads (20 to 60 percent of maximum for arms, shoulders and upper body and 40 to 75 percent of maximum for lower back, hips and legs) using a moderate number of repetitions (10 to 12), one or two sets, at a medium fast cadence consistent with safety.

(d). Speed-dominated imitative power development requires use of very light to medium light weights (2 to 10 percent of maximum for arms, shoulders and upper body and 15 to 25 percent of maximum for lower back, hips and legs) using a moderate number of repetitions (10 to 15), one or two sets, at as fast a cadence as possible, consistent with good form and safety. This type of training is associated with the skills of the event such as the shot putter practicing with 8 lb., 12 lb. and 25 lb. shots, the discus thrower with an underweight or overweight discus, the javelin thrower practicing with 2 kg. (4½ lb.) iron balls or a lighter javelin.

DEPTH JUMP TRAINING

The system of depth jump training was developed in Russia for jumpers, sprinters, throwers and steeplechasers. It is described as reactive-ability training in that country, plyometric training by Fred Wilt, imitative power training by Doherty and elastic energy transfer by the physiologists. The physiological explanation is beyond the scope of this chapter.

This type of training is not for the adolescent athlete or the older beginning athlete. Russian experiments have shown that it has few benefits for the young athlete but that it provides great benefits for the older, experienced athlete.

The Russians use depth jump training as a "shock" method of improving the reactive ability of the nerve-muscle apparatus. During take-off in a jump, the extensor muscles fulfill yielding work in the beginning and later overcoming work (phase of active take-off). Verhoshanskiy (1973) points out that for the development of reactive abilities, it is best to jump straight from a height of 75-100 cm. (30-40 in.). Most important is a fast, active take-off after landing. Special investigations have shown that at the first height (30 in.) maximum speed is achieved in switching the muscles from yielding work to overcoming work and that the second height (40 in.) corresponds to the maximum strength developed. The body is not loaded in using this type of training. The kinetic energy used is only that of the falling body.

Verhoshanskiy states the best methods of preparation for depth jumps appear to be jumping with weights of 32 kg. (70 lb.) between gymnastic benches and jumping (squat) exercises in place.

The number of jumps depends upon the qualifications and preparation of the athlete—twice per week for prepared athletes and once per week for those less prepared. The optimal number of take-offs after the depth jump in one session for prepared athletes should not be greater than 40 and for less prepared athletes 20-30 repetitions. The jumps are executed in series (10 reps from a height of 30 in. and 10 reps from a height of 40 in.) and are repeated two times. Between series, running exercises and exercises for relaxation are practiced.

Number of Workouts Each Week

Accepted practice for beginners is three times per week with a day of rest between each workout. This provides an opportunity for the body to recuperate. When a weight training program is integrated into the overall training program, this approach is modified to meet the demands of time and energy expended on the development of stamina, speed, flexibility, timing, skill and competitive events.

Length of Workout Period

The average total use of muscular force against resistance accomplished in a one-hour workout is 12 to 15 minutes.

Time of Day

The late afternoon or evening is generally the best time to work out. The athlete should never engage in weight training prior to training for endurance, speed or skill.

Selection of Exercises

Three points should be taken into consideration in meeting the objectives of a weight training program: (a) development of strength, power and/or muscular endurance in all the movement patterns of the athlete's event; (b) development of similar qualities in the antagonistic muscles to ensure a balanced development;

and (c) exercises should be changed periodically (every 8 weeks) in order to involve different movement patterns of the muscle groups and to avoid boredom.

Exercise Cadence

Strength development exercises should be carried out at a slow, controlled pace (4 counts) in a strict manner with complete flexion and extension of the muscle groups involved. Under no circumstances should "cheating" or "swinging" body movements be used in performing localized strength development exercises. Power type movements should be done at an increased pace, using a definite rhythm, consistent with the amount of weight used and the form requirements of the exercise.

Rest Pauses

In performing strength development exercises, rest periods between exercises or sets should be based on the muscle groups involved, For arms, shoulders and neck, the rest period should be 1-1½ min.; for the trunk, back and legs, 2-2½ min. In performing power movements, the rest period should vary from 3-4 min.; depending on the number of repetitions and the resistance used.

Exercise Loads

Maximum load is the amount of weight that can be lifted or pushed from one repetition of a specific movement. Near maximum loads would be 85 to 99 percent of maximum; heavy weights, 60 to 85 percent of maximum; moderate weights, 25 to 60 percent of maximum; light weights, 5 to 25 percent of maximum.

Starting Weights

In determining the initial starting weight for a strength development exercise, trial and error is still the best method. Various methods have been tried, but involve a great deal of time and effort. Where the exercise calls for a specific number of repetitions and the weight the exerciser is using does not force her to strain during the final one or two repetitions, she is not using enough weight. The resistance should be increased.

Increasing Resistance

Add weight to bar, dumbbell handles or iron boots when you can complete the required number of repetitions, or the required number of repetitions in the last set, without strain for three successive workouts. It is the last set that provides the greatest gain in strength.

Repetitions

The number of repetitions or sets is based on the weight training being used and the objects being sought (development of strength, different types of power, or muscular endurance).

Dumbbells

Dumbbells allow for natural movements that closely simulate many arm and shoulder movements used in track and field. They provide for a more equitable distribution of resistance to both sides of the body.

Weight Training Systems

All systems are based on the principle of progressive resistance.

(a). Double progressive—combines strength development and muscular endurance development. To be used by prospective athletes in the age group of 12 through the second year of high school. The range of repetitions would be 8 through 12 for arm, chest and shoulder exercises, and 12 to 15 through 20 to 24 for leg and back exercises. Begin with the minimum repetitions and every other workout, add one repetition for arm, chest and shoulder exercises and two repetitions for leg and back exercises until the maximum repetitions are attained. At that point add resistance and start over with minimum repetitions.

(b). Set System—also known as a single progressive system. To be used by the athlete with previous weight training experience or athletes in the age group of third year high school through college. A designated number of repetitions is established for a specific exercise. This is known as a set. When the athlete begins the program, perform one set of repetitions per exercise for the four to six workouts, then add a second set, and where recommended, a third set for performing the second set for four to six workouts. When the athlete is able to complete all repetitions of the three sets without too much strain, add weight to the bar but continue with the same number of sets and repetitions.

Weight Increases

In general 2½-5 lb. (1-2 kg.) are added for arm, chest and shoulder exercises, 5 lb. (2 kg.) for lower back, sides and abdomen and 10 lb. (4 kg.) for the legs. The exception to this rule is straight arm or leg leverage exercises with dumbbells or iron boots. The weight increase would be 1¼, 2½ or 5 lb. (½, 1 or 2 kg.) for each dumbbell or iron boot.

WEIGHT TRAINING PROGRAMS

Exercises for development of strength in the upper arm flexors (biceps) are not included in the programs. The lifting of barbell and dumbbells to the shoulders, and in addition the rowing movement exercises, provide sufficient exercise for this group of muscles.

SPRINTS	SETS	REPS	FIG. NO.
1. Wide grip rowing	3	6	13-4
2. Wide grip bench press	3	6	13-1
3. Squat	3	6	13-18
4. Upright rowing	3	6	13-5

		SETS	REPS	FIG. NO.
5.	Bent leg knee raise	3	6	13-15
6.	Leg extension	3	6	13-20
7.	Leg curl	3	6	13-21
8.	Straight leg dead lift	3	8	13-13
9.	Bent knee sit-up	3	8	13-9
10.	Bouncing split squat	1	1	13-22
11.	Seated heel raise*	8	10	13-24

HURDLES		SETS	REPS	FIG. NO.
1.	Wide grip rowing	3	6	13-4
2.	Wide grip bench press	3	6	13-1
3.	Squat	3	6	13-18
4.	Upright rowing	3	6	13-5
5.	Bent leg knee raise	3	6	13-15
6.	Leg extension	3	6	13-20
7.	Leg curl	3	6	13-21
8.	Straight leg dead lift	3	8	13-13
9.	Bent knee sit-up	3	8	13-9
10.	Bouncing split squat	1	16	13-22
11.	Seated heel raise	3	10	13-24

MIDDLE AND LONG DISTANCE		SETS	REPS	FIG NO.
1.	Wide grip rowing	3	6	13-4
2.	Wide grip bench press	3	6	13-1
3.	Upright rowing	3	6	13-5
4.	Bent leg knee raise	3	6	13-15
5.	Leg extension	3	6	13-20
6.	Leg curl	3	6	13-21
7.	Straight leg dead lift	3	8	13-13
8.	Bent knee sit-up	3	8	13-9
9.	Bouncing split squat	1	16	13-22

LONG JUMP		SETS	REPS	FIG NO.
1.	Alternate forward raise	3	6	13-6
2.	Wide grip rowing	3	6	13-4
3.	Squat	3	6	13-18
4.	Upright rowing	3	6	13-5
5.	Bent leg knee raise	3	6	13-15
6.	Twisting sit-up	3	6	13-10
7.	Bend over twist	3	6	13-11
8.	Leg extension	3	6	13-20
9.	Leg curl	3	6	13-21
10.	Straight leg dead lift	3	8	13-13
11.	Seated heel raise	3	10	13-24
12.	Bouncing split squat	1	16	13-22

HIGH JUMP		SETS	REPS	FIG NO.
1.	Alternate forward raise	3	6	13-6
2.	Wide grip rowing	3	6	13-4
3.	Squat	3	6	13-18
4.	Upright rowing	3	6	13-5

*When the knee is bent the primary plantar flexor muscle is the soleus. The major calf muscle (gastroenemius) does not become activated until the knee is locked. When performing the seated heel raise for the soleus muscle always do so with the toes pointed inwards, in a pigeon toed position.

5.	Bent leg knee raise	3	6	13-15
6.	Twisting sit-up	3	6	13-10
7.	Bend over twist	3	6	13-11
8.	Leg extension	3	6	13-20
9.	Leg curl	3	6	13-21
10.	Straight leg dead lift	3	8	13-13
11.	Seated heel raise	3	10	13-24

SPECIAL EXERCISES FOR RUNNERS—HURDLERS—JUMPERS

EVENT	EXERCISE	SETS	REPS	FIG NO.
Hurdlers	Side leg raise	3	10	13-16
High Jumpers (Fosbury style)	Internal-external leg rotation	3	10	13-17
High Jumpers (Straddle type)	Internal leg rotation	3	10	13-17
All Athletes	Ankle dorsiflexion	3	10	13-25
All Athletes	Ankle balance exercise	3	10	13-27

PREPARATORY EXERCISE FOR DEPTH JUMPING

Sprinters-Hurdlers-Jumpers	Jumping squats	3	10	13-23

FIGURE 13-1   Wide Grip Bench Press. *Extend arms completely.*

FIGURE 13-2:   Incline Bench Press. *Extend arms completely.*

FIGURE 13-3:   Bent Arm Lateral Raise. *Arms slightly bent.*

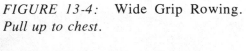

FIGURE 13-4: Wide Grip Rowing. *Pull up to chest.*

FIGURE 13-5: Upright Rowing. *Vary hand spacing.*

FIGURE 13-6: Alternate Dumbbell Forward Raise. *Keep arms straight.*

FIGURE 13-7: Standing Triceps Extension. *Keep elbow in same position throughout triceps extension movements.*

FIGURE 13-8: One Arm Press. *Bend to side as weight goes overhead.*

FIGURE 13-9: Bent Knee Sit-up. *Knees bent, chin on chest.*

FIGURE 13-10: Twisting Sit-up. *One end unloaded, repeat on the other side.*

FIGURE 13-11: Bend Over Twist. *One end unloaded.*

FIGURE 13-12: Round Back Forward Bend. *Bend knees, round back.*

FIGURE 13-13: Straight Leg Dead Lift. *Perform exercise slowly.*

FIGURE 13-14: Barbell Swing. *Hold weight in hands at hip level. Raise weight to overhead position, twisting trunk and hips in a swinging motion. Lower weight and repeat to the opposite side.*

FIGURE 13-15: Bent Knee Leg Raise. *Attempt to touch chest.*

FIGURE 13-16: Standing Side Leg Raise. *Keep leg straight.*

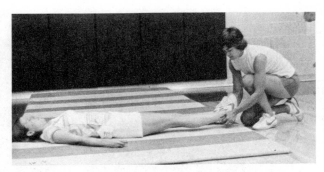

FIGURE 13-17: Internal-External Leg
Rotation. *Exerciser keeps leg locked at
knee. Partner holds heel of foot with one
hand and forefoot with other hand.
Partner rotates entire leg outward
against exerciser's resistance to
strengthen internal thigh rotators. Rotate leg inwards to strengthen external
thigh rotators.*

FIGURE 13-18: Parallel Squat. *Place
2-inch block under heels to provide balance.*

FIGURE 13-19: One-third Squat.
*Place 2-inch block under heels to pro-
vide balance.*

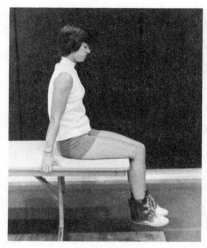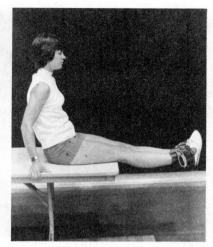

FIGURE 13-20: Leg Extension. *Lock knees for count of one, when legs are extended.*

FIGURE 13-21: Leg Curl. *Raise weight to right angle only.*

FIGURE 13-22: Bouncing Split Squat. *Leap into air, splitting legs forwards and backwards. When landing, get hips as low as possible.*

FIGURE 13-23: Jumping Squat. *Begin with thighs parallel with the ground. Leap as high as possible. Do not hesitate between jumps.*

FIGURE 13-24: Seated Heel Raise. *Exercises soleus muscle.*

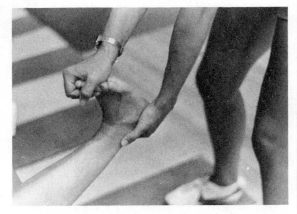

FIGURE 13-25: Ankle Dorsi Flexion. *Partner raises foot towards shin while exerciser resists. Partner places free hand behind the heel to stabilize the ankle.*

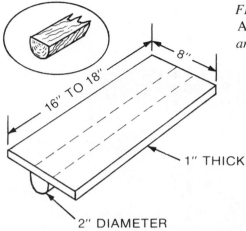

16" TO 18"

8"

1" THICK

2" DIAMETER

FIGURE 13-26:
Ankle Balance Board. *Two ankle boards are required for the exercise.*

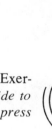

FIGURE 13-27: Ankle Balance Exercise. *Tilting balance board from side to side. Keep feet flat on boards and press down with toes.*

FIGURE 13-28: Shoulder Push. *Raise weight upward with shoulder movement only.*

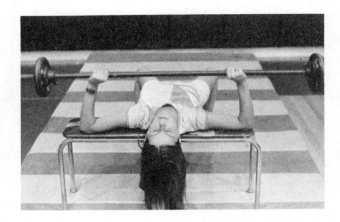

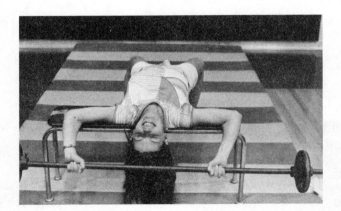

FIGURE 13-29: Forearm Pullover.
Without moving elbows from bench,
lower weight backwards and down-
wards. As the weight is pulled upwards
and forward, a strong pull is felt on the
inside of the elbow. Begin with a light
weight.

FIGURE 13-30: Close Hand Bench Press. *Grasp bar with hands 2 inches apart, elbows pointed outward. Press weight upwards.*

FIGURE 13-31: Wrist Lever Extension. *Perform repetitions in both positions.*

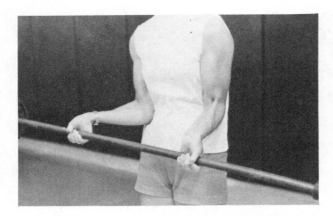

FIGURE 13-32: Wrist Curl. *Perform repetitions with palms up, and with palms down (Reverse Wrist Curl). Raise weight slowly as high as possible in both positions.*

FIGURE 13-33: Wrist Rotation. *Do exercise slowly with weighted end of bar in a downwards and upwards position.*

FIGURE 13-34 Finger Exercises. *Drop a heavy barbell plate with one hand and catch it with the opposite hand. Pick up loaded end of a heavy barbell with a pinch grip.*

WEIGHT TRAINING AND THE THROWING EVENTS

During the past 20 years, this writer has maintained that athletes in the throwing events, both men and women, along with their coaches have over-emphasized the development of great body strength and total body power in the vertical plane. Little attention has been given to the development of strength and related power in the horizontal and rotational planes. From the type of exercise movements used in their training programs, one could easily gather the impression they are training to become Olympic champions in weight lifting, the world's strongest power lifters or American football interior linemen.

They could well ask themselves two questions. How much total body strength and power in the vertical plane is required to project a shot, discus or javelin the greatest possible distance using the horizontal and rotational movements common to all three events? How do you condition the nervous system to display its maximum efficiency in the expression of strength, power and skill in horizontal and rotational movements when it has only been conditioned to display its maximum efficiency in the vertical plane?

Much greater attention should be given to the development of strength and power in the muscles of the trunk that supply the force for the rotational movements of the body; the development of related and imitative power; the coordination of linear velocity (momentum) with rotational velocity and the development of skill.

The javelin thrower should spend more time on developing the ability to transfer great linear velocity (run-up momentum) to the rotational velocity in throwing, without any hesitation in the transition phase. This was the fundamental weakness of America's premier female javelin thrower, who had natural talent and size and had developed speed, strength, and skill of the throw from a standing position.

Shot-putters and discus throwers, instead of concentrating on body size and great strength, should spend more time on development of speed across the ring (horizontal and linear velocity) and its transfer to rotational velocity during the put or throw. The U.S. shot putters at Montreal clearly demonstrated a lack of speed across the ring. They were all carrying 25-30 lb. of excessive body weight that contributed nothing to their performances.

SHOT PUT	SETS	REPS	FIG NO.
1. Upright rowing	3	6	13-5
2. Incline bench press	3	6	13-3
3. Wide grip rowing	3	6	13-4
4. Squat	3	8	13-18
5. Leg curl	3	6	13-21
6. Straight leg dead lift	3	8	13-13
7. Twisting sit-up	3	8	13-10
8. Bend over twist	3	8	13-11
9. Bouncing split squat	1	16	13-22
10. Round back bend over	3	6	13-12
11. One arm press	3	6	13-8

DISCUS	SETS	REPS	FIG NO.
1. Upright rowing	3	6	13-5
2. Bent arm lateral raise	3	8	13-3
3. Wide grip rowing	3	8	13-4
4. Squat	3	8	13-18
5. Twisting sit-up	3	8	13-10
6. Bend over twist	3	8	13-11
7. Incline bench press	3	6	13-2
8. Round back bend over	3	6	13-12
9. Bouncing split squat	1	16	13-22
10. Barbell swing	3	6	13-14

JAVELIN	SETS	REPS	FIG NO.
1. Upright rowing	3	6	13-5
2. Bent arm lateral raise	3	8	13-3
3. Wide grip rowing	3	8	13-4
4. ⅓ squat	3	6	13-19
5. Twisting sit-up	3	8	13-10
6. Bend over twist	3	8	13-11
7. Triceps extension	3	6	13-7
8. Round back bend over	3	6	13-12
9. Bouncing split squat	1	16	13-22

SPECIAL EXERCISES FOR SHOT-PUT—DISCUS—JAVELIN

EVENT	EXERCISE	SETS	REPS	FIG NO.
1. All Throwers	Shoulder push*	3	10	13-28
2. Javelin	Forearm pullover	3	10	13-29
3. Shot-Put	Close hand bench press	3	6	13-30
4. Discus	Wrist levers	3	10	13-31
5. Shot-Put	Wrist curls	3	10	13-32
6. Javelin	Wrist curls and rotations	3	10	13-32 & 13-33
7. Shot-Put	Hand and finger exercises	3	10	13-34

---

*The prime mover in the forward movement of the scapula in all throwing movements is the serratus anterior muscle. The shoulder push exercise develops this muscle. Partners are required in performing this exercise as the weight must be at least 120% of the maximum bench press ability.

BIBLIOGRAPHY

CHAPTER 1

Alabin, B. and Maishutovich, M. "How Do Hurdlers Run?" *Athletic Asia,* 5(1), March 1975.

Brooks, C. "Characteristics of Top U.S. Female Sprinters," unpublished report, 1976.

Cooper, J.M.; Ward, R.; Taylor, P. and Barlow, D. "Kinesiology of the Long Jump," in *Biomechanics III* (ed. by S. Cerguiglini; A. Venerando and J. Wartenweiler). Baltimore: University Park Press, 1973. 381-386.

Doherty, K., *Track and Field Omnibook.* Swarthmore, PA: Tafmop Publishers, 1971.

Gagnon, M., *Biomechanical Comparison of the Standing and Kneeling Sprint Starts,* Ph.D. dissertation, The Pennsylvania State University, 1976.

Henry, F.M., "Research on Sprint Running," *The Athletic Journal,* Feb. 1952.

Henry, F.M., "Force-Time Characteristics of the Sprint Start," *Research Quarterly,* 23(3):301-318, 1952.

Hoffman, K., "Stride Length and Frequency of Female Sprinters," *Track Technique,* No. 48, June 1972.

Ikai, M., "Biomechanics of Sprint Running with Respect to the Speed Curve," in *Biomechanics: Technique of Drawings of Movement and Movement Analysis* (ed. by J. Wartenweiler, E. Jokl and M. Hebbelinck). Basel, Switzerland: S. Karger AG, 1968, 282-290.

Jackson, A.S. and Cooper, J.M., "Effect of Hand Spacing and Rear Knee Angle on the Sprinter's Start," *Research Quarterly,* 41(3).

Lance, J.F., *The Relationship Existing Between the Time Spent in Executing the Spring and the Height of a Jump,* M.A. thesis, State University of Iowa, 1935.

Marhold, G., "Biomechanical Analysis of the Shot Put," in *Biomechanics IV* (ed. by R.C. Nelson and C.A. Morehouse). Baltimore: University Park Press, 1974.

Nelson, R.C., "Biomechanical Aspects of Distance Running," *Track and Field Quarterly Review,* 75(4), 1976.

Nelson, R.C.; Aegerter, J. and Tait, T., "Comparison of Two Take-off Methods in the Volleyball Spike," unpublished report, 1976.

Nelson, R.C. and Gregor, R.J., "The Biomechanics of Distance Running: A Longitudinal Study," *Research Quarterly,* 46(2), 1975.

Slater-Hammel, A., "Possible Neuromuscular Mechanism as a Limiting Factor for Rate of Leg Movement in Sprinting," *Research Quarterly,* 12(4), 1941.

Smith, H.K., Speech to the USTCA Executive Board, June 4, 1976.

Winter, Lloyd. *The Rocket Sprint Start.* Winter Enterprises, 1430 Cherrydale, San José, CA.

CHAPTER 2

American College of Sports Medicine, "Position Statement: Prevention of Heat Injuries During Distance Running," *Medicine and Science in Sports,* 7: vii (Spring), 1975.

Astrand, P.O., L. Engstrom, B.O. Eriksson, P. Karlberg, I. Nylander, B. Saltin and C. Thoren, "Girl Swimmers," *Acta Paediatrica* Supplement, 147, 1963.

Astrand, P.O. and K. Rodahl, *Textbook of Work Physiology.* New York: McGraw-Hill Book Company, 1970.

Buskirk, E.R. and W.C. Grasley, "Heat Injury and Conduct of Athletics," in *Science and Medicine of Exercise and Sports,* 2d. ed. (ed. by W.R. Johnson and E.R. Buskirk). New York: Harper and Row, 1974.

Costill, D.L., W.F. Kammer and A. Fisher, "Fluid Ingestion during Distance Running," *Archives of Environmental Health,* 21: 520, 1970.

Drinkwater, B.L. and S.M. Horvath, "Detraining Effects on Young Women," *Medicine and Science in Sports,* 4:91, 1972.

Erdelyi, G., "Gynecological Survey of Female Athletes," *Journal of Sports Medicine and Physical Fitness,* 2: 174, 1962.

Gollnick, P.D. and L. Hermansen, "Biochemical Adaptations to Exercise: Anaerobic Metabolism," in *Exercise and Sport Sciences Reviews,* Vol. 1 (ed. by J.H. Wilmore). New York: Academic Press, 1973.

Lundegren, H.M., "Changes in Skinfold and Girth Measures of Women Varsity Basketball and Field Hockey Players," *Research Quarterly,* 39: 1020, 1968.

Mathews, D.K. and E.L. Fox, *The Physiological Basis of Physical Education and Athletics.* Philadelphia: W.B. Saunders Company, 1971.

Saltin, B., "Metabolic Fundamentals in Exercise," *Medicine and Science in Sports,* 5: 137, 1973.

White, H.S., "Iron Nutriture of Girls and Women—A Review. 1. Dietary Iron and Hemoglobin Concentration," *Journal of American Dietary Association,* 53: 563, 1968.

Wilmore, J.H., "Alterations in Strength, Body Composition and Anthropometric Measurements Consequent to a 10-week Weight Training Program," *Medicine and Science in Sport,* 6: 133, 1974.

Wilt, F., "Training for Competitive Running," in *Exercise Physiology,* (ed. by H.B. Falls). New York: Academic Press, 1968.

Zaharieva, E., "Survey of Sportswomen at the Tokyo Olympics," *Journal of Sports Medicine and Physical Fitness,* 5: 215, 1965.

CHAPTER 3

Atkinson, J. W., "Motivational Determinants of Risk-Taking Behavior," *Psychological Review,* 1957, *64*, 359-372.

Atkinson, J. W., *An Introduction to Motivation.* Princeton: D. Van Nostrand, 1964.

Bandura, A., *Principles of Behavior Modification.* New York: Holt, Rinehart & Winston, 1969.

Bandura, A., Grusec, J. E., & Menlove, F. L., "Vicarious Extinction of Avoidance Behavior," *Journal of Personality and Social Psychology,* 1967, *5*, 16-23.

Bandura, A., & Jeffery, R. W., "Role of Symbolic Coding and Rehearsal Processes in Observational Learning," *Journal of Personality and Social Psychology,* 1973, *26,* 122-130.

Bandura, A., & Kupers, C. J., "Transmission of Patterns of Self-Reinforcement Through Modeling," *Journal of Abnormal and Social Psychology,* 1964, *69,* 1-9.

Baron, R. A., "Attraction Toward the Model and Model's Competence as Determinants of Adult Imitative Behavior," *Journal of Personality and Social Psychology,* 1970, *14,* 345-351.

Bilodeau, E. A., *Some Effects of Various Degrees of Supplemental Information Given at Two Levels of Practice upon the Acquisition of Complex Motor Skill.* (Hum RRD Tech. Rep. 52-15) Lackland Air Force Base, San Antonio, Texas: Human Resources Research Center, 1952.

Bilodeau, E. A. (ed.), *Acquisition of Skill.* New York: Academic Press, 1966.

Bilodeau, E. A., & Bilodeau, I. McD., "Variable Frequency of Knowledge of Results and the Learning of a Simple Skill," *Journal of Experimental Psychology,* 1958, *55,* 379-383. (a)

Bilodeau, E. A., & Bilodeau, I. McD., "Variation of Temporal Intervals Among Critical Events in Five Studies of Knowledge of Results," *Journal of Experimental Psychology,* 1958, *55,* 603-612. (b)

Bilodeau, E. A., Bilodeau, I. McD., & Schumsky, D. A., "Some Effects of Introducing and Withdrawing Knowledge of Results Early and Late in Practice," *Journal of Experimental Psychology,* 1959, *58,* 142-144.

Bradtke, M., & Oberste, W., "Equality of the Start in Races with a Staggered Start," *Die Lehre der Leichtathletik,* 1975, *43,* 1565-1568.

Brown, H. S., & Messersmith, L., "An Experiment in Teaching Tumbling with and Without Motion Pictures," *Research Quarterly,* 1948, *19,* 304-307.

Burwitz, L., & Newell, K. M., "The Effects of the Mere Presence of Coactors on Learning a Motor Skill," *Journal of Motor Behavior,* 1972, *4,* 99-102.

Chansky, N., "Learning: A Function of Schedule and Type of Feedback," *Psychological Reports,* 1960, *7,* 362.

Cottrell, N. B., "Performance in the Presence of Other Human Beings: Mere Presence, Audience and Affiliation Effects," in E. C. Simmel, R. A. Hoppe, & G. A. Milton (eds.), *Social Facilitation and Imitative Behavior.* Boston: Allyn & Bacon, 1968.

Cottrell, N. B., "Social Facilitation," in C. G. McClintock (ed.), *Experimental Social Psychology.* New York: Holt, Rinehart & Winston, 1972.

Crandall, R., "Social Facilitation Theories and Research," in A. Harrison (ed.), *Explorations in Psychology.* Monterey, Calif.: Brooks/Cole Publishing Co., 1974.

Cratty, B. J., *Psychology in Contemporary Sport.* Englewood Cliffs, N. J.: Prentice Hall, Inc., 1973.

Deutsch, M. "The Effects of Cooperation and Competition upon Group Process," *Human Relations,* 1949, *2,* 129-152, 199-231.

Duffy, E., *Activation and Behavior.* New York: Wiley, 1962.

Easterbrook, J. A., "The Effect of Emotion on Cue Utilization and the Organization of Behavior," *Psychological Review,* 1959, *66,* 183-201.

Fenz, W. D., "Coping Mechanisms and Performance under Stress," in D. M. Landers (ed.), *Psychology of Sport and Motor Behavior II.* Penn State HPER Series No. 10, 1975, 3-24.

Flanders, J. P., "A Review of Research on Imitative Behavior," *Psychological Bulletin,* 1968, *69,* 316-337.

Fouts, G. T., *Imitation in Children: The Effects of Audience and Number of Presentations* (Doctoral dissertation, University of Iowa, 1970), *Dissertation Abstracts International,* 1970, *31,* 3-4, 1563-B. (University Microfilms No. 70-15, 598).

Frost, R. B., *Psychological Concepts Applied to Physical Education and Coaching.* Reading, Mass.: Addison-Wesley, 1971.

Gelfand, D. M., "The Influence of Self-Esteem on Rate of Verbal Conditioning and Social Matching Behavior," *Journal of Abnormal and Social Psychology,* 1962, *65,* 259-265.

Gerst, M. S., "Symbolic Coding Processes in Observational Learning," *Journal of Personality and Social Psychology,* 1971, *19,* 7-17.

Gill, D. L., "Knowledge of Results Precision and Motor Skill Acquisition," *Journal of Motor Behavior,* 1975, *7,* 191-198.

Gill, D., "Competitive Trait Anxiety and Success-Failure as Predictors of State Anxiety in Competition." Paper presented at the American Alliance of Health, Physical Education and Recreation, Milwaukee, April 1976.

Gill, D. L., & Martens, R., "The Informational and Motivational Influence of Social Reinforcement on Motor Performance," *Journal of Motor Behavior, 1975, 7,* 171-182.

Goodenough, F. L., & Brian, C. R., "Certain Factors Underlying the Acquisition of Motor Skill by Pre-School Children," *Journal of Experimental Psychology,* 1929, *12,* 127-155.

Gray, C. A., & Brumbach, W. B., "Effect of Daylight Projection of Film Loops on Learning Badminton," *Research Quarterly,* 1967, *38,* 562-569.

Green, R. F., Zimilies, H. L., & Spragg, S. D. S., *The Effects of Varying Degrees of Knowledge of Results on Knob Setting Performance,* Special Devices Center Technical Report 241-6-20. Orlando, Florida: Naval Training Device Center, 1955.

Haas, J., & Roberts, G. C., "Effects of Evaluative Others upon Learning and Performance of a Complex Motor Skill," *Journal of Motor Behavior,* 1975, *7,* 81-90.

Hammond, L. K., & Goldman, M., "Competition and Non-Competition and its Relationship to Individual and Group Productivity," *Sociometry,* 1961, *24,* 46-60.

Harney, D. M., & Parker, R., "Effects of Social Reinforcement, Subject Sex, and Experimenter Sex on Children's Motor Performance," *Research Quarterly,* 1972, *43,* 187-196.

Herbert, M. J., & Harsch, C. H., "Observational Learning in Cats," *Journal of Comparative Psychology,* 1944, *37,* 81-95.

Hunt, P. J., & Hillery, J. M., "Social Facilitation in a Coaction Setting: An Examination of the Effects over Learning Trials," *Journal of Experimental Social Psychology,* 1973, *9,* 563-571.

Julian J. W., & Perry, F. A., "Cooperation Contrasted with Intra-group and Inter-Group Competition," *Sociometry,* 1067, *30,* 79-90.

Landers, D. M., "Observational Learning of a Motor Skill: Temporal Spacing of Demonstrations and Audience Presence," *Journal of Motor Behavior,* 1975, *7,* 281-287.

Landers, D. M., "Social Facilitation and Human Performance: A Review of Contemporary and Past Research," in D. M. Landers (ed.), *Psychology of Sport and Motor Behavior II*. Penn State HPER Series No. 10, 1975, 197-208.

Landers, D. M., & Landers, D. M., "Teacher Versus Peer Models: Effects of Model's Presence and Performance Level on Motor Behavior," *Journal of Motor Behavior,* 1973, *5,* 129-139.

Landers, D. M., & McCullagh, P. D., "Social Facilitation of Motor Performance," in J. Keogh (ed.), *Exercise and Sports Sciences Reviews* (Vol. 4). Santa Barbara, Calif.: Journal Publishing Affiliates, 1976.

Lewin, K., "Psychology of Success and Failure," in C. L. Stacey & M. F. DeMartino (eds.), *Understanding Human Motivation* (Rev. Ed.). Cleveland: Allen, 1963, 317-322.

Lockhart, A., "The Value of Motion Picture as an Instrumental Device in Learning a Motor Skill," *Research Quarterly,* 1944, *15,* 181-187.

Lowe, R. H., *A New Look at the Relationship Between Arousal and Performance* (Doctoral dissertation, University of Illinois, 1973), *Dissertation Abstracts International,* 1973, *34,* 876 B. (University Microfilms No. 73-17590)

Lynn, R., "An Achievement Motivation Questionnaire," *British Journal of Psychology,* 1969, *60,* 529-534.

Malmo, R. B., "Activation: A Neurophysiological Dimension," *Psychological Review,* 1959, *66,* 367-386.

Margolius, G. J., & Sheffield, F. D., "Optimum Methods of Combining Practice with Filmed Demonstration in Teaching Complex Response Sequences: Serial Learning of a Mechanical-Assembly Task," in A. A. Lumsdaine (ed.), *Student Response in Programmed Instruction.* Washington, D. C.: National Academy of Sciences— National Research Council, 1961.

Marteniuk, R. G., *Information Processing in Motor Skills.* New York: Holt, Rinehart & Winston, 1976.

Martens, R., *The Effects of an Audience on Learning and Performance of a Complex Motor Skill,* (Doctoral dissertation, University of Illinois, 1968). *Dissertation Abstracts International,* 1968, *30,* 156 A. (University Microfilms No. 69-10, 785).

Martens, R., "Effect of an Audience on Learning and Performance of a Complex Motor Skill," *Journal of Personality and Social Psychology,* 1969, *12,* 252-260.

Martens, R., "Social Reinforcement Effects on Preschool Children's Motor Performance," *Perceptual and Motor Skills,* 1970, *31,* 787-792.

Martens, R., "Internal-External Control and Social Reinforcement Effects on Motor Performance," *Research Quarterly,* 1971, *42,* 307-313. (a)

Martens, R., "Competition: In Need of a Theory." Paper presented at the Conference on Sport and Social Deviancy, Brockport, N.Y., December 1971, p. 8. (b)

Martens, R., "Social Reinforcement Effects on Motor Performance as a Function of Socio-Economic Status," *Perceptual and Motor Skills,* 1972, *35,* 215-218.

Martens, R., "Arousal and Motor Performance," in J. H. Wilmore (ed.), *Exercise and Sport Sciences Review* (Vol. 2). New York: Academic Press, 1974.

Martens, R., *Social Psychology and Physical Activity.* New York: Harper & Row, 1975.

Martens, R., *Sport Competition Anxiety Test.* Urbana, Ill.: Human Kinetics Publishers, in press.

Martens, R., Burwitz, L., & Newell, K., "Money and Praise: Do They Improve Motor Learning and Performance?" *Research Quarterly,* 1972, *43,* 429-442.

Martens, R., Burwitz, L., & Zuckerman, J., "Modeling Effects on Motor Performance," *Research Quarterly,* 1976, *47,* 277-291.

Martens, R., Gill, D. L., Simon, J. A., & Scanlon, T., "Competitive Anxiety: Theory and Research," *Mouvement,* 1975, *7,* 289-292.

Martens, R., & Landers, D. M., "Motor Performance under Stress: A Test of the Inverted-U Hypothesis," *Journal of Personality and Social Psychology,* 1970, *16,* 29-37.

Martens, R., & Landers, D. M., "Evaluation Potential as a Determinant of Coaction Effects," *Journal of Experimental Social Psychology,* 1972, *8,* 347-359.

McClelland, D. C., Atkinson, J. W., Clark, R. A., & Lowell, E. L., *The Achievement Motive.* New York: Appleton-Century-Crofts, 1953.

McCullagh, P. D., & Landers, D. M., "A Comparison of the Audience and Coaction Paradigms," in D. M. Landers (ed.), *Psychology of Sport and Motor Behavior II.* Penn State HPER Series No. 10, 1975, 209-220.

McCullagh, P. D., & Landers, D. M. "Size of Audience and Social Facilitation," *Perceptual and Motor Skills,* 1976, *42,* 1067-1070.

McGuigan, F. J., "The Effect of Precision, Delay, and Schedule of Knowledge of Results on Performance," *Journal of Experimental Psychology,* 1959, *58,* 79-84.

McGuire, W. J., "Interpolated Motivational Statements Within a Programmed Series of Instructions as a Distribution-of-Practice Factor," in A. A. Lumsdaine (ed.), *Student Response in Programmed Instruction.* Washington, D. C.: National Academy of Sciences—National Research Council, 1961.

McTavish, C. L., "Effects of Repetitive Film Showings on Learning," (SDC 269-17-12), Instructional Film Research Program, The Pennsylvania State University, 1949.

Miller, D. M., *Coaching the Female Athlete.* Philadelphia: Lea & Febiger, 1974.

Mischel, W., & Grusec, J., "Determinants of the Rehearsal and Transmission of Neutral and Aversive Behaviors," *Journal of Personality and Social Psychology,* 1966, *3,* 197-205.

Myers, A., "Team Competition, Success, and the Adjustment of Group Members," *Journal of Abnormal and Social Psychology,* 1962, *65,* 325-332.

Nelson, D. O., "Effects of Slow-Motion Loop Films on the Learning of Golf," *Research Quarterly,* 1958, *29,* 37-45.

Newell, K. M., "Knowledge of Results and Motor Learning," *Journal of Motor Behavior,* 1974, *6,* 235-243.

Newell, K. M., "Knowledge of Results and Children's Motor Learning." Paper presented at the American Alliance for Health, Physical Education and Recreation, Milwaukee, April 1976.

Obermeir, G. E., Landers, D. M., & Ester, M. A., "Social Facilitation of Speed Events: The Coaction Effect in Racing Dogs and Trackmen," In D. M. Landers & R. W. Christina (eds.), *Psychology of Sport and Motor Behavior III.* Penn State HPER Series, 1976.

Oxendine, J. B., "Emotional Arousal and Motor Performance," *Quest,* 1970, *13,* 23-32.

Paulus, P. B., Shannon, J. C., Wilson, D. L., & Boone, T. C., "The Effect of Spectator

Presence on Gymnastic Performance in a Field Situation," *Psychonomic Science,* 1972, *29*, 88-90.

Roberts, G. C., "Effect of Achievement Motivation and Social Environment on Performance of a Motor Task," *Journal of Motor Behavior,* 1972, *4*, 37-46.

Roberts, G. C., "Effect of Achievement Motivation and Social Environment on Risk Taking," *Research Quarterly,* 1974, *45*,, 42-55.

Roberts, G. C., "Sex and Achievement Motivation Effects on Risk Taking," *Research Quarterly,* 1975, *46*, 58-70.

Roberts, G. C., "Social Facilitation: Mere Presence or Evaluation Apprehension," *Mouvement,* 1975, *7*, 4-5-411.

Roberts, G. C., & Martens, R., "Social Reinforcement and Complex Motor Performance," *Research Quarterly,* 1970, *41*, 175-181.

Rogers, C. A., Jr., "Feedback Precision and Postfeedback Interval Duration," *Journal of Experimental Psychology,* 1974, *102*, 604-608.

Ross, D., "Relation Between Dependency, Intentional Learning and Incidental Learning in Preschool Children," *Journal of Personality and Social Psychology,* 1966, *4*, 374-381.

Ryan, E. D., & Lakie, W. L. "Competitive and Noncompetitive Performance in Relation to Achievement Motive and Manifest Anxiety," *Journal of Personality and Social Psychology,* 1965, *1*, 342-345.

Sasfy, J., & Okun, M., "Form of Evaluation and Audience Expertness as Joint Determinants of Audience Effects," *Journal of Experimental Social Psychology,* 1974, *10*, 461-467.

Singer, R. N., "Effect of an Audience on Performance of a Motor Task," *Journal of Motor Behavior,* 1970, *2*, 88-95.

Singer, R. N., *Coaching, Athletics, and Psychology.* New York: McGraw-Hill, 1972.

Smoll, F. L., "Effects of Precision of Information Feedback upon Acquisition of a Motor Skill," *Research Quarterly,* 1972, *43*, 489-493.

Spence, J. T., & Spence, K. W., "The Motivational Components of Manifest Anxiety: Drive and Drive Stimuli," in C. D. Speilberger (ed.), *Anxiety and Behavior.* New York: Academic Press, 1966, 291-326.

Thayer, R. E., "Measurement of Activation Through Self-Report," *Psychological Reports,* 1967, 663-678.

Triplett, N., "The Dynamogenic Factors of Pace-Making and Competition," *American Journal of Psychology,* 1897-1898, *9*, 507-533.

Trowbridge, M. H., & Carson, H., "An Experimental Study of Thorndike's Theory of Learning," *Journal of General Psychology,* 1932, *7*, 245-258.

Wakefield, F., Harkins, D., & Cooper, J. M., *Track and Field Fundamentals for Girls and Women.* Saint Louis: C. V. Mosby, 1966.

Wallace, S. A., DeOreo, K. L., & Roberts, G. C., "Memory and Perceptual Trace Development in Ballistic Timing," *Journal of Motor Behavior,* in press.

Weinberg, D. R., Guy, D. E., & Tupper, R. W., "Variations of Postfeedback Interval in Simple Motor Learning," *Journal of Experimental Psychology,* 1964, *67*, 98-99.

Welsh, R., "Achieving a Performance Peak Through Psychological and Physiological Readiness," *Athletic Journal,* 1973, *54*, 60-63.

Yussen, S. R., "Determinants of Visual Attention and Recall in Observational Learning by Preschoolers and Second Graders," *Developmental Psychology,* 1974, *10,* 93-100.

Zajonc, R. B., "Social Facilitation," *Science,* 1965, *149,* 269-274.

Zander, A., "Motivation and Performance of Sport Groups," in D. M. Landers (ed.), *Psychology of Sport and Motor Behavior II.* Penn State HPER Series No. 10, 1975, 25-40.

CHAPTER 13

Doherty, Dr. J. Kenneth, "Power-Skill Training in Field Events—Part I," *Track Technique,* No. 45, September 1971.

Valik, B., "Strength Preparation for Young Track and Fielders," *Physical Culture in Schools,* Moscow, Vol. 4, 1966.

Verhoshanskiy, Yoriy, "Depth Jumping in the Training of Jumpers," *Track Technique,* No. 51, March 1973.